Exploring Arduino®

Tools and Techniques for
Engineering Wizardry

Jeremy Blum

WILEY

Exploring Arduino®: Tools and Techniques for Engineering Wizardry

Published by
John Wiley & Sons, Inc.
10475 Crosspoint Boulevard
Indianapolis, IN 46256
www.wiley.com

Published simultaneously in Canada

ISBN: 978-1-118-54936-0
ISBN: 978-1-118-54948-3 (ebk)
ISBN: 978-1-118-78616-1 (ebk)

Manufactured in the United States of America

10 9 8 7 6 5 4 3 2 1

For general information on our other products and services please contact our Customer Care Department within the United States at (877) 762-2974, outside the United States at (317) 572-3993 or fax (317) 572-4002.

Wiley publishes in a variety of print and electronic formats and by print-on-demand. Some material included with standard print versions of this book may not be included in e-books or in print-on-demand. If this book refers to media such as a CD or DVD that is not included in the version you purchased, you may download this material at http://booksupport.wiley.com. For more information about Wiley products, visit www.wiley.com.

Library of Congress Control Number: 2013937652

*To my grandmother, whose lifelong curiosity and encouragement
inspires me to be a better person every day.*

Credits

Acquisitions Editor
Mary James

Project Editor
Jennifer Lynn

Technical Editor
Scott Fitzgerald

Production Editor
Daniel Scribner

Copy Editor
Keith Cline

Editorial Manager
Mary Beth Wakefield

Freelancer Editorial Manager
Rosemarie Graham

Associate Director of Marketing
David Mayhew

Marketing Manager
Ashley Zurcher

Business Manager
Amy Knies

Production Manager
Tim Tate

Vice President and Executive Group Publisher
Richard Swadley

Vice President and Executive Publisher
Neil Edde

Associate Publisher
Jim Minatel

Project Coordinator, Cover
Katie Crocker

Compositor
Cody Gates,
Happenstance Type-O-Rama

Proofreader
James Saturnio, Word One

Indexer
John Sleeva

Cover Designer
Ryan Sneed

Cover Image
Courtesy of Jeremy Blum

About the Author

Jeremy Blum recently received his Master's degree in Electrical and Computer Engineering from Cornell University, where he previously received his Bachelor's degree in the same field. At Cornell, he oversaw the design and creation of several sustainable buildings around the world and domestically through his founding and leadership of Cornell University Sustainable Design, a nationally recognized sustainable design organization that has been specifically lauded by the CEO of the U.S. and World Green Building Councils. In that vein, Jeremy has applied his passion for electrical engineering to design solar home energy monitoring systems, revolutionary fiber-optic LED lighting systems, and sun-tracking smart solar panels. He is also responsible for helping to start a first-of-its-kind entrepreneurial co-working space that contributes to the development of dozens of student start-ups (including some of his own creation) every year.

Jeremy has designed award-winning prosthetic control methods, gesture-recognition systems, and building-automation systems, among many other things. He designed the electronics for the MakerBot Replicator 3D printers (which are used by people around the world, and by notable organizations such as NASA), and the prototype electronics and firmware for the MakerBot Digitizer 3D Scanner. As a researcher in the renowned Creative Machines Lab, he has contributed to the creation of robots that can assemble themselves, self-learning quadrupedal robots, and 3D printers that redefine personal manufacturing. He has presented this research in peer-reviewed journals and at conferences as far away as India.

Jeremy produces YouTube videos that have introduced millions of people to engineering and are among the most popular Arduino tutorials on the Internet. He is well known within the international open source and "maker" communities for his development of open source hardware projects and tutorials that have been featured on the Discovery Channel, and have won several awards and hack-a-thons. Jeremy was selected by the American Institute of Electrical and Electronics Engineers as the 2012 New Face of Engineering.

He offers engineering consulting services through his firm, Blum Idea Labs LLC, and he teaches engineering and sustainability to young students in New York City. Jeremy's passion is improving people's lives and our planet through creative engineering solutions. You can learn more about Jeremy and his work at his website: `www.jeremyblum.com`.

About the Technical Editor

Scott Fitzgerald is an artist and educator who has been using the Arduino platform as a teaching tool and in his practice since 2006. He has taught physical computing in the Interactive Telecommunications Program (ITP) of New York University since 2005, introducing artists and designers to microcontrollers. Scott works for the Arduino team, documenting new products and creating tutorials to introduce people to the platform. He was technical editor of the second edition of *Making Things Talk* in 2011, and he authored the book that accompanies the official Arduino Starter Kit in 2012.

Acknowledgments

First, I must thank my friends at Wiley publishing for helping to make this possible: Mary James, for encouraging me to write this book in the first place; and Jennifer Lynn, for keeping me on track as I worked through writing all the chapters. I also owe a big thanks to Scott Fitzgerald for his critical eye in the technical editing of this book.

Had it not been for the great folks at element14, I may never have gotten into producing my Arduino Tutorial Series, a prelude to the book you are about to read. Sabrina Deitch and Sagar Jethani, in particular, have been wonderful partners with whom I've had the privilege to work.

I wrote the majority of this book while simultaneously completing my Master's degree and running two companies, so I owe a tremendous amount of gratitude to my professors and peers who put up with me while I tried to balance all of my responsibilities.

Finally, I want to thank my family, particularly my parents and my brother, David, whose constant encouragement reminds me why I do the things I do.

Contents at a Glance

Contents

Introduction

You have excellent timing. As I often like to say, "We're living in the future." With the tools available to you today, many of which you'll learn about in this book, you have the opportunity and the ability to bend the physical world to your whim. Until very recently, it has not been possible for someone to pick up a microcontroller and have it controlling his or her world within minutes. As you may have guessed, a *microcontroller* is a programmable platform that gives you the power to define the operation of complex mechanical, electrical, and software systems using relatively simple commands. The possibilities are endless, and the Arduino microcontroller platform will become your new favorite tool as you explore the world of electronics, programming, human-computer interaction, art, control systems, and more. Throughout the course of this book, you'll use the Arduino to do everything from detecting motion to creating wireless control systems to communicating over the Internet.

Whether you are completely new to any kind of engineering or are a seasoned veteran looking to get started with embedded systems design, the Arduino is great place to start. Are you looking for a general reference for Arduino development? This book is perfect for you, too. This book walks you through a number of particular projects, but you'll also find it easy to return to the book for code snippets, best practices, system schematics, and more. The electrical engineering, systems design, and programming practices that you'll learn while reading this book are widely applicable beyond the Arduino platform and will prepare you to take on an array of engineering projects, whether they use the Arduino or some other platform.

Who This Book Is For

This book is for Arduino enthusiasts of all experience levels. Chapters build upon each other, utilizing concepts and project components from previous chapters to develop more complex ideas. But don't worry. Whenever you face new, complex ideas, a cross-reference reminds you where you first encountered any relevant building-block concepts so that you can easily refresh your memory.

This book assumes that you have little or no previous experience working with programming or electrical engineering. To facilitate readers of various experience levels, the book features a number of optional sections and sidebars, or short excerpts, that explain a particular concept in greater detail. Although these sidebars are not obligatory for you to gain a good understanding of how to use the Arduino, they do provide a closer look at technical topics for the more curious reader.

What You'll Learn in This Book

This book is not a recipe book. If you want to follow step-by-step instructions that tell you exactly how to build a particular project without actually explaining why you are doing what you are doing, this book is not for you. You can think of this book as an introduction to electrical engineering, computer science, product design, and high-level thinking using the Arduino as a vehicle to help you experience these concepts in a hands-on manner.

When building hardware components of the Arduino projects demonstrated in this book, you'll learn not just how to wire things together, but how to read schematics, why particular parts are used for particular functions, and how to read datasheets that will allow you to choose appropriate parts to build your own projects. When writing software, I provide complete program code, but you will first be stepped through several iterative processes to create the final program. This will help to reinforce specific program functions, good code-formatting practices, and algorithmic understanding.

This book will teach physics concepts, algorithms, digital design principles, and Arduino-specific programming concepts. It is my hope that working through the projects in this book will not just make you a well-versed Arduino developer, but that it will also give you the skills you need to develop more-complex electrical systems, and to pursue engineering endeavors in other fields, and with different platforms.

Features Used in This Book

The following features and icons are used in this book to help draw your attention to some of the most important or useful information in the book:

WARNING Be sure to take heed when you see one of these asides. When particular steps could cause damage to your electronics if performed incorrectly, you'll see one of these asides.

TIP These asides contain quick hints about how to perform simple tasks that might prove useful for the task at hand.

NOTE These asides contain additional information that may be of importance to you, including links to videos and online material that will make it easier to following along with the development of a particular project.

SAMPLE HEADING

These asides go into additional depth about the current topic or a related topic.

Getting the Parts

Lucky for you, you can easily obtain the components you need to execute the projects in this book. This book's partner, Newark element14, has created kits specially designed for the contents of this book. You can even use the coupon code at the back of this book to get a discount!

You should order the basic kit first. You can then purchase add-on kits as you progress through the book. Don't want to buy a kit? Don't worry. At the beginning of each chapter, you'll find a detailed list of parts that you need to complete that chapter. The companion website for this book, www.exploringarduino.com, also provides links to where you can find the parts for each chapter.

NOTE Did you already buy this book as a bundle from Newark? If so, you're good to go.

What You'll Need

In addition to the actual parts that you'll use to build your Arduino projects, there are a few other tools and materials that you'll need on your Arduino adventures. Most importantly, you'll need a computer that is compatible with the Arduino integrated development environment (IDE) (Max OSX 10.4+, Windows XP+, or a Linux Distro). I will provide instructions for all operating systems when warranted.

You may also want some additional tools that will be used throughout the book to debug, assemble hardware, etc. These are not explicitly necessary to complete the projects in this book. As you develop your electrical engineering skillset, these tools will come in handy for other projects. I recommend the following:

- A soldering iron and solder (Note: You will not need to solder to complete the projects in this book, but you may wish to assemble your own circuits on a protoboard, or you may wish to purchase shields that require soldering assembly.)

- A multimeter (This will be useful for debugging concepts within this book, but is not explicitly required.)

- A set of small screwdrivers

- A hot glue gun

Source Code and Digital Content

The primary companion site for this book is www.exploringarduino.com, and it is maintained by the author. You will find code downloads for each chapter on this site (along with videos, links, and other useful materials). Wiley also maintains a repository of digital content that accompanies this book at www.wiley.com. Specifically for this book, the code download is on the Download Code tab at www.wiley.com/go/exploringarduino.

You can also search for the book at www.wiley.com by ISBN (the ISBN for this book is 978-1-118-54936-0) to find the code.

At the beginning of each chapter, you can find the location of the major code files for the chapter. Throughout each chapter, you can also find references to the names of code files as needed in listing titles and text.

The code available at www.exploringarduino.com and www.wiley.com is provided in compressed ZIP archives. After you download the code, just decompress it with an appropriate compression tool.

NOTE Because many books have similar titles, you may find it easiest to search by ISBN; this book's ISBN is 978-1-118-54936-0.

Errata

We make every effort to ensure that there are no errors in the text or in the code. However, no one is perfect, and mistakes do occur. If you find an error in this book, such as a spelling mistake or faulty piece of code, we would be grateful for your feedback. By sending in errata, you may save another reader hours of frustration, and at the same time, you can help us provide even higher quality information.

To find the errata page for this book, go to www.wiley.com/go/exploringarduino and click the Errata link. On this page you can view all errata that has been submitted for this book and posted by Wiley editors.

Supplementary Material and Support

During your adventures with your Arduino, you'll inevitably have questions and perhaps run into problems. One of the best parts about using the Arduino is the excellent support community that you can find on the Web. This extremely active base of Arduino users will readily help you along your way. The following are just a few resources that you'll find helpful on your journey:

- Official Arduino Reference

  www.arduino.cc/en/Reference/HomePage

- My Arduino Tutorial Series

  www.jeremyblum.com/category/arduino-tutorials

- adafruit Industries' Arduino Tutorial Series

  learn.adafruit.com/category/learn-arduino

- SparkFun's Electronics Tutorials

  learn.sparkfun.com/tutorials

- The Official Arduino Forum

  www.arduino.cc/forum

- The element14 Arduino Community

  www.element14.com/community/groups/arduino

If you've exhausted all of those resources and still cannot solve your problem, reach out to me on Twitter (@sciguy14); maybe I can help. You can also get in touch with me directly via the contact page on my website (www.jeremyblum.com/contact), but I generally don't guarantee fast response times.

What Is an Arduino?

The best part about the Arduino prototyping platform is that it's whatever you want it to be. The Arduino could be an automatic plant-watering control system. It can be a web server. It could even be a quadcopter autopilot.

The Arduino is a microcontroller development platform paired with an intuitive programming language that you develop using the Arduino integrated development environment (IDE). By equipping the Arduino with sensors, actuators, lights, speakers, add-on modules (called *shields*), and other integrated circuits, you can turn the Arduino into a programmable "brain" for just about any control system.

It's impossible to cover everything that the Arduino is capable of, because the possibilities are limited only by your imagination. Hence, this book serves as a guide to get you acquainted with the Arduino's functionality by executing a number of projects that will give you the skills you need to develop your own projects.

You'll learn more about the Arduino and the available variations of the board in Chapter 1, "Getting Up and Blinking with the Arduino." If you're eager to know all the inner workings of the Arduino, you're in luck: It is completely open source, and all the schematics and documentation are freely available on the Arduino website. Appendix A, "Deciphering the ATMega Datasheet and Arduino Schematics," covers some of the Arduino's technical specifications.

An Open Source Platform

If you're new to the world of open source, you are in for a treat. This book does not go into detail about the open source hardware movement, but it is worth knowing a bit about the ideologies that make working with the Arduino so wonderful. If you want a full rundown of what open source hardware is, check out the official definitions on the Open Source Hardware Association website (www.oshwa.org/definition).

NOTE Learn all about the open source movement from my TEDx Talk: www.jeremyblum.com/portfolio/tedx-cornell-university-2011/. You can also find this video on the Wiley website shown at the beginning of this Introduction.

Because the Arduino is open source hardware, all the design files, schematics, and source code are freely available to everybody. Not only does this mean that you can more easily hack the Arduino to serve a very particular function, but you can also even integrate the Arduino platform into your designs, make and sell Arduino clones, and use the Arduino software libraries in other projects. Although this book focuses mostly on using official Arduino hardware, you could also use hundreds of Arduino derivative boards (often with particular functions added on to them) to create the projects in this book.

The Arduino open source license also permits commercial reuse of their designs (so long as you don't utilize the Arduino trademark on your designs). So, if you use an Arduino to prototype an exciting project and you want to turn it into a commercial product, you can do that. For example, you'll read about products like the MakerBot Replicator 3D printer, which uses electronics based on the Arduino Mega platform (www.thingiverse.com/thing:16058). (Full disclosure: I designed that motherboard.)

Be sure to respect the licenses of the source code and hardware that you use throughout this book. Some licenses require that you provide attribution to the original author when you publish a design based on their previous work. Others require that you always share improvements that you make under an equivalent license. This sharing helps the community grow, and leads to all the amazing online documentation and support that you'll undoubtedly refer to often during your Arduino adventures. All code examples that I've written for this book (unless otherwise specified) are licensed under the GNU General Public License (GPL), enabling you to use them for anything you want.

Beyond This Book

Some of you might already be familiar with my popular series of YouTube Arduino and electronics tutorials (www.youtube.com/sciguy14). I refer to them throughout this book as a way to see more-detailed walkthroughs of the topics covered here. If you're curious about some of the remarkable things that you can do with clever combinations of electronics, microcontrollers, computer science, and creativity, check out my portfolio (www.jeremyblum.com/portfolio) for a sampling of projects. Like Arduino, most of what I do is released via open source licenses that allow you to easily duplicate my work for your own needs.

I'm anxious to hear about what you do with the skills you acquire from this book. I encourage you to share them with me and with the rest of the world. Good luck on your Arduino adventures!

Arduino Engineering Basics

In This Part

Getting Up and Blinking with the Arduino

Parts You'll Need for This Chapter:

Arduino Uno

USB cable

CODE AND DIGITAL CONTENT FOR THIS CHAPTER

Code downloads, videos, and other digital content for this chapter can be found at `www.exploringarduino.com/content/ch1`.

In addition, all code can be found at `www.wiley.com/go/exploringarduino` on the Download Code tab. The code is in the chapter 01 download and individually named according to the names throughout the chapter.

Now that you have some perspective on the Arduino platform and its capabilities, it's time to explore your options in the world of Arduino. In this chapter, you examine the available hardware, learn about the programming environment and language, and get your first program up and running. Once you have a grip on the functionality that the Arduino can provide, you'll write your first program and get the Arduino to blink!

NOTE To follow along with a video that introduces the Arduino platform, visit www.jeremyblum.com/2011/01/02/arduino-tutorial-series-it-begins/. You can also find this video on the Wiley website shown at the beginning of this chapter.

Exploring the Arduino Ecosystem

In your adventures with the Arduino, you'll depend on three main components for your projects:

- The Arduino board itself
- External hardware (including both shields and hand-made circuits, which you'll explore throughout this book)
- The Arduino integrated development environment, or Arduino IDE

All these system components work in tandem to enable you do just about anything with your Arduino.

You have a lot of options when it comes to Arduino development boards, but this book focuses on using official Arduino boards. Because the boards are all designed to be programmable via the same IDE, you can generally use any of the modern Arduino boards to complete the projects in this book with zero or minor changes. However, when necessary, you'll see caveats about using different boards for various projects. The majority of the projects use the Arduino Uno.

You start by exploring the basic functionality baked in to every Arduino board. Then you examine the differences between each modern board so that you can make an informed decision when choosing a board to use for your next project.

Arduino Functionality

All Arduino boards have a few key capabilities and functions. Take a moment to examine the Arduino Uno (see Figure 1-1); it will be your base configuration. These are some key components that you'll be concerning yourself with:

- Atmel microcontroller
- USB programming/communication interface(s)
- Voltage regulator and power connections
- Breakout I/O pins
- Debug, Power, and RX/TX LEDs
- Reset button
- In-circuit serial programmer (ICSP) connector(s)

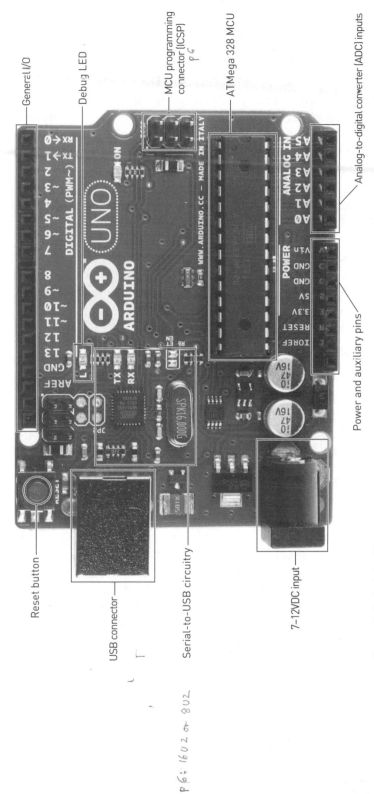

Figure 1-1: Arduino Uno components

Credit: Arduino, www.arduino.cc

Atmel Microcontroller

At the heart of every Arduino is an Atmel microcontroller unit (MCU). Most Arduino boards, including the Arduino Uno, use an AVR ATMega microcontroller. The Arduino Uno in Figure 1-1 uses an ATMega 328p. The Due is an exception; it uses an ARM Cortex microcontroller. This microcontroller is responsible for holding all of your compiled code and executing the commands you specify. The Arduino programming language gives you access to microcontroller peripherals, including analog-to-digital converters (ADCs), general-purpose input/output (I/O) pins, communication buses (including I²C and SPI), and serial interfaces. All of this useful functionality is broken out from the tiny pins on the micro-controller to accessible female headers on the Arduino that you can plug wires or shields into. A 16 MHz ceramic resonator is wired to the ATMega's clock pins, which serves as the reference by which all program commands execute. You can use the Reset button to restart the execution of your program. Most Arduino boards come with a debug LED already connected to pin 13, which enables you to run your first program (blinking an LED) without connecting any additional circuitry.

Programming Interfaces

Ordinarily, ATMega microcontroller programs are written in C or Assembly and programmed via the ICSP interface using a dedicated programmer (see Figure 1-2). Perhaps the most important characteristic of an Arduino is that you can program it easily via USB, without using a separate programmer. This functionality is made possible by the Arduino bootloader. The bootloader is loaded onto the ATMega at the factory (using the ICSP header), which allows a serial USART (Universal Synchronous/Asynchronous Receiver/Transmitter) to load your program on the Arduino without using a separate programmer. (You can learn more about how the bootloader functions in "The Arduino Bootloader and Firmware Setup" sidebar.)

In the case of the Arduino Uno and Mega 2560, a secondary microcontroller (an ATMega 16U2 or 8U2 depending on your revision) serves as an interface between a USB cable and the serial USART pins on the main microcontroller. The Arduino Leonardo, which uses an ATMega 32U4 as the main microcontroller, has USB baked right in, so a secondary microcontroller is not needed. In older Arduino boards, an FTDI brand USB-to-serial chip was used as the interface between the ATMega's serial USART port and a USB connection.

@ 108

Figure 1-2: AVR ISP MKII programmer

General I/O and ADCs

The part of the Arduino that you'll care the most about during your projects is the general-purpose I/O and ADC pins. All of these pins can be individually addressed via the programs you'll write. All of them can serve as digital inputs and outputs. The ADC pins can also act as analog inputs that can measure voltages between 0 and 5V (usually from resistive sensors). Many of these pins are also multiplexed to serve additional functions, which you will explore during your projects. These special functions include various communication interfaces, serial interfaces, pulse-width-modulated outputs, and external interrupts.

Power Supplies

For the majority of your projects, you will simply use the 5V power that is provided over your USB cable. However, when you're ready to untether your project from a computer, you have other power options. The Arduino can accept between 6V and 20V (7-12V recommend) via the direct current (DC) barrel jack connector, or into the V_{in} pin. The Arduino has built-in 5V and 3.3V regulators:

- 5V is used for all the logic on the board. In other words, when you toggle a digital I/O pin, you are toggling it between 5V and 0V.

- 3.3V is broken out to a pin to accommodate 3.3V shields and external circuitry.

THE ARDUINO BOOTLOADER AND FIRMWARE SETUP

A *bootloader* is a chunk of code that lives in a reserved space in the program memory of the Arduino's main MCU. In general, AVR microcontrollers are programmed with an ICSP, which talks to the microcontroller via a serial peripheral interface (SPI). Programming via this method is fairly straightforward, but necessitates the user having a hardware programmer such as an STK500 or an AVR ISP MKII programmer (see Figure 1-2).

When you first boot the Arduino board, it enters the bootloader, which runs for a few seconds. If it receives a programming command from the IDE over the MCU's UART (serial interface) in that time period, it loads the program that you are sending it into the rest of the MCU's program memory. If it does not receive a programming command, it starts running your most recently uploaded sketch, which resides in the rest of the program memory.

When you send an "upload" command from the Arduino IDE, it instructs the USB-to-serial chip (an ATMega 16U2 or 8U2 in the case of the Arduino Uno) to reset the main MCU, hence forcing it into the bootloader. Then, your computer immediately begins to send the program contents, which the MCU is ready to receive over its UART connection (facilitated by the USB-to-serial converter).

Bootloaders are great because they enable simple programming via USB with no external hardware. However, they do have two downsides:

- First, they take up valuable program space. If you have written a complicated sketch, the approximately 2KB of space taken up by the bootloader might be really valuable.

- Second, using a bootloader means that your program will always be delayed by a few seconds at boot as the bootloader checks for a programming request.

If you have a programmer (or another Arduino that can be programmed to act as a programmer), you can remove the bootloader from your ATMega and program it directly by connecting your programmer to the ICSP header and using the File ⇨ Upload Using Programmer command from within the IDE.

Arduino Boards

This book cannot possibly cover all the available Arduino boards; there are many, and manufacturers are constantly releasing new ones with various features. The following section highlights some of the features in the official Arduino boards.

The Uno (see Figure 1-3) is the flagship Arduino and will be used heavily in this book. It uses a 16U2 USB-to-serial converter chip and an ATMega 328p as the main MCU. It is available in both DIP and SMD versions (which defines whether the MCU is removable).

Atmega 32U4

Credit: Arduino, www.arduino.cc

Figure 1-3: The Arduino Uno

The Leonardo (see Figure 1-4) uses the 32U4 as the main microcontroller, which has a USB interface built in. Therefore, it doesn't need a secondary MCU to perform the serial-to-USB conversion. This cuts down on the cost and enables you to do unique things like emulate a joystick or a keyboard instead of a simple serial device. You will learn how to use these features in Chapter 6, "USB and Serial Communication."

@6

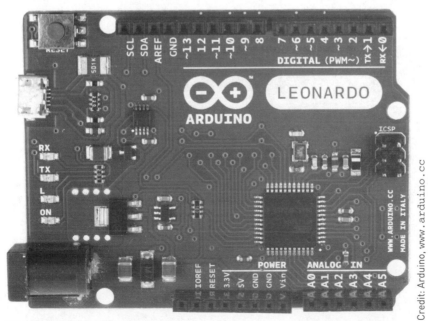

Credit: Arduino, www.arduino.cc

Figure 1-4: The Arduino Leonardo

The Mega 2560 (see Figure 1-5) employs an ATMega 2560 as the main MCU, which has 54 general I/Os to enable you to interface with many more devices. The Mega also has more ADC channels, and has four hardware serial interfaces (unlike the one serial interface found on the Uno).

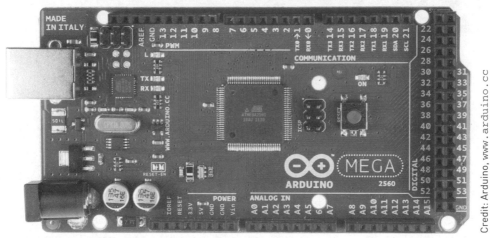

Figure 1-5: The Arduino Mega 2560

Unlike all the other Arduino variants, which use 8-bit AVR MCUs, the Due (see Figure 1-6) uses a 32-bit ARM Cortex M3 SAM3X MCU. The Due offers higher-precision ADCs, selectable resolution pulse-width modulation (PWM), Digital-to-Analog Converters (DACs), a USB host connector, and an 84 MHz clock speed.

Figure 1-6: The Arduino Due

The Nano (see Figure 1-7) is designed to be mounted right into a breadboard socket. Its small form factor makes it perfect for use in more finished projects.

Credit: Cooking Hacks, www.cookinghacks.com.

Figure 1-7: The Arduino Nano

The Mega ADK (see Figure 1-8) is very similar to the Mega 2560, except that it has USB host functionality, allowing it to connect to an Android phone so that it can communicate with apps that you write.

ala Leonardo p9

Credit: Arduino, www.arduino.cc

Figure 1-8: The Arduino Mega ADK

The LilyPad (see Figure 1-9) is unique because it is designed to be sewn into clothing. Using conductive thread, you can wire it up to sewable sensors, LEDs, and more. To keep size down, you need to program it using an FTDI cable.

p6 USB ⟷ serial chip

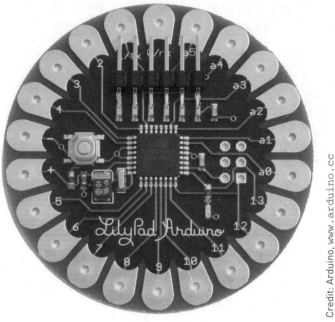

Credit: Arduino, www.arduino.cc

Figure 1-9: The LilyPad Arduino

As explained in this book's introduction, the Arduino is open source hardware. As a result, you can find dozens and dozens of "Arduino compatible" devices available for sale that will work just fine with the Arduino IDE and all the projects you'll do in this book. Some of the popular third-party boards include the Seeeduino, the adafruit 32U4 breakout board, and the SparkFun Pro Mini Arduino boards. Many third-party boards are designed for very particular applications, with additional functionality already built in to the board. For example, the ArduPilot is an autopilot board for use in autonomous DIY quadcopters (see Figure 1-10). You can even find Arduino-compatible circuitry baked in to consumer devices like the MakerBot Replicator and Replicator 2 3D printers.

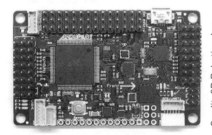

Credit: 3D Robotics, Inc., www.3drobotics.com

Figure 1-10: Quadcopter and ArduPilot Mega controller

Creating Your First Program

Now that you understand the hardware that you'll be using throughout this book, you can install the software and run your first program. Start by downloading the Arduino software to your computer.

Downloading and Installing the Arduino IDE

Access the Arduino website at www.arduino.cc and download the newest version of the IDE from the Download page (see Figure 1-11).

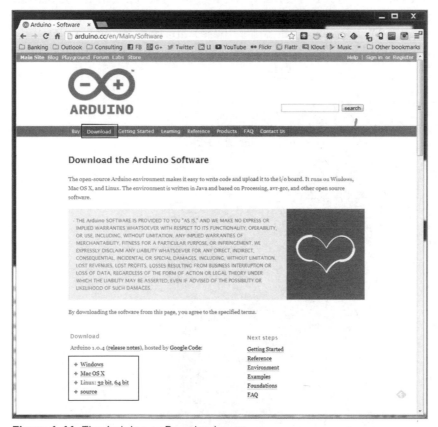

Figure 1-11: The Arduino.cc Download page

After completing the download, unzip it. Inside, you'll find the Arduino IDE. New versions of the Windows IDE are available as an installer that you can download and run, instead of downloading a ZIP file.

Running the IDE and Connecting to the Arduino

Now that you have the IDE downloaded and ready to run, you can connect the Arduino to your computer via USB, as shown in Figure 1-12. Mac and Linux machines install the drivers (mostly) automatically.

If you are using OS X, the first time you plug in an Uno or a Mega 2560, you will get a notification that a new network device has been added. Click the Network Preferences button. In the new window, click Apply. Even though the board will appear as "Not Configured" in the network device list, it will be ready to use. Now, quit System Preferences.

If you are using a modern Arduino on a Windows computer, you will probably need to install drivers. You can skip the following directions if you are not using a Windows computer that needs to have drivers installed. If you installed the IDE using the Windows installer, then these steps have been completed for you. If you downloaded the ZIP on your Windows machine, then you will need to follow the directions shown next.

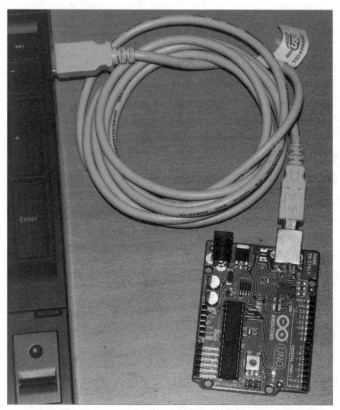

Figure 1-12: Arduino Uno connected to a computer via USB

On your Windows computer, follow these steps to install the drivers (instructions adapted from the Arduino.cc website):

1. Wait for the automatic install process to fail.

2. Open the Start menu, right-click My Computer, and select Properties.

3. Choose Device Manager.

4. Look under Ports (COM and LPT) for the Arduino that you connected.

5. Right-click it and choose Update Driver Software.

6. Choose to browse your computer for software.

7. Select the appropriate driver from the drivers directory of the Arduino IDE that you just downloaded (not the FTDI drivers directory).

8. Windows will now finish the driver installation.

Now, launch the Arduino IDE. You're ready to load your first program onto your Arduino. To ensure that everything is working as expected, you'll load the Blink example program, which will blink the onboard LED. Most Arduinos have an LED connected to pin 13. Navigate to File ➪ Examples ➪ Basic, and click the Blink program. This opens a new IDE window with the Blink program already written for you. First, you'll program the Arduino with this example sketch, and then you'll analyze the program to understand the important components so that you can start to write your own programs in the next chapter.

Before you load the program, you need to tell the IDE what kind of Arduino you have connected and what port it is connected to. Go to Tools ➪ Board and ensure that the right board is selected. This example uses the Uno, but if you are using a different board, select that one (assuming that it also has an LED connected to pin 13).

The last step before programming is to tell the IDE what port your board is connected to. Navigate to Tools ➪ Serial Port and select the appropriate port. On Windows machines, this will be com*, where * is some number representing the serial port number.

TIP If you have multiple serial devices attached to your computer, try unplugging your board to see which COM port disappears from the menu; then plug it back in and select that COM port.

On Linux and Mac computers, the serial port looks something like /dev/tty .usbmodem* or /dev/tty.usbserial*, where * is a string of alphanumeric characters.

You're finally ready to load your first program. Click the Upload button (➡) on the top left of the IDE. The status bar at the bottom of the IDE shows a progress bar as it compiles and uploads your program. When the upload completes, the yellow LED on your Arduino should be blinking once per second. Congratulations! You've just uploaded your first Arduino program.

Breaking Down Your First Program

Take a moment to deconstruct the Blink program so that you understand the basic structure of programs written for the Arduino. Consider Figure 1-13. The numbered callouts shown in the figure correspond to the following list.

Here's how the code works, piece by piece:

1. This is a multiline comment. Comments are important for documenting your code. Everything you write between these symbols will not be compiled or even seen by your Arduino. Multiline comments start with `/*` and end with `*/`. Multiline comments are generally used when you have to say a lot (like the description of this program).

2. This is a single-line comment. When you put `//` on any line, the compiler ignores all text after that symbol on the same line. This is great for annotating specific lines of code or for "commenting out" a particular line of code that you believe might be causing problems.

3. This code is a variable declaration. A variable is a place in the Arduino's memory that holds information. Variables have different types. In this case, it's of type `int`, which means it will hold an integer. In this case, an integer variable called `led` is being set to the value of `13`, the pin that the LED is connected to on the Arduino Uno. Throughout the rest of the program, we can simply use `led` whenever we want to control pin 13. Setting variables is useful because you can just change this one line if you hook up your LED to a different I/O pin later on; the rest of the code will still work as expected.

4. `void setup()` is one of two functions that must be included in every Arduino program. A *function* is a piece of code that does a specific task. Code within the curly braces of the `setup()` function is executed once at the start of the program. This is useful for one-time settings, such as setting the direction of pins, initializing communication interfaces, and so on.

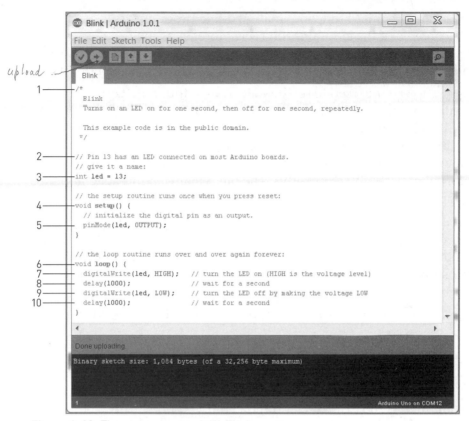

upload

1
2
3
4
5
6
7
8
9
10

Figure 1-13: The components of the Blink program

5. The Arduino's digital pins can function as input or outputs. To configure their direction, use the command pinMode(). This command takes two arguments. An *argument* gives commands information on how they should operate. Arguments are placed inside the parentheses following a command. The first argument to pinMode determines which pin is having its direction set. Because you defined the led variable earlier in the program, you are telling the command that you want to set the direction of pin 13. The second argument sets the direction of the pin: INPUT or OUTPUT. Pins are inputs by default, so you need to explicitly set them to outputs if you want them to function as outputs. Because you want to light an LED, you have set the led pin to an output (current is flowing out of the I/O pin). Note that you have to do this only one time. It will then function as an output for the rest of the program, or until you change it to an input.

6. The second required function in all Arduino programs is `void loop()`. The contents of the loop function repeat forever as long as the Arduino is on. If you want your Arduino to do something once at boot only, you still need to include the loop function, but you can leave it empty.

7. `digitalWrite()` is used to set the state of an output pin. It can set the pin to either 5V or 0V. When an LED and resistor is connected to a pin, setting it to 5V will enable you to light up the LED. (You learn more about this in the next chapter.) The first argument to `digitalWrite()` is the pin you want to control. The second argument is the value you want to set it to, either `HIGH` (5V) or `LOW` (0V). The pin remains in this state until it is changed in the code.

8. The `delay()` function accepts one argument: a delay time in milliseconds. When calling `delay()`, the Arduino stops doing anything for the amount of time specified. In this case, you are delaying the program for 1000ms, or 1 second. This results in the LED staying on for 1 second before you execute the next command.

9. Here, `digitalWrite()` is used to turn the LED off, by setting the pin state to `LOW`.

10. Again, we delay for 1 second to keep the LED in the off state before the loop repeats and switches to the on state again.

That's all there is to it. Don't be intimidated if you don't fully understand all the code yet. As you put together more examples in the following chapters, you'll become more and more proficient at understanding program flow, and writing your own code.

Summary

In this chapter you learned about the following:

- All the components that comprise an Arduino board
- How the Arduino bootloader allows you to program Arduino firmware over a USB connection
- The differences between the various available Arduino boards
- How to connect and install the Arduino with your system
- How to load and run your first program

CHAPTER 2

Digital Inputs, Outputs, and Pulse-Width Modulation

Parts You'll Need for This Chapter:

Arduino Uno

Small breadboard

Jumper wires

1 10kΩ resistor

3 220Ω resistors

USB cable

Pushbutton

5mm single-color LED

5mm common-cathode RGB LED

CODE AND DIGITAL CONTENT FOR THIS CHAPTER

Code downloads, videos, and other digital content for this chapter can be found at www.exploringarduino.com/content/ch2.

In addition, all code can be found at www.wiley.com/go/exploringarduino on the Download Code tab. The code is in the chapter 02 download and individually named according to the names throughout the chapter.

Blinking an LED is great, as you learned in the preceding chapter, but what makes the Arduino microcontroller platform so useful is that the system is equipped with both inputs and outputs. By combining both, your opportunities are nearly limitless. For example, you can use a magnetic reed switch to play music when your door opens, create an electronic lockbox, or build a light-up musical instrument!

In this chapter, you start to learn the skills you need to build projects like these. You explore the Arduino's digital input capabilities, learn about pullup and pulldown resistors, and learn how to control digital outputs. Most Arduinos do not have analog outputs, but it is possible to use digital pulse-width modulation to emulate it in many scenarios. You learn about generating pulse-width modulated signals in this chapter. You will also learn how to debounce digital switches, a key skill when reading human input. By the end of the chapter, you will be able to build and program a controllable RGB (Red, Green, Blue) LED nightlight.

NOTE You can follow along with a video as I teach you about digital inputs and outputs, debouncing, and pulse-width modulation (PWM): www.jeremyblum.com/ 2011/01/10/arduino-tutorial-2-now-with-more-blinky-things/. You can also find this video on the Wiley website shown at the beginning of this chapter.

If you want to learn more about some of the basics of electrical engineering touched on in this chapter, watch this video: www.jeremyblum.com/2011/01/17/ electrical-engineering-basics-in-arduino-tutorial-3/. You can also find this video on the Wiley website shown at the beginning of this chapter.

Digital Outputs

In Chapter 1, "Getting Up and Blinking with the Arduino," you learned how to blink an LED. In this chapter, you will further explore Arduino digital output capabilities, including the following topics:

- Setting pins as outputs
- Wiring up external components
- New programming concepts, including `for` loops and constants
- Digital versus analog outputs and pulse-width modulation (PWM)

Wiring Up an LED and Using Breadboards

In Chapter 1, you learned how to blink the onboard LED, but what fun is that? Now it is time to whip out the breadboard and wire up an external LED to pin 9 of your Arduino. Adding this external LED will be a stepping-stone towards helping you to understand how to wire up more complex external circuits in the coming chapters. What's more, pin 9 is PWM-enabled, which will enable you to pursue the analog output examples later in this chapter.

Working with Breadboards

It is important to understand how breadboards work so that you can use them effectively for the projects in this book. A *breadboard* is a simple prototyping tool that easily allows you to wire up simple circuits without having to solder together parts to a custom printed circuit board. First, consider the blue and red lines that run the length of the board. The pins adjacent to these color-coded lines are designed to be used as power and ground buses. All the red pins are electrically connected, and are generally used for providing power. In the case of most Arduinos and the projects in this book, this will generally be at 5V. All the blue pins are electrically connected and are used for the ground bus. All the vertically aligned pins are also connected in rows, with a division in the middle to make it easy to mount integrated circuits on the breadboard. Figure 2-1 highlights how the pins are electrically connected, with all the thick lines representing connected holes.

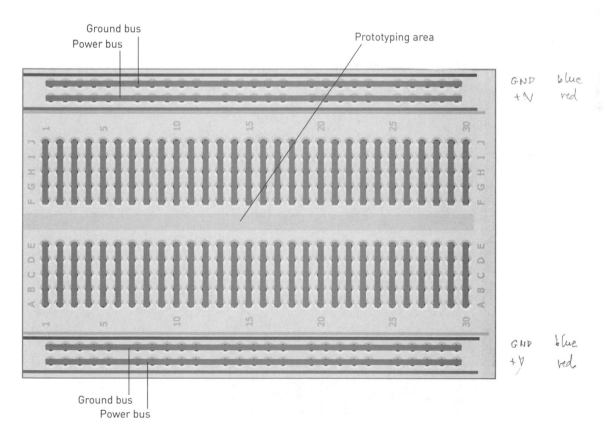

Figure 2-1: Breadboard electrical connections

Wiring LEDs

LEDs will almost certainly be one of the most-used parts in your projects through-out this book. LEDs are polarized; in other words, it matters in what direction you hook them up. The positive lead is called the *anode*, and the negative lead is called the *cathode*. If you look at the clear top of the LED, there will usually be a flat side on the lip of the casing. That side is the cathode. Another way to determine which side is the anode and which is the cathode is by examining the leads. The shorter lead is the cathode.

As you probably already know, LED stands for light-emitting diode. Like all diodes, LEDs allow current to flow in only one direction—from their anode to their cathode. Because current flows from positive to negative, the anode of the LED should be connected to the current source (a 5V digital signal in this case), and the cathode should be connected to ground. The resistor can be inserted in series on either side of the LED. Resistors are not polarized, and so you do not have to worry about their orientation.

You'll wire the LED into pin 9 in series with a resistor. LEDs must always be wired in series with a resistor to serve as a current limiter. The larger the resistor value, the more it restricts the flow of current and the dimmer the LED glows. In this scenario, you use a 220Ω resistor. Wire it up as shown in Figure 2-2.

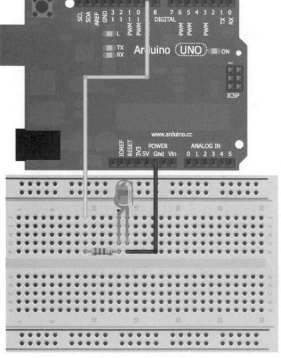

Image created with Fritzing.

Figure 2-2: Arduino Uno wired to an LED

OHM'S LAW AND THE POWER EQUATION

The most important equation for any electrical engineer to know is Ohm's law. Ohm's law dictates the relationship between voltage (measured in volts), current (measured in amps), and resistance (measured in ohms or Ω) in a circuit. A circuit is a closed loop with a source of electrical energy (like a 9V battery) and a load (something to use up the energy, like an LED). Before delving into the law, it is important to understand what each term means, at least at a basic level:

■ *Voltage* represents the potential electrical difference between two points.

■ *Current* flows from a point of higher potential energy to lower potential energy. You can think of current as a flow of water, and voltage as elevation. Water (or current) always flows from high elevation (higher voltage) to lower elevation (ground, or a lower voltage). Current, like water in a river, will always follow the path of least resistance in a circuit.

■ *Resistance*, in this analogy, is representative of how easy it is for current to flow. When the water (the current) is flowing through a narrow pipe, less can pass through in the same amount of time as through a larger pipe. The narrow pipe is equivalent to a high resistance value because the water will have a harder time flowing through. The wider pipe is equivalent to a low resistance value (like a wire) because current can flow freely through it.

Ohm's law is defined as follows:

V = IR

Where V is Voltage difference in volts, I is Current in amps, and R is the Resistance in ohms.

In a circuit, all voltage gets used up, and each component offers up some resistance that lowers the voltage. Knowing this, the above equation comes in handy for things like figuring out what resistor value to match up with an LED. LEDs have a predefined voltage drop across them and are designed to operate at a particular current value. The larger the current through the LED, the brighter the LED glows, up to a limit. For the most common LEDs, the maximum current designed to go through an LED is 20milliamps (a milliamp is 1/1000 of an amp and is typically abbreviated as mA). The voltage drop across an LED is defined in its datasheet. A common value is around 2V. Consider the LED circuit shown in Figure 2-3.

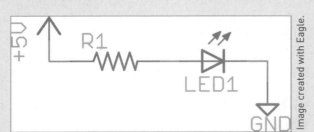

Figure 2-3: Simple LED circuit

Continues

continued

You can use Ohm's law to decide on a resistor value for this circuit. Assume that this is a standard LED with 20mA forward current and a 2V drop across it. Because the source voltage is 5V and it ends at ground, a total of 5V must drop across this circuit. Since the LED has a 2V drop, the other 3V must drop across the resistor. Knowing that you want approximately 20mA to flow through these components, you can find the resistor value by solving for R:

$R = V/I$

Where V = 3V and I = 20mA.

Solving for R, R = 3V / 0.02A = 150Ω. So, with a resistor value of 150Ω, 20mA flows through both the resistor and LED. As you increase the resistance value, less current is allowed to flow through. 220Ω is a bit more than 150Ω, but still allows the LED to glow sufficiently bright, and is a very commonly available resistor value.

Another useful equation to keep in mind is the power equation. The power equation tells you how much power, in watts, is dissipated across a given resistive component. Because increased power is associated with increased heat dissipation, components generally have a maximum power rating. You want to ensure that you do not exceed the maximum power rating for resistors because otherwise they might overheat. A common power rating for resistors is 1/8 of a watt (abbreviated as W, milliwatts as mW). The power equation is as follows:

$P = IV$

Where P is power in watts, and I and V are still defined as the current and voltage.

For the resistor defined earlier with a voltage drop of 3V and a current of 20mA, P = 3V × 0.02A = 60mW, well under the resistor's rating of 1/8W, or 125mW. So, you do not have to worry about the resistor overheating; it is well within its operating limits.

Programming Digital Outputs

By default, all Arduino pins are set to inputs. If you want to make a pin an output, you need to first tell the Arduino how the pin should be configured. In the Arduino programming language, the program requires two parts: the setup() and the loop().

As you learned in Chapter 1, the setup() function runs one time at the start of the program, and the loop() function runs over and over again. Because you'll generally dedicate each pin to serve as either an input or an output, it is common practice to define all your pins as inputs or outputs in the setup. You start by writing a simple program that sets pin 9 as an output and turns it on when the program starts.

To write this program, use the `pinMode()` command to set the direction of pin 9, and use `digitalWrite()` to make the output high (5V). See Listing 2-1.

Listing 2-1: Turning on an LED—led.ino

```
const int LED=9;                //define LED for pin 9
void setup()
{
  pinMode (LED, OUTPUT);    //Set the LED pin as an output
  digitalWrite(LED, HIGH);  //Set the LED pin high
}

void loop()
{
  //we are not doing anything in the loop!
}
```

Load this program onto your Arduino, wired as shown in Figure 2-2. In this program, also notice that I used the `const` operator before defining the pin integer variable. Ordinarily, you'll use variables to hold values that may change during program execution. By putting `const` before your variable declaration, you are telling the compiler that the variable is "read only" and will not change during program execution. All instances of LED in your program will be "replaced" with 9 when they are called. When you are defining values that will not change, using the `const` qualifier is recommended. In some of the examples later in this chapter, you will define non-constant variables that may change during program execution.

You must specify the type for any variable that you declare. In the preceding case, it is an integer (pins will always be integers), so you should set it as such. You can now easily modify this sketch to match the one you made in Chapter 1 by moving the `digitalWrite()` command to the loop and adding some delays. Experiment with the delay values and create different blink rates.

Using For Loops

It's frequently necessary to use loops with changing variable values to adjust parameters of a program. In the case of the program you just wrote, you can implement a `for` loop to see how different blink rates impact your system's operation. You can visualize different blink rates by using a `for` loop to cycle through various rates. The code in Listing 2-2 accomplishes that.

Listing 2-2: LED with Changing Blink Rate—blink.ino

```
const int LED=9;              //define LED for Pin 9
void setup()
{
  pinMode (LED, OUTPUT); //Set the LED pin as an output
}

void loop()
{
  for (int i=100; i<=1000; i=i+100)
  {
    digitalWrite(LED, HIGH);
    delay(i);
    digitalWrite(LED, LOW);
    delay(i);
  }
}
```

Compile the preceding code and load it onto your Arduino. What happens? Take a moment to break down the for loop to understand how it works. The for loop declaration always contains three semicolon-separated entries:

- The first entry sets the index variable for the loop. In this case, the index variable is i and is set to start at a value of 100.

- The second entry specifies when the loop should stop. The contents of the loop will execute over and over again while that condition is true. <= indicates less than or equal to. So, for this loop, the contents will continue to execute as long as the variable i is still less than or equal to 1000.

- The final entry specifies what should happen to the index variable at the end of each loop execution. In this case, i will be set to its current value plus 100.

To better understand these concepts, consider what happens in two passes through the for loop:

1. i equals 100.

2. The LED is set high, and stays high for 100ms, the current value of i.

3. The LED is set low, and stays low for 100ms, the current value of i.

4. At the end of the loop, i is incremented by 100, so it is now 200.

5. 200 is less than or equal to 1000, so the loop repeats again.

6. The LED is set high, and stays high for 200ms, the current value of i.

7. The LED is set low, and stays low for 200ms, the current value of i.

8. At the end of the loop, i is incremented by 100, so it is now 300.

9. This process repeats until i surpasses 1000 and the outer loop function repeats, setting the i value back to 100 and starting the process again.

Now that you've generated digital outputs from your Arduino, you'll learn about using PWM to create analog outputs from the I/O pins on your Arduino.

Pulse-Width Modulation with analogWrite()

So, you have mastered digital control of your pins. This is great for blinking LEDs, controlling relays, and spinning motors at a constant speed. But what if you want to output a voltage other than 0V or 5V? Well, you can't—unless you are using the digital-to-analog converter (DAC) pins on the Due or are using an external DAC chip.

However, you can get pretty close to generating analog output values by using a trick called *pulse-width modulation* (PWM). Select pins on each Arduino can use the analogWrite() command to generate PWM signals that can emulate a pure analog signal when used with certain peripherals. These pins are marked with a ~ on the board. On the Arduino Uno, Pins 3, 5, 6, 9, 10, and 11 are PWM pins. If you're using an Uno, you can continue to use the circuit from Figure 2-1 to test out the analogWrite() command with your LED. Presumably, if you can decrease the voltage being dropped across the resistor, the LED should glow more dimly because less current will flow. That is what you will try to accomplish using PWM via the analogWrite() command. The analogWrite() command accepts two arguments: the pin to control and the value to write to it.

The PWM output is an 8-bit value. In other words, you can write values from 0 to 2^8-1, or 0 to 255. Try using a similar for loop structure to the one you used previously to cycle through varying brightness values (see Listing 2-3).

Listing 2-3: LED Fade Sketch—fade.ino

```
const int LED=9;     //define LED for Pin 9
void setup()
{
  pinMode (LED, OUTPUT);     //Set the LED pin as an output
}

void loop()
{
  for (int i=0; i<256; i++)
  {
    analogWrite(LED, i);
    delay(10);
```

```
    }
    for (int i=255; i>=0; i--)
    {
      analogWrite(LED, i);
      delay(10);
    }
}
```

What does the LED do when you run this code? You should observe the LED
fading from off to on, then from on to off. Of course, because this is all in the
main loop, this pattern repeats ad infinitum. Be sure to note a few differences
in this `for` loop. In the first loop, `i++` is just shorthand code to represent `i=i+1`.
Similarly, `i--` is functionally equivalent to `i=i-1`. The first `for` loop fades the
LED up, and the second loop fades it down.

PWM control can be used in lots of circumstances to emulate pure analog control, but it cannot always be used when you actually need an analog signal. For
instance, PWM is great for driving direct current (DC) motors at variable speeds
(you experiment with this in later chapters), but it does not work well for driving
speakers unless you supplement it with some external circuitry. Take a moment
to examine how PWM actually works. Consider the graphs shown in Figure 2-4.

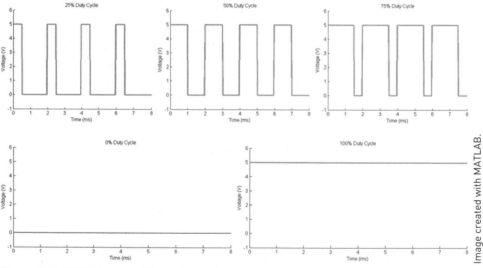

Figure 2-4: PWM signals with varying duty cycles

PWM works by modulating the duty cycle of a square wave (a signal that
switches on and off). *Duty cycle* refers to the percentage of time that a square
wave is high versus low. You are probably most familiar with square waves that
have a duty cycle of 50%—they are high half of the time, and low half of the time.

The `analogWrite()` command sets the duty cycle of a square wave depending on the value you pass to it:

- Writing a value of 0 with `analogWrite()` indicates a square wave with a duty cycle of 0 percent (always low).

- Writing a 255 indicates a square wave with a duty cycle of 100 percent (always high).

- Writing a 127 indicates a square wave with a duty cycle of 50 percent (high half of the time, low half of the time).

The graphs in Figure 2-4 show that for a signal with a duty cycle of 25 percent, it is high 25 percent of the time, and low 75 percent of the time. The frequency of this square wave, in the case of the Arduino, is about 490Hz. In other words, the signal varies between high (5V) and low (0V) about 490 times every second.

So, if you are not actually changing the voltage being delivered to an LED, why do you see it get dimmer as you lower the duty cycle? It is really a result of your eyes playing a trick on you! If the LED is switching on and off every 1ms (which is the case with a duty cycle of 50 percent), it appears to be operating at approximately half brightness because it is blinking faster than your eyes can perceive. Therefore, your brain actually averages out the signal and tricks you into believing that the LED is operating at half brightness.

Reading Digital Inputs

Now it is time for the other side of the equation. You've managed to successfully *generate* both digital and analog(ish) outputs. The next step is to *read* digital inputs, such as switches and buttons, so that you can interact with your project in real time. In this section, you learn to read inputs, implement pullup and pulldown resistors, and debounce a button in software.

Reading Digital Inputs with Pulldown Resistors

You should start by modifying the circuit that you first built from Figure 2-1. Following Figure 2-5, you'll add a pushbutton and a pulldown resistor connected to a digital input pin.

> **TIP** Be sure to also connect the power and ground buses of the breadboard to the Arduino. Now that you're using multiple devices on the breadboard, that will come in handy.

Before you write the code to read from the pushbutton, it is important to understand the significance of the pulldown resistor used with this circuit. Nearly all digital inputs use a pullup or pulldown resistor to set the "default state" of the input pin. Imagine the circuit in Figure 2-5 without the 10kΩ resistor. In this scenario, the pin would obviously read a high value when the button is pressed.

But, what happens when the button is not being pressed? In that scenario, the input pin you would be reading is essentially connected to nothing—the input pin is said to be "floating." And because the pin is not physically connected to 0V or 5V, reading it could cause unexpected results as electrical noise on nearby pins causes its value to fluctuate between high and low. To remedy this, the pulldown resistor is installed as shown in Figure 2-5.

Now, consider what happens when the button is not pressed with the pulldown resistor in the circuit: The input pin will be connected through a 10kΩ resistor to ground. While the resistor will restrict the flow of current, there is still enough current flow to ensure that the input pin will read a low logic value. 10kΩ is a fairly common pulldown resistor value. Larger values are said to be *weak pulldowns* because it easier to overcome them, and smaller resistor values are said to be *strong pulldowns* because it is easier for more current to flow through them to ground. When the button is pressed, the input pin is directly connected to 5V through the button.

Now, the current has two options:

- It can flow through a nearly zero resistance path to the 5V rail.

- It can flow through a high resistance path to the ground rail.

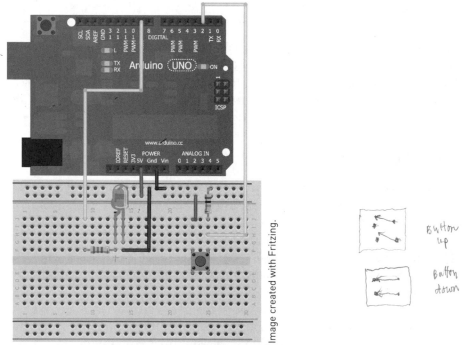

Image created with Fritzing.

Figure 2-5: Wiring an Arduino to a button and an LED

Recall from the previous sidebar on Ohm's law and the power equation that current will always follow the path of the least resistance in a circuit. In this scenario, the majority of the current flows through the button, and a high logic level is generated on the input pin, because that is the path of least resistance.

> **NOTE** This example uses a pulldown resistor, but you could also use a pullup resistor by connecting the resistor to 5V instead of ground and by connecting the other side of the button to ground. In this setup, the input pin reads a high-logic value when the button is unpressed and a low-logic value when the button is being pressed.

Pulldown and pullup resistors are important because they ensure that the button does not create a short circuit between 5V and ground when pressed and that the input pin is never left in a floating state.

Now it is time to write the program for this circuit! In this first example, you just have the LED stay on while the button is held down, and you have it stay off while the button is unpressed (see Listing 2-4).

Listing 2-4: Simple LED Control with a Button—led_button.ino

```
const int LED=9;        //The LED is connected to pin 9
const int BUTTON=2;       //The Button is connected to pin 2

void setup()
{
  pinMode (LED, OUTPUT);     //Set the LED pin as an output
  pinMode (BUTTON, INPUT);   //Set button as input (not required)
}

void loop()
{
  if (digitalRead(BUTTON) == LOW)      // if button pressed . . .
  {
    digitalWrite(LED, LOW);            // . . . turn LED on when pressed
  }
  else
  {
    digitalWrite(LED, HIGH);          // . . . else turn LED off
  }
}
```

Notice here that the code implements some new concepts, including `digitalRead` and `if/else` statements. A new `const int` statement has been added for the button pin. Further, this code defines the button pin as an input in the `setup` function. This is not explicitly necessary, though, because pins are inputs by default; it is shown for completeness. `digitalRead()` reads the value of an input. In this case, it is reading the value of the BUTTON pin. If the button is being pressed, digitalRead() returns a value of HIGH, or 1. If it is not being pressed, it returns LOW, or 0. When placed in the if() statement, you're checking the state of the pin and evaluating if it matches the condition you've declared. In this if() statement, you're checking to see if the value returned by digitalRead() is LOW. The == is a comparison operator that tests whether the first item (digitalRead()) is equal to the second (LOW). If this is true (that is, the button is not being pressed), the code inside the brackets executes, and the LED set to LOW. If this is not true (the button is being pressed), the else statement is executed, and the LED is turned HIGH.

That's it! Program your circuit with this code and confirm that it works as expected.

Working with "Bouncy" Buttons

When was the last time you had to hold a button down to keep a light on? Probably never. It makes more sense to be able to click the button once to turn it on and to click the button again to turn it off. This way, you do not have to hold the button down to keep the light on. Unfortunately, this is not quite as easy as you might first guess. You cannot just look for the value of the switch to change from low to high; you need to worry about a phenomenon called *switch bouncing*.

Buttons are mechanical devices that operate as a spring-damper system. In other words, when you push a button down, the signal you read does not just go from low to high, it bounces up and down between those two states for a few milliseconds before it settles. Figure 2-6 illustrates the expected behavior next to the actual behavior you might see when probing the button using an oscilloscope (though this figure was generated using a MATLAB script):

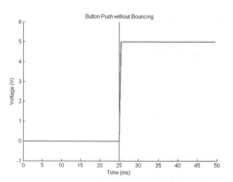
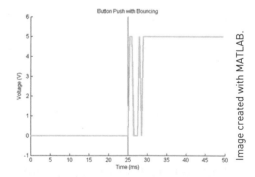

Figure 2-6: Bouncing button effects.

The button is physically pressed at the 25ms mark. You would expect the button state to be immediately read as a high logic level as the graph on the left shows. However, the button actually bounces up and down before settling, as the graph on the right shows.

If you know that the switch is going to do this, it is relatively straightforward to deal with it in software. Next, you write switch-debouncing software that looks for a button state change, waits for the bouncing to finish, and then reads the switch state again. This program logic can be expressed as follows:

1. Store a previous button state and a current button state (initialized to LOW).

2. Read the current button state.

3. If the current button state differs from the previous button state, wait 5ms because the button must have changed state.

4. After 5ms, reread the button state and use that as the current button state.

5. If the previous button state was low, and the current button state is high, toggle the LED state.

6. Set the previous button state to the current button state.

7. Return to step 2.

This is a perfect opportunity to explore using *functions* for the first time. *Functions* are blocks of code that can accept input arguments, execute code based on those arguments, and optionally return a result. Without realizing it, you've already been using predefined functions throughout your programs. For example, digitalWrite() is a function that accepts a pin and a state, and writes that state to the given pin. To simplify your program, you can define your own functions to encapsulate actions that you do over and over again.

Within the program flow (listed in the preceding steps) is a series of repeating steps that need to be applied to changing variable values. Because you'll want to repeatedly debounce the switch value, it's useful to define the steps for debouncing as a function that can be called each time. This function will accept the previous button state as an input and outputs the current debounced button state. The following program accomplishes the preceding steps and switches the LED state every time the button is pressed. You'll use the same circuit as the previous example for this. Try loading it onto your Arduino and see how it works (see Listing 2-5).

Listing 2-5: Debounced Button Toggling—debounce.ino

```
const int LED=9;            //The LED is connected to pin 9
const int BUTTON=2;         //The Button is connected to pin 2
boolean lastButton = LOW;   //Variable containing the previous
                            //button state
boolean currentButton = LOW; //Variable containing the current
                            //button state
```

global vars

```
boolean ledOn = false;          //The present state of the LED (on/off)

void setup()
{
  pinMode (LED, OUTPUT);        //Set the LED pin as an output
  pinMode (BUTTON, INPUT);      //Set button as input (not required)
}

/*
 * Debouncing Function
 * Pass it the previous button state,
 * and get back the current debounced button state.
 */
boolean debounce(boolean last)        // Caller keeps the last reading
{
  boolean current = digitalRead(BUTTON);      //Read the button state
  if (last != current)                        //if it's different…
  {
    delay(5);                                 //wait 5ms
    current = digitalRead(BUTTON);            //read it again
  }
  return current;                             //return the current value
}

void loop()
{
  currentButton = debounce(lastButton);                //read deboucned state
  if (lastButton == LOW && currentButton == HIGH) //if it was pressed...
  {
    ledOn = !ledOn;                                    //toggle the LED value
  }
  lastButton = currentButton;                          //reset button value

  digitalWrite(LED, ledOn);                            //change the LED state

}
```

Now, break down the code in Listing 2-5. First, constant values are defined for the pins connected to the button and LED. Next, three Boolean *variables* are declared. When the const qualifier is not placed before a variable declaration, you are indicating that this variable can change within the program. By defining these values at the top of the program, you are declaring them as *global* variables that can be used and changed by any function within this sketch. The three Boolean variables declared at the top of this sketch are *initialized* as well, meaning that they have been set to an initial value (LOW, LOW, and false respectively). Later in the program, the values of these variables can be changed with an assignment operator (a single equals sign: =).

Consider the function definition in the preceding code: `boolean debounce(boolean last)`. This function accepts a Boolean (a data type that has only two states: true/false, high/low, on/off, 1/0) input variable called `last` and returns a Boolean value representing the current debounced pin value. This function compares the current button state with the previous (`last`) button state that was passed to it as an argument. The `!=` represents inequality and is used to compare the present and previous button values in the `if` statement. If they differ, then the button must have been pressed and the `if` statement will execute its contents. The `if` statement waits 5ms before checking the button state again. This 5ms gives sufficient time for the button to stop bouncing. The button is then checked again to ascertain its stable value. As you learned earlier, functions can optionally return values. In the case of this function, the `return current` statement returns the value of the `current` Boolean variable when the function is called. `current` is a *local* variable—it is declared and used only within the debounce function. When the debounce function is called from the main loop, the returned value is written to the *global* `currentButton` variable that was defined at the top of the sketch. Because the function was defined as `debounce`, you can call the function by writing `currentButton = debounce(lastButton)` from within the `setup` or `loop` functions. `currentButton` will be set equal to the value that is returned by the `debounce` function.

After you've called the function and populated the `currentButton` variable, you can easily compare it to the previous button state by using the `if` statement in the code. The `&&` is a logical operator that means "AND". By joining two or more equality statements with an `&&` in an `if` statement, you are indicating that the contents of the `if` statement block should execute only if both of the equalities evaluate to `true`. If the button was previously `LOW`, and is now `HIGH`, you can assume that the button has been pressed, and you can invert the value of the `ledOn` variable. By putting an `!` in front of the `ledOn` variable, you reset the variable to the opposite of whatever it currently is. The loop is finished off by updating the previous button variable and writing the updated LED state.

This code should change the LED state each time the button is pressed. If you try to accomplish the same thing without debouncing the button, you will find the results unpredictable, with the LED sometimes working as expected and sometimes not.

Building a Controllable RGB LED Nightlight

In this chapter, you have learned how to control digital outputs, how to read debounced buttons, and how to use PWM to change LED brightness. Using those skills, you can now hook up an RGB LED and a debounced button to cycle through some colors for a controllable RGB LED nightlight. It's possible to mix colors with an RGB LED by changing the brightness of each color.

In this scenario, you use a common cathode LED. That means that the LED has four leads. One of them is a cathode pin that is shared among all three diodes, while the other three pins connect to the anodes of each diode color. Wire that LED up to three PWM pins through current-limiting resistors on the Arduino as shown in the wiring diagram in Figure 2-7.

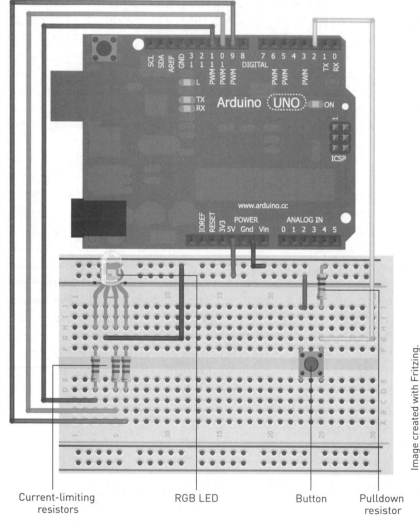

Figure 2-7: Nightlight wiring diagram

You can configure a debounced button to cycle through a selection of colors each time you press it. To do this, it is useful to add an additional function to set the RGB LED to the next state in the color cycle. In the following program (see Listing 2-6), I have defined seven total color states, plus one off state for the LED. Using the `analogWrite()` function, you can choose your own color-mixing combinations. The only change to the `loop()` from the previous example is that instead of flipping a single LED state, an LED state counter is incremented each time the button is pressed, and it is reset back to zero when you cycle through all the options. Upload this to your Arduino connected to the circuit you just built and enjoy your nightlight. Modify the color states by changing the values of `analogWrite()` to make your own color options.

Listing 2-6: Toggling LED Nightlight—rgb_nightlight.ino

```
const int BLED=9;      //Blue LED on Pin 9
const int GLED=10;     //Green LED on Pin 10
const int RLED=11;     //Red LED on Pin 11
const int BUTTON=2;      //The Button is connected to pin 2

boolean lastButton = LOW;    //Last Button State
boolean currentButton = LOW; //Current Button State
int ledMode = 0;             //Cycle between LED states

void setup()
{
  pinMode (BLED, OUTPUT);    //Set Blue LED as Output
  pinMode (GLED, OUTPUT);    //Set Green LED as Output
  pinMode (RLED, OUTPUT);    //Set Red LED as Output
  pinMode (BUTTON, INPUT);   //Set button as input (not required)
}

/*
 * Debouncing Function
 * Pass it the previous button state,
 * and get back the current debounced button state.
 */
boolean debounce(boolean last)
{
  boolean current = digitalRead(BUTTON);       //Read the button state
  if (last != current)                         //if it's different...
  {
    delay(5);                                  //wait 5ms
    current = digitalRead(BUTTON);             //read it again
  }
  return current;                              //return the current value
}

/*
 * LED Mode Selection
 * Pass a number for the LED state and set it accordingly.
 */
void setMode(int mode)
```

[handwritten margin notes: "1st read" pointing to `boolean current = digitalRead(BUTTON);`; "delay if diff from prev state" pointing to `delay(5);`; "2nd read" pointing to `return current;`; "Green = 5"; "220 Ω : Red Red Brown"]

```
{
  //RED
  if (mode == 1)
  {
    digitalWrite(RLED, HIGH);
    digitalWrite(GLED, LOW);
    digitalWrite(BLED, LOW);
  }
  //GREEN
  else if (mode == 2)
  {
    digitalWrite(RLED, LOW);
    digitalWrite(GLED, HIGH);
    digitalWrite(BLED, LOW);
  }
  //BLUE
  else if (mode == 3)
  {
    digitalWrite(RLED, LOW);
    digitalWrite(GLED, LOW);
    digitalWrite(BLED, HIGH);
  }
  //PURPLE (RED+BLUE)
  if (mode == 4)
  {
    analogWrite(RLED, 127);
    analogWrite(GLED, 0);
    analogWrite(BLED, 127);
  }
  //TEAL (BLUE+GREEN)
  else if (mode == 5)
  {
    analogWrite(RLED, 0);
    analogWrite(GLED, 127);
    analogWrite(BLED, 127);
  }
  //ORANGE (GREEN+RED)
  else if (mode == 6)
  {
    analogWrite(RLED, 127);
    analogWrite(GLED, 127);
    analogWrite(BLED, 0);
  }
  //WHITE (GREEN+RED+BLUE)
  else if (mode == 7)
  {
    analogWrite(RLED, 85);
    analogWrite(GLED, 85);
    analogWrite(BLED, 85);
  }
```

```
  //OFF (mode = 0)
  else
  {
    digitalWrite(RLED, LOW);
    digitalWrite(GLED, LOW);
    digitalWrite(BLED, LOW);
  }
}

void loop()
{
  currentButton = debounce(lastButton);            //read deboucned state
  if (lastButton == LOW && currentButton == HIGH) //if it was pressed
  {
    ledMode++;                                     //increment the LED value
  }
  lastButton = currentButton;                      //reset button value
  //if you've cycled through the different options,
  //reset the counter to 0
  if (ledMode == 8) ledMode = 0;
  setMode(ledMode);                                //change the LED state
}
```

This might look like a lot of code, but it is nothing more than a conglomeration of code snippets that you have already written throughout this chapter.

How else could you modify this code? You could add additional buttons to independently control one of the three colors. You could also add blink modes, using code from Chapter 1 that blinked the LED. The possibilities are limitless.

Summary

In this chapter you learned about the following:

- How a breadboard works
- How to pick a resistor to current-limit an LED
- How to wire an external LED to your Arduino
- How to use PWM to write "analog" values to LEDs
- How to read a pushbutton
- How to debounce a pushbutton
- How to use `for` loops
- How to utilize pullup and pulldown resistors

CHAPTER 3

Reading Analog Sensors

Parts You'll Need for This Chapter

Arduino Uno

Small breadboard

Jumper wires

10kΩ potentiometer

10kΩ resistor (×2)

220Ω resistor (×3)

USB cable

Photoresistor

TMP36 temperature sensor (or any other 5V analog sensor)

5mm common-cathode RGB LED

CODE AND DIGITAL CONTENT FOR THIS CHAPTER

Code downloads, video, and other digital content for this chapter can be found at www.exploringarduino.com/content/ch3.

In addition, all code can be found at www.wiley.com/go/exploringarduino on the Download Code tab. The code is in the chapter 03 download and individually named according to the names throughout the chapter.

The world around you is analog. Even though you might hear that the world is "going digital," the majority of observable features in your environment will always be analog in nature. The world can assume an infinite number of potential states, whether you are considering the color of sunlight, the temperature of the ocean, or the concentration of contaminants in the air. This chapter focuses on developing techniques for discretizing these infinite possibilities into palatable digital values that can be analyzed with a microcontroller system like the Arduino.

In this chapter, you will learn about the differences between analog and digital signals and how to convert between the two, as well as a handful of the analog sensors that you can interface with your Arduino. Using skills that you acquired in the preceding chapter, you will add light sensors for automatically adjusting your nightlight. You will also learn how to send analog data from your Arduino to your computer via a USB-to-serial connection, which opens up enormous possibilities for developing more complex systems that can transmit environmental data to your computer.

NOTE You can follow along with a video as I teach you about reading from analog inputs: `www.jeremyblum.com/2011/01/24/arduino-tutorial-4-analog-inputs/`. You can also find this video on the Wiley website shown at the beginning of this chapter.

If you want to learn more about the differences between analog and digital signals, check out this video that explains each in depth: `www.jeremyblum.com/2010/06/20/lets-get-digital-or-analog/`. You can also find this video on the Wiley website shown at the beginning of this chapter.

Understanding Analog and Digital Signals

If you want your devices to interface with the world, they will inevitably be interfacing with analog data. Consider the projects you completed in the preceding chapter. You used a switch to control an LED. A switch is a digital input—it has only two possible states: on or off, high or low, 1 or 0, and so on. Digital information (what your computer or the Arduino processes) is a series of binary (or digital) data. Each bit has only has one of two values.

The world around you, however, rarely expresses information in only two ways. Take a look out the window. What do you see? If it's daytime, you probably see sunlight, trees moving in the breeze, and maybe cars passing or people walking around. All these things that you perceive cannot readily be classified as binary data. Sunlight is not on or off; its brightness varies over the course of a day. Similarly, wind does not just have two states; it gusts at different speeds all the time.

Comparing Analog and Digital Signals

The graphs in Figure 3-1 show how analog and digital signals compare to each other. On the left is a square wave that varies between only two values: 0 and 5 volts. Just like with the button that you used in the preceding chapter, this signal is only a "logic high" or "logic low" value. On the right is part of a cosine wave. Although its bounds are still 0 and 5 volts, the signal takes on an infinite number of values between those two voltages.

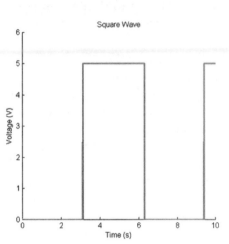
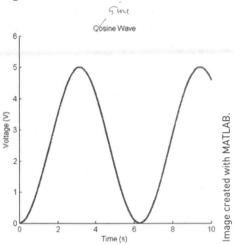

Figure 3-1: Analog and digital signals

Analog signals are those that cannot be discretely classified; they vary within a range, theoretically taking on an infinite number of possible values within that range. Think about sunlight as an example of an analog input you may want to measure. Naturally, there is a reasonable range over which you might measure sunlight. Often measured in lux, or luminous flux per unit area, you can reasonably expect to measure values between 0 lux (for pitch black) and 130,000 lux in direct sunlight. If your measuring device were infinitely accurate, you could measure an infinite number of values between those two. An indoor setting might be 400 lux. If it were slightly brighter, it could be 401 lux, then 401.1 lux, then 401.11 lux, and so on. A computer system could never feasibly measure an infinite number of decimal places for an analog value because memory and computer power must be finite values. If that's the case, how can you interface your Arduino with the "real world?" The answer is analog-to-digital converters (ADC), which can convert analog values into digital representations with a finite amount of precision and speed.

Converting an Analog Signal to a Digital One

Suppose that you want to measure the brightness of your room. Presumably, a good light sensor could produce a varying output voltage that changes with the brightness of the room. When it is pitch black, the device would output 0V, and when it's completely saturated by light, it would output 5V, with values in between corresponding to the varying amount of light. That's all well and good, but how do you go about reading those values with an Arduino to figure out how bright the room is? You can use the Arduino's analog-to-digital converter (ADC) pins to convert analog voltage values into number representations that you can work with.

The accuracy of an ADC is determined by the resolution. In the case of the Arduino Uno, there is a 10-bit ADC for doing your analog conversions. "10-bit" means that the ADC can subdivide (or quantize) an analog signal into 2^{10} different values. If you do the math, you'll find that $2^{10} = 1024$; hence, the Arduino can assign a value from 0 to 1023 for any analog value that you give it. Although it is possible to change the reference voltage, you'll be using the default 5V reference for the analog work that you do in this book. The reference voltage determines the max voltage that you are expecting, and, therefore, the value that will be mapped to 1023. So, with a 5V reference voltage, putting 0V on an ADC pin returns a value of 0, 2.5V returns a value of 512 (half of 1023), and 5V returns a value of 1023. To better understand what's happening here, consider what a 3-bit ADC would do, as shown in Figure 3-2.

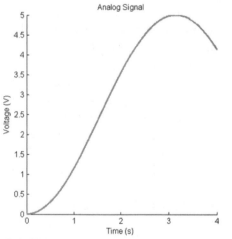
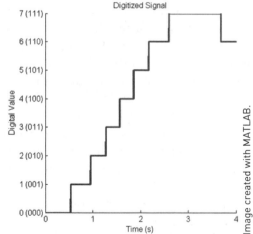

Figure 3-2: 3-bit analog quantization

NOTE If you want to learn more about using your own reference voltage or using a different internal voltage reference, check out the *analogReference()* page on the Arduino website: www.arduino.cc/en/Reference/AnalogReference.

A 3-bit ADC has 3 bits of resolution. Because $2^3=8$, there are 8 total logic levels, from 0 to 7. Therefore, any analog value that is passed to a 3-bit ADC will have to be assigned a value from 0 to 7. Looking at Figure 3-2, you can see that voltage levels are converted to discrete digital values that can be used by the microcontroller. The higher the resolution, the more steps that are available for representing each value. In the case of the Arduino Uno, there are 1024 steps rather than the 8 shown here.

Reading Analog Sensors with the Arduino: analogRead()

Now that you understand how to convert analog signals to digital values, you can integrate that knowledge into your programs and circuits. Different Arduinos have different numbers of analog input pins, but you read them all the same way, using the analogRead() command. First, you'll experiment with a potentiometer and a packaged analog sensor. Then, you'll learn how voltage dividers work, and how you can use them to make your own analog sensors from devices that vary their resistance in response to some kind of input.

Reading a Potentiometer

The easiest analog sensor to read is a simple potentiometer (a pot, for short). Odds are that you have tons of these around your home in your stereos, speakers, thermostats, cars, and elsewhere. Potentiometers are variable voltage dividers (discussed later in this chapter) that look like knobs. They come in lots of sizes and shapes, but they all have three pins. You connect one of the outer pins to ground, and the other to the 5V. Potentiometers are symmetrical, so it doesn't matter which side you connect the 5V and ground to. You connect the middle pin to analog input 0 on your Arduino. Figure 3-3 shows how to properly hook up your potentiometer to an Arduino.

As you turn the potentiometer, you vary the voltage that you are feeding into analog input 0 between 0V and 5V. If you want, you can confirm this with a multimeter in voltage measurement mode by hooking it up as shown Figure 3-4 and reading the display as you turn the knob. The red (positive) probe should be connected to the middle pin, and the black (negative) probe should be connected to whichever side is connected to ground. Note that your potentiometer and multimeter might look different than shown here.

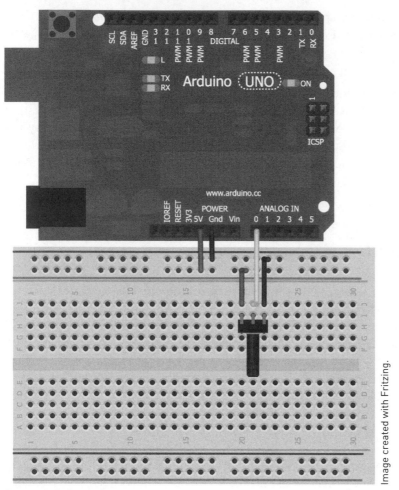

Figure 3-3: Potentiometer circuit

Before you use the potentiometer to control another piece of hardware, use the Arduino's serial communication functionality to print out the potentiometer's ADC value on your computer as it changes. Use the analogRead() function to read the value of the analog pin connected to the Arduino and the Serial .println() function to print it to the Arduino IDE serial monitor. Start by writing and uploading the program in Listing 3-1 to your Arduino.

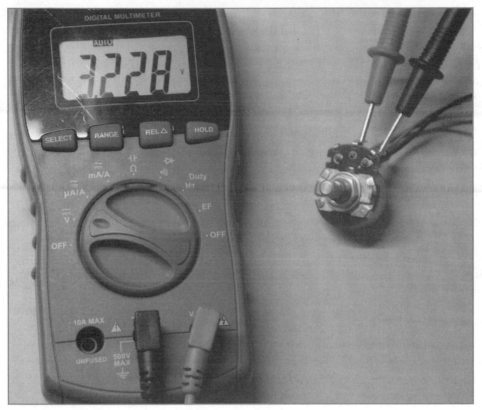

Figure 3-4: Multimeter measurement

Listing 3-1: Potentiometer Reading Sketch—pot.ino

```
//Potentiometer Reading Program

const int POT=0;   //Pot on analog pin 0
int val = 0;       //variable to hold the analog reading from the POT

void setup()
{
  Serial.begin(9600);
}

void loop()
{
  val = analogRead(POT);
  Serial.println(val);
  delay(500);
}
```

You'll investigate the functionality of the serial interface more in later chapters. For now, just be aware that the serial interface to the computer must be started in the setup. Serial.begin() takes one argument that specifies the communication speed, or baud rate. The *baud rate* specifies the number of bits being transferred per second. Faster baud rates enable you to transmit more data in less time, but can also introduce transmission errors in some communication systems. 9600 baud is a common value, and it's what you use throughout this book.

In each iteration through the loop, the val variable is set to the present value that the ADC reports from analog pin 0. The analogRead() command requires the number of the ADC pin to be passed to it. In this case, it's 0 because that's what you hooked the potentiometer up to. You can also pass A0, though the analogRead() function knows you must be passing it an analog pin number, so you can pass 0 as shorthand. After the value has been read (a number between 0 and 1023), Serial.println() prints that value over serial to the computer's serial terminal, followed by a "newline" that advances the cursor to the next line. The loop then delays for half a second (so that the numbers don't scroll by faster than you can read them), and the process repeats.

After loading this onto your Arduino, you'll notice that the TX LED on your Arduino is blinking every 500ms (at least it should be). This LED indicates that your Arduino is transmitting data via the USB connection to the serial terminal on your computer. You can use a variety of terminal programs to see what your Arduino is sending, but the Arduino IDE conveniently has one built right in! Click the circled button shown in Figure 3-5 to launch the serial monitor.

Figure 3-5: Serial monitor button

After launching the serial monitor, you should see a window with numbers streaming by. Turn the dial and you'll see the numbers go up and down to correspond with the position of the potentiometer. If you turn it all the way in one direction, the numbers should approach 0, and if you turn it all the way in the other direction, the numbers should approach 1023. It will look like the example shown in Figure 3-6.

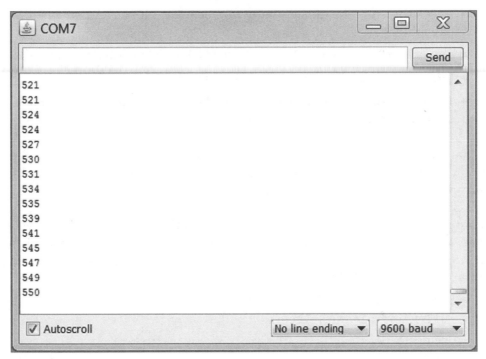

Figure 3-6: Incoming serial data

NOTE If you're getting funky characters, make sure that you have the baud rate set correctly. Because you set it to 9600 in the code, you need to set it to 9600 in this window as well.

You've now managed to successfully turn a dial and make some numbers change; pretty exciting, right? No? Well, this is the just the first step. Next, you learn about other types of analog sensors and how you can use the data from analog sensors to control other pieces of hardware. For now, you use the familiar LED, but in later chapters you use motors and other output devices to visualize your analog inputs.

Using Analog Sensors

Although potentiometers generate an analog voltage value on a pin, they aren't really sensors in the traditional sense. They "sense" your turning of the dial, but that gets boring pretty quickly. The good news is that all kinds of sensors generate analog output values corresponding to "real-world" action. Examples of such include the following:

- Accelerometers that detect tilting (many smartphones and tablets now have these)

- Magnetometers that detect magnetic fields (for making digital compasses)

- Infrared sensors that detect distance to an object

- Temperature sensors that can tell you about the operating environment of your project

Many of these sensors are designed to operate in a manner similar to the potentiometer you just experimented with: You provide them with a power (VCC) and ground (GND) connection, and they output an analog voltage between VCC and GND on the third pin that you hook up to your Arduino's ADC.

For this next experiment, you get to choose what kind of analog sensor you want to use. They all output a value between 0V and 5V when connected to an Arduino, so they will all work the same for your purposes. Here are some examples of sensors that you can use:

- **Sharp Infrared Proximity Sensor**

  www.exploringarduino.com/parts/IR-Distance-Sensor

  Connector: www.exploringarduino.com/parts/JST-Wire

  The Sharp infrared distance sensors are popular for measuring the distance between your project and other objects. As you move farther from the object you are aiming at, the voltage output decreases. Figure 5 in the datasheet from the part webpage linked above shows the relationship between voltage and measured distance.

- **TMP36 Temperature Sensor**

  www.exploringarduino.com/parts/TMP36

  The TMP36 temperature sensor easily correlates temperature readings in Celsius with voltage output levels. Since every 10mV corresponds to 1°C, you can easily create a linear correlation to convert from the voltage you measure back to the absolute temperature of the ambient environment: °C = [(Vout in mV) − 500]/10. The offset of −500 is for dealing with temperatures below 0°C. The graph in Figure 3-7 (extracted from the datasheet) shows this conversion.

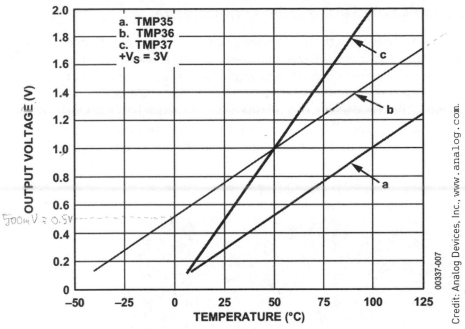

Figure 3-7: Voltage to Temperature Correlation

- **Triple Axis Analog Accelerometer**

  www.exploringarduino.com/parts/TriAxis-Analog-Accelerometer

  Triple axis accelerometers are great for detecting orientation. Analog accelerometers output an analog value corresponding to each axis of movement: X, Y, and Z (each on a different pin). Using some clever math (trigonometry and knowledge of gravity), you can use these voltage values to ascertain the position of your project in 3D space! Importantly, many of these sensors are 3.3V, so you will need to use the analogReference() command paired with the AREF pin to set a 3.3V voltage reference to enable you to get the full resolution out of the sensor.

- **Dual Axis Analog Gyroscope**

  www.exploringarduino.com/parts/DualAxis-Analog-Gyroscope

  Gyroscopes, unlike accelerometers, are not affected by gravity. Their analog output voltages fluctuate in accordance with angular acceleration around an axis. These prove particularly useful for detecting twisting motions. For an example of a gyroscope in action with an Arduino, check out my SudoGlove, a glove I designed that captures hand gestures to control hardware like music synthesizers and RC cars: www.sudoglove.com. Like accelerometers, be aware that many gyroscopes are 3.3V parts.

Now that you've chosen a sensor, it's time to put that sensor to use.

Working with Analog Sensors to Sense Temperature

This simple example uses the TMP36 temperature sensor mentioned in the previous section. However, feel free to use any analog sensor you can get your hands on. Experiment with one of the examples listed earlier, or find your own. (It should be 5V compliant if you are using the Arduino Uno.) The following steps are basically the same for any analog sensor you might want to use.

To begin, wire up your RGB LED as you did in the preceding chapter, and wire the temperature sensor up to analog input 0 as shown in the Figure 3-8.

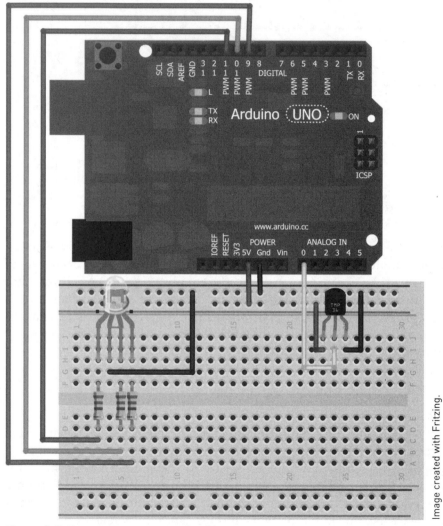

Image created with Fritzing.

Figure 3-8: Temperature sensor circuit

Using this circuit, you'll make a simple temperature alert system. The light will glow green when the temperature is within an acceptable range, will turn red when it gets too hot, and will turn blue when it gets too cold.

First things first, you need to ascertain what values you want to use as your cutoffs. Using the exact same sketch from Listing 3-1, use the serial monitor to figure out what analog values correspond to the temperature cutoffs you care about. My room is about 20°C, which corresponds to an analog reading of about 143. These numbers might differ for you, so launch the sketch from before, open the serial terminal, and take a look at the readings you are getting. You can confirm the values mathematically using the graph from Figure 3-7. In my case, a value of 143/1023 corresponds to a voltage input of about 700mV. Deriving from the datasheet, the following equation can be used to convert between the temperature (°C) and the voltage (mV):

$$\text{Temperature}(°C) \times 10 = \text{voltage (mV)} - 500$$

Plugging in the value of 700mV, you can confirm that it equates to a temperature of 20°C. Using this same logic (or by simply observing the serial window and picking a value), you can determine that 22°C is a digital value of 147 and 18°C is a digital value of 139. Those values will serve as the cutoffs that will change the color of the LED to indicate that it is too hot or too cold. Using the if statements, the digitalWrite function, and the analogRead function that you have now learned about, you can easily read the temperature, determine what range it falls in, and set the LED accordingly.

NOTE Before you copy the code in Listing 3-2, try to write this yourself and see whether you can make it work. After giving it a shot, compare it with the code here. How did you do?

Listing 3-2: Temperature Alert Sketch—tempalert.ino

```
//Temperature Alert!
const int BLED=9;            //Blue LED on pin 9
const int GLED=10;           //Green LED on pin 10
const int RLED=11;           //Red LED on pin 11
const int TEMP=0;            //Temp Sensor is on pin A0

const int LOWER_BOUND=139;   //Lower Threshold
const int UPPER_BOUND=147;   //Upper Threshold

int val = 0;                 //Variable to hold analog reading


void setup()
{
  pinMode (BLED, OUTPUT); //Set Blue LED as Output
  pinMode (GLED, OUTPUT); //Set Green LED as Output
```

```
    pinMode (RLED, OUTPUT); //Set Red LED as Output
}

void loop()
{
  val = analogRead(TEMP);

  if (val < LOWER_BOUND)
  {
    digitalWrite(RLED, LOW);
    digitalWrite(GLED, LOW);
    digitalWrite(BLED, HIGH);
  }
  else if (val > UPPER_BOUND)
  {
    digitalWrite(RLED, HIGH);
    digitalWrite(GLED, LOW);
    digitalWrite(BLED, LOW);
  }
  else
  {
    digitalWrite(RLED, LOW);
    digitalWrite(GLED, HIGH);
    digitalWrite(BLED, LOW);
  }
}
```

This code listing doesn't introduce any new concepts; rather, it combines what you have learned so far to make a system that uses both inputs and outputs to interact with the environment. To try it out, squeeze the temperature sensor with your fingers or exhale on it to heat it up. Blow on it to cool it down.

Using Variable Resistors to Make Your Own Analog Sensors

Thanks to physics, tons of devices change resistance as a result of physical action. For example, some conductive inks change resistance when squished or flexed (force sensors and flex sensors), some semiconductors change resistance when struck by light (photoresistors), and some polymers change resistance when heated or cooled (thermistors). These are just a few examples of components that you can take advantage of to build your own analog sensors. Because these sensors are changing resistance and not voltage, you need to create a voltage divider circuit so that you can measure their resistance change.

Using Resistive Voltage Dividers

A resistive voltage divider uses two resistors to output a voltage that is some fraction of the input voltage. The output voltage is a function directly related to the value of the two resistors. So, if one of the resistors is a variable resistor, you can monitor the change in voltage from the voltage divider that results from the varying resistance. The size of the other resistor can be used to set the sensitivity of the circuit, or you can use a potentiometer to make the sensitivity adjustable.

First, consider a fixed voltage divider and the equations associated with it, as shown in Figure 3-9. A0 in the Figure 3-9 refers to analog pin 0 on the Arduino.

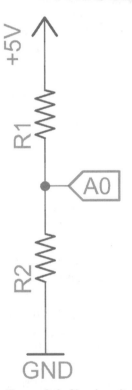

Figure 3-9: Simple voltage divider circuit

The equation for a voltage divider is as follows:

$$Vout = Vin(R2/(R1 + R2))$$

In this case, the voltage input is 5V, and the voltage output is what you'll be feeding into one of the analog pins of the Arduino. In the case where R1 and R2 are matched (both 10kΩ for example), the 5V is divided by 2 to make 2.5V at the analog input. Confirm this by plugging values into the equation:

$$Vout = 5V(10k/(10k + 10k)) = 5V \times .5 = 2.5V$$

Now, suppose one of those resistors is replaced with a variable resistor, such as a photoresistor. Photoresistors (see Figure 3-10) change resistance depending on the amount of light that hits them. In this case, I'll opt to use a 200kΩ photoresistor. When in complete darkness, its resistance is about 200kΩ; when saturated with light, the resistance drops nearly to zero. Whether you choose to replace R1 or R2 and what value you choose to make the fixed resistor will affect the scale and precision of the readings you receive. Try experimenting with different configurations and using the serial monitor to see how your values change. As an example, I will choose to replace R1 with the photoresistor, and I'll make R2 a 10kΩ resistor (see Figure 3-11). You can leave the RGB LED in place for now, though you'll only use one of the colors for this exercise.

Credit: element14, www.element14.com

Figure 3-10: Photoresistor

Load up your trusty serial printing sketch again (Listing 3-1) and try changing the lighting conditions over the photoresistor. Hold it up to a light and cup it with your hands. Odds are, you aren't going to be hitting the full range from 0 to 1023 because the variable resistor will never have a resistance of zero. Rather, you can probably figure out the maximum and minimum values that you are likely to receive. You can use the data from your photoresistor to make a more intelligent nightlight. The nightlight should get brighter as the room gets darker, and vice versa. Using your serial monitor sketch, pick the values that represent when your room is at full brightness or complete darkness. In my case, I found that a dark room has a value of around 200 and a completely bright room has a value around 900. These values will vary for you based upon your lighting conditions, the resistor value you are using, and the value of your photoresistor.

Using Analog Inputs to Control Analog Outputs

Recall that you can use the analogWrite() command to set the brightness of an LED. However, it is an 8-bit value; that is, it accepts values between 0 and 255 only, whereas the ADC is returning values as high as 1023. Conveniently, the Arduino programming language has two functions that are useful for mapping between two sets of values: the map() and constrain() functions. The map() function looks like this:

```
output = map(value, fromLow, fromHigh, toLow, toHigh)
```

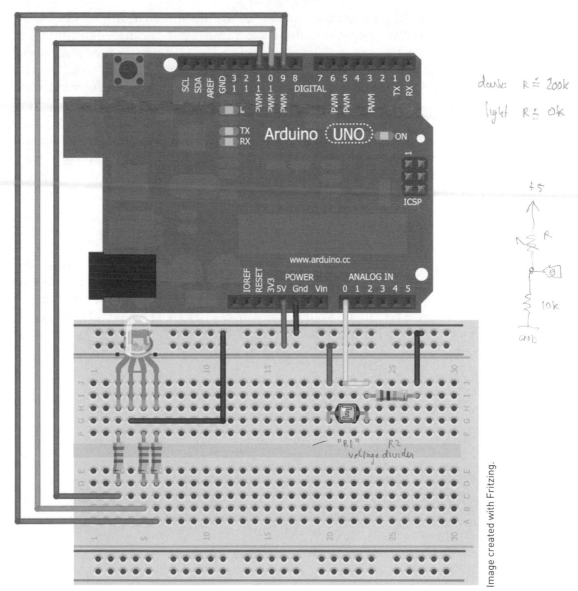

Figure 3-11: Photoresistor circuit

`value` is the information you are starting with. In your case, that's the most recent reading from the analog input. `fromLow` and `fromHigh` are the input boundaries. These are values you found to correspond to the minimum and maximum brightness in your room. In my case, they were `200` and `900`. `toLow` and `toHigh` are the values you want to map them to. Because `analogWrite()` expects value between `0` and `255`, you use those values. However, we want a darker room to map to a brighter LED. Therefore, when the input from the ADC is a low value, you want the output to the LED to be a high value, and vice versa.

Conveniently, the map function can handle this automatically; simply swap the high and low values so that the low value is 255 and the high value is 0. The map() function creates a linear mapping. For example, if your fromLow and fromHigh values are 200 and 900, respectively, and your toLow and toHigh values are 255 and 0, respectively, 550 maps to 127 because 550 is halfway between 200 and 900 and 127 is halfway between 255 and 0. Importantly, however, the map() function does not constrain these values. So, if the photoresistor does measure a value below 200, it is mapped to a value above 255 (because you are inverting the mapping). Obviously, you don't want that because you can't pass a value greater than 255 to the analogWrite() function. You can deal with this by using the constrain() function. The constrain() function looks like this:

```
output = constrain(value, min, max)
```

If you pass the output from the map function into the constrain function, you can set the min to 0 and the max to 255, ensuring that any numbers above or below those values are constrained to either 0 or 255. Finally, you can then use those values to command your LED! Now, take a look at what that final sketch will look like (see Listing 3-3).

Listing 3-3: Automatic Nightlight Sketch—nightlight.ino

```
//Automatic Nightlight

const int RLED=9;         //Red LED on pin 9 (PWM)
const int LIGHT=0;        //Lght Sensor on analog pin 0
const int MIN_LIGHT=200;  //Minimum expected light value
const int MAX_LIGHT=900;  //Maximum Expected Light value
int val = 0;              //variable to hold the analog reading

void setup()
{
  pinMode(RLED, OUTPUT); //Set LED pin as output
}

void loop()
{
  val = analogRead(LIGHT);                      //Read the light sensor
  val = map(val, MIN_LIGHT, MAX_LIGHT, 255, 0); //Map the light reading
  val = constrain(val, 0, 255);                 //Constrain light value
  analogWrite(RLED, val);                       //Control the LED
}
```

Note that this code reuses the val variable. You can alternatively use a different variable for each function call. In functions such as map() where val is both the input and the output, the previous value of val is used as the input, and its value is reset to the updated value when the function has completed.

Play around with your nightlight. Does it work as expected? Remember, you can adjust the sensitivity by changing the minimum and maximum bounds of the mapping function or changing the fixed resistor value. Use the serial monitor to observe the differences with different settings until you find one that works the best. Can you combine this sketch with the color-selection nightlight that you designed in the preceding chapter? Try adding a button to switch between colors, and use the photoresistor to adjust the brightness of each color.

Summary

In this chapter you learned about the following:

- The differences between analog and digital signals
- How to convert analog signals to digital signals
- How to read an analog signal from a potentiometer
- How to display data using the serial monitor
- How to interface with packaged analog sensors
- How to create your own analog sensors
- How to map and constrain analog readings to drive analog outputs

Controlling Your Environment

In This Part

Using Transistors and Driving Motors

Parts You'll Need for This Chapter:

Arduino Uno

USB cable

9V battery

9V battery clip

5V L4940V5 linear regulator

22uF electrolytic capacitor

.1uF electrolytic capacitor

1uF ceramic capacitor

Blue LEDs (×4)

1kΩ resistors (×4)

PN2222 NPN BJT transistor

Jumper wires

Sharp GP2Y0A41SK0F IR distance sensor with cable

Hot glue or tape

Standard servo motor

DC motor

Breadboard

Potentiometer

SN754410 H-Bridge IC

CODE AND DIGITAL CONTENT FOR THIS CHAPTER

Code downloads, videos, and other digital content for this chapter can be found at www.exploringarduino.com/content/ch4.

The wiley.com code downloads for this chapter are found at www.wiley.com/go/exploringarduino on the Download Code tab. The code is in the chapter 04 download and individually named according to the names throughout the chapter.

You're now a master of *observing* information from the world around you. But how can you *control* that world? Blinking LEDs and automatically adjusting nightlights are a good start, but you can do so much more. Using assorted types of motors and actuators, and with the help of transistors, you can use your Arduino to generate physical action in the real world. By pairing motors with your Arduino, you can drive robots, build mechanical arms, add an additional degree of freedom to distance sensors, and much more.

In this chapter, you learn how to control inductive loads like direct current (DC) motors, how to use transistors to switch high-current devices, and how to interface with precision actuators (namely, servo motors). At the end of this chapter, you build a sweeping distance sensor capable of identifying the location of nearby obstacles. This sensor is perfect for mounting on a self-driving robotic car, for example. Having completed this chapter, you'll have all the skills you need to build a machine that you can really interact with!

NOTE If you want to learn all about motors and transistors, check out this video: www.jeremyblum.com/2011/01/31/arduino-tutorial-5-motors-and-transistors/. You can also find this video on the Wiley website shown at the beginning of this chapter.

WARNING In this chapter, you use a 9V battery so that you can power motors that require more power than what the Arduino can provide. These voltages are still not high enough to pose a danger to you, but if hooked up improperly, these batteries can damage your electronics. As you make your way through the exercises in this chapter, follow the diagrams and instructions carefully. Avoid short circuits (connecting power directly to ground), and while you'll be sharing the ground line between power supplies, don't try to connect two separate voltage sources to each other. For example, don't try to hook both the 9V supply and the Arduino's 5V supply into the same supply row on the breadboard.

Driving DC Motors

DC motors, which you can find in numerous devices around your home, rotate continuously when a DC voltage is applied across them. Such motors are commonly found as the driving motors in radio control (RC) cars, and as the motors that make the discs spin in your DVD player. DC motors are great because they come in a huge array of sizes and are generally very cheap. By adjusting the voltage you apply to them, you can change their rotation speed. By reversing the direction of the voltage applied to them, you can change their direction of rotation as well. This is generally done using an H bridge, which you learn about later in this chapter.

Brushed DC motors, such as the one you are using for this chapter, employ stationary magnets and a spinning coil. Electricity is transferred to the coil using "brushes," hence the reason they are called *brushed* DC motors. Unlike *brushless* DC motors (such as stepper motors), brushed DC motors are cheap and have easier speed control. However, brushed DC motors do not last as long because the brushes can wear out over time. These motors work through an inductive force. When current passes through the spinning coil, it generates a magnetic field that is either attracted to or repelled by the stationary magnets depending on the polarity. By using the brushes to swap the polarity each half-rotation, you can generate angular momentum. The exact same configuration can be used to create a generator if you manually turn the armature. This will generate a fluctuating magnetic field that will, in turn, generate current. This is how hydroelectric generators work—falling water turns the shaft, and a current is produced. This capability to create current in the opposite direction is why you will use a diode later in this chapter to ensure that the motor cannot send current back into your circuit when it is forcibly turned.

Handling High-Current Inductive Loads

DC motors generally require more current than the Arduino's built-in power supply can provide, and they can create harmful voltage spikes due to their inductive nature. To address this issue, you first learn how to effectively isolate a DC motor from your Arduino, and then how to power it using a secondary supply. A transistor will allow the Arduino to switch the motor on and off safely, as well as to control the speed using the pulse-width modulation (PWM) techniques that you learned about in Chapter 3, "Reading Analog Sensors." Reference the schematic shown in Figure 4-1 as you learn about the various components that go into connecting a DC motor to an Arduino with a secondary power supply. Make sure you understand all of these concepts before you actually start wiring.

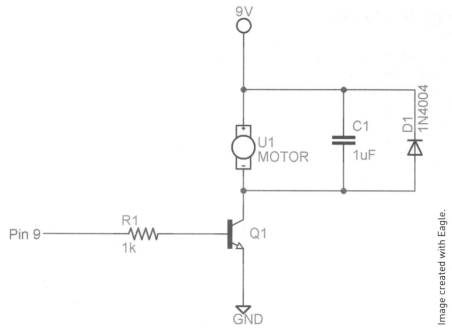

Figure 4-1: DC motor control schematic

Before you hook up your DC motor, it's important to understand what all these components are doing:

- Q1 is an NPN bipolar-junction transistor (BJT) used for switching the separate 9V supply to the motor. There are two types of BJTs, NPN and PNP, which refer to the different semiconductor "doping" techniques used to create the transistor. This book will focus on using NPN BJTs. You can simplistically think of an NPN transistor as a voltage-controlled switch that allows you to inhibit or allow current flow.

- A 1kΩ resistor is used to separate the transistor's base pin from the control pin of the Arduino.

- U1 is the DC motor.

- C1 is for filtering noise caused by the motor.

- D1 is a diode used to protect the power supply from reverse voltage caused by the motor acting like an inductor.

Using Transistors as Switches

Transistors can do an exceptional number of tasks, from making amplifiers to making up the CPU inside your computer and smartphone. You can use a single transistor to make a simple electrically controlled switch. Every BJT has three pins (see Figure 4-2): the emitter (E), the collector (C), and the base (B).

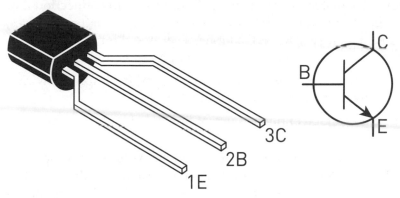

Figure 4-2: An NPN BJT

Current flows in through the collector and out of the emitter. By modulating the base pin, you can control whether current is permitted to flow. When a sufficiently high voltage is applied to the base, current is allowed to flow through the transistor, and the motor spins as a result. The 5V generated by the Arduino I/O pins more than suffices to turn on the transistor. By taking advantage of PWM, you can control the speed of the motor by rapidly turning the transistor on and off. Because the motor can maintain momentum, the duty of the cycle of the PWM signal determines the motor's speed. The transistor is essentially connecting and disconnecting one terminal of the motor from the ground and determining when a complete circuit can be made with the battery.

Using Protection Diodes

It is important to consider issues caused by DC motors acting like inductors. (*Inductors* are electrical devices that store energy in their magnetic fields and resist changes in current.) As the DC motor spins, energy is built up and stored in the inductance of the motor coils. If power is instantaneously removed from the motor, the energy is dissipated in the form of an inverted voltage spike, which could prove harmful to the power supply. That's where protection diodes come in. By putting the diode across the motor, you ensure that the current generated by the motor flows through the diode and that the reverse voltage cannot exceed the forward voltage of the diode (because diodes allow current to flow in one direction only). This will also absorb any current generated by you forcibly turning the motor.

Using a Secondary Power Source

Note, as well, from the circuit diagram shown in Figure 4-1 that the power supply to the motor is 9V, instead of the usual 5V from the USB connection that you've been using. For the purposes of this experiment, a 9V battery suffices, but you could also use an AC-DC wall adapter. The reason for using a power source separate from the Arduino's built-in 5V supply is twofold:

1. By using a separate supply, you reduce the chances that improper wiring of a higher-power circuit could harm your Arduino.

2. You can take advantage of higher current limits and higher voltages.

Some DC motors can consume more current than the Arduino 5V supply can source. Further, many motors are rated at voltages higher than 5V. Although they might spin at 5V, you can reach their max speed at only 9V or 12V (depending on the motor specifications).

Note that you must connect the ground of both your secondary power supply and the Arduino ground. This connection ensures a common reference point between the voltage levels in the two parts of the circuit.

Wiring the Motor

Now that you understand the intricacies of controlling a brushed DC motor, it's time to get it wired up on your breadboard. Try to wire it by only referencing the previous schematic (shown in Figure 4-1). After you've tried to assemble the circuit using only the schematic, reference the graphical version shown in Figure 4-3 to confirm that you wired it correctly.

It's important to get good at reading electrical schematics without having to look at a graphical layout. Did you wire it correctly? Remember to check for the following as you wire up the circuit:

1. Make sure that you've connected the ground from your 9V battery to the ground from your Arduino. You might want to use the horizontal bus on the breadboard to accomplish this, as shown in Figure 4-3.

2. Make sure that the 9V supply is not connected to the 5V supply. In fact, you don't even need to wire the 5V supply to the breadboard.

3. Make sure that the orientation of your transistor is correct. If you aren't using the same NPN BJT listed in the parts list for this chapter, reference the datasheet to ensure that the emitter, base, and collector are connected to the same pins. If they are not, adjust your wiring.

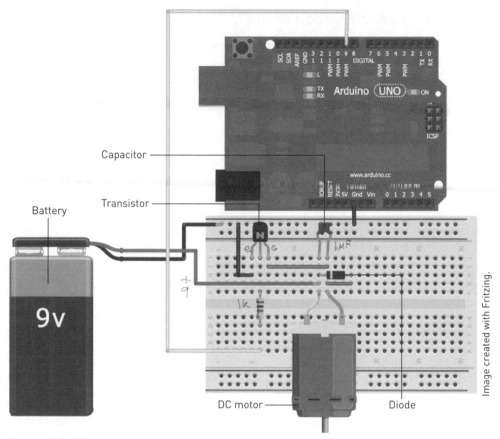

Figure 4-3: DC Motor wiring

4. Make sure that the orientation of the diode is correct. Current flows from the side with no stripe to the side with the stripe. The stripe on the physical device matches the line in the schematic symbol. You use a ceramic capacitor for this exercise, so the polarity doesn't matter.

Next up, it's time to get this motor spinning. You might want to attach a piece of tape or a wheel to the end of the motor so that you can more easily see the speed at which it is spinning. Before you write the program, you can confirm that the circuit is working correctly by providing power to the Arduino over the USB connection, plugging in the 9V battery, and connecting the transistor's base pin (after the resistor) directly to 5V from the Arduino. This simulates a logic high command and should make the motor spin. Connecting that same wire to ground will ensure that it does not spin. If this doesn't work, check your wiring before moving on to the next step: programming.

Controlling Motor Speed with PWM

First up, you can use a program very similar to the one you used to adjust LED brightness of your nightlight in Chapter 3 to adjust the speed of your motor. By sending varying duty-cycle signals to the transistor, the current flow through the motor rapidly starts and stops resulting in a change in velocity. Try out the program in Listing 4-1 to repeatedly ramp the motor speed up and down.

Listing 4-1: Automatic Speed Control—motor.ino

```
//Simple Motor Speed Control Program

const int MOTOR=9;      //Motor on Digital Pin 9
                        // Ie, pin 9 is connected to base of transistor,
void setup()            // which turns on/turns off the motor
{
    pinMode (MOTOR, OUTPUT);
}

void loop()
{
    for (int i=0; i<256; i++)
    {
        analogWrite(MOTOR, i);      # pwm output w. i varying the duty cycle
        delay(10);
    }
    delay(2000);
    for (int i=255; i>=0; i--)
    {
        analogWrite(MOTOR, i);
        delay(10);
    }
    delay(2000);
}
```

If everything is hooked up correctly, this code should slowly ramp the motor speed up, then back down again in a loop. Using these techniques, you could easily make a simple roving robot.

Next up, you can combine your new knowledge of DC motors with your knowledge of analog sensors. Using a potentiometer, you can manually adjust the motor speed. To begin, add a potentiometer to analog pin 0, as shown in Figure 4-4. Note that you must connect the 5V pin from the Arduino to the power rail on the breadboard if you want to connect the potentiometer to that row on the board.

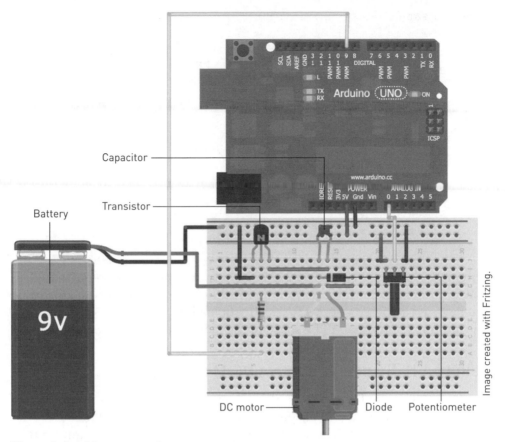

Figure 4-4: Adding a potentiometer

You can now modify the program to control the motor speed based on the present setting of the potentiometer. With the potentiometer at zero, the motor stops; with the potentiometer rotated fully, the motor runs at full speed. Recall that the Arduino is running quite fast; it's actually running through the loop several thousand times every second! Therefore, you can simply check the potentiometer speed each time through the loop and adjust the motor speed after each check. It checks often enough that motor speed adjusts in real time with the potentiometer. The code in Listing 4-2 does the trick. Create a new sketch (or update your previous sketch to match this code) and upload it to your Arduino from the integrated development environment (IDE).

Listing 4-2: Adjustable Speed Control—motor_pot.ino

```
//Motor Speed Control with a Pot

const int MOTOR=9;  //Motor on Digital Pin 9
```

```
const int POT=0;   //POT on Analog Pin 0

int val = 0;

void setup()
{
    pinMode (MOTOR, OUTPUT);
}

void loop()
{
    val = analogRead(POT);
    val = map(val, 0, 1023, 0, 255);
    analogWrite(MOTOR, val);
}
```

A lot of this code should look familiar from your previous experience dealing with analog sensors. Note that the constrain function is not required when using a potentiometer, because you can use the entire input range, and the value will never go below 0 or above 1023. After uploading the code to your Arduino, adjust the pot and observe the speed of the motor changing accordingly.

Using an H-Bridge to Control DC Motor Direction

So, you can change DC motor speed. This is great for making wheels on an Arduino-controlled robot… as long as you only want it to drive forward. Any useful DC motor needs to be able to spin in two directions. To accomplish this, you can use a handy device called an *H-bridge*. The operation of an H-bridge can best be explained with a diagram (see Figure 4-5).

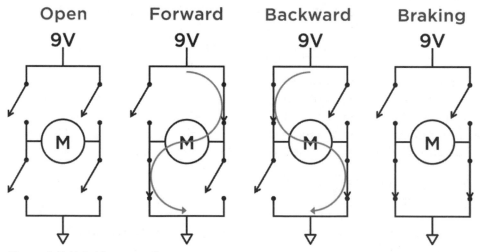

Figure 4-5: H-bridge operation

Can you figure out why it's called an H-bridge? Notice that the motor in combination with the four switches forms an uppercase *H*. Although the diagram shows them as switches, the switching components are actually transistors, similar to the ones you used in the previous exercise. Some additional circuitry, including protection diodes, is also built in to the H-bridge integrated circuit.

The H-bridge has four main states of operation: open, braking, forward, and backward. In the open state, all the switches are open and the motor won't spin. In the forward state, two diagonally opposing switches are engaged, causing current to flow from 9V, through the motor, and down to ground. When the opposing switches are flipped, current then runs through the motor in the opposite direction, causing it to spin in the opposite direction. If the H-bridge is put in the braking state, all residual motion caused by momentum is ceased, and the motor stops.

CREATING SHORT CIRCUITS WITH H-BRIDGES

Be aware of one extremely important consideration when using H-bridges. What would happen if both switches on the left or both switches on the right were opened? It would cause a direct short between 9V and ground. If you've ever shorted a 9V battery before, you know that this is not something you want to do. A shorted battery heats up very quickly, and, in rare circumstances, could burst or leak. Furthermore, a short could destroy the H-bridge or other parts of the circuit. An H-bridge is a rare scenario where you could potentially destroy a piece of hardware by programming something wrong. For this experiment, you use SN754410 Quadruple Half-H Driver. This chip has a built-in thermal shutdown that should kick in before a short circuit destroys anything, but it's still a good idea to be cautious.

To ensure that you don't blow anything up, *always* disable the chip before flipping the states of any of the switches. This ensures that a short cannot be created even when you quickly switch between motor directions. You'll use three control pins: one for controlling the top two gates, one for controlling the bottom two gates, and one for enabling the circuit.

Building an H-bridge Circuit

With the preceding considerations in mind, it's time to build the circuit. The H-bridge chip you use is the SN754410 Quadruple Half-H driver. Two Half-H drivers are combined into one Full-H driver, such as the one shown in Figure 4-5. For this exercise, you just use two of the four Half-H drivers to drive one DC motor. If you want to make an RC car, for example, you could use this chip to control two DC motors (one for the left wheels and one for the right wheels). Before you actually get it wired up, take a look at the pin-out and logic table from the part's datasheet (see Figure 4-6).

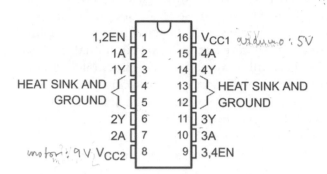

FUNCTION TABLE
(each driver)

INPUTS[†]		OUTPUT
A	EN	Y
H	H	H
L	H	L
X	L	Z

H = high-level, L = low-level
X = irrelevant
Z = high-impedance (off)
[†] In the thermal shutdown mode, the output is in a high-impedance state regardless of the input levels.

Image used with permission courtesy of Texas Instruments.

Figure 4-6: H-bridge pin-out and logic table

Pin numbering on integrated circuits (ICs) always starts at the top-left pin and goes around the part counter-clockwise. Chips will always have some kind of indicator to show which pin is Pin 1, so that you don't plug the IC in upside-down. On through-hole parts (which is what you will use exclusively in this chapter), a half circle on one end of the chip indicates the top of the chip (where Pin 1 is located). Some chips may have a small circle marked next to pin one on the plastic casing in addition to, or instead of, the half-circle.

Let's run through the pins and how you'll be using them:

- **GND (Pins 4, 5, 12, & 13):** The four pins in the middle connect to a shared ground between your 9V and 5V supplies.

- **V_{CC2} (Pin 8):** V_{CC2} supplies the motor current, so you connect it to 9V.

- **V_{CC1} (Pin 16):** V_{CC1} powers the chip's logic, so you connect it to 5V.

- **1Y and 2Y (Pins 3 and 6):** These are the outputs from the left driver. The motor wires connect to these pins.

- **1A and 2A (Pins 2 and 7):** The states of the switches on the left are controlled by these pins, so they are connected to I/O pins on the Arduino for toggling.

- **1,2EN (Pin 1):** This pin is used to enable or disable the left driver. It is connected to a PWM pin on the Arduino, so that speed can be controlled dynamically.

- **3Y and 4Y (Pins 11 and 14):** These are the outputs from the right driver. Because you are using the left driver only, you can leave these disconnected.

- **3A and 4A (Pins 10 and 15):** The states of the switches on the right are controlled by these pins, but you are using only the left driver in this example, so you can leave them disconnected.

- **3,4EN (Pin 9):** This pin is used to enable or disable the right driver. Because you will not be using the right driver, you can disable it by connecting this pin directly to GND.

For reference, confirm your wiring with Figure 4-7. Keep the potentiometer wired as it was before.

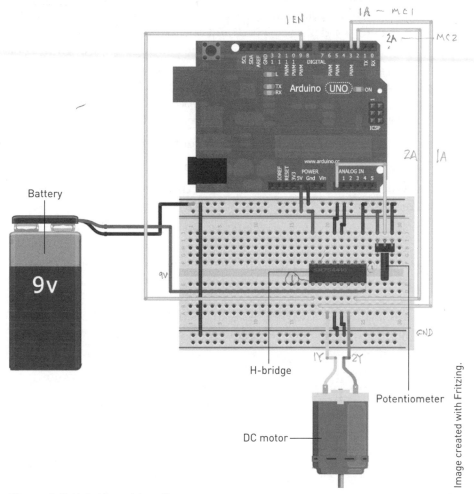

Figure 4-7: H-bridge wiring diagram

You can confirm that the circuit is working before you program it by hooking up the enable pin to 5V, hooking up one of the *A* pins to ground, and the other *A* pin to 5V. You can reverse direction by swapping what the *A* pins are connected to.

WARNING You should disconnect the 9V battery while swapping the *A* pins to ensure that you can't possibly cause an accidental short circuit within the H-bridge.

Operating an H-bridge Circuit

Next up, you write a program to control the motor's direction and speed using the potentiometer and the H-bridge. Setting the potentiometer in a middle range stops the motor, setting the potentiometer in a range above the middle increases the speed forward, and setting the potentiometer in a range below the middle increases the speed backward. This is another perfect opportunity to employ functions in your Arduino program. You can write a function to stop the motor, one to cause it spin forward at a set speed, and one to cause it to spin backward at a set speed. Ensure that you correctly disable the H-bridge at the beginning of the function before changing the motor mode; doing so reduces the probability that you will make a mistake and accidentally short out the H-bridge.

Following the logic diagram from Figure 4-6, you can quickly figure out how you need to control the pins to achieve the desired results:

- To stop current flow through the device, set the enable pin low.

- To set the switches for rotation in one direction, set one high, the other low.

- To set switches for rotation in the opposite direction, swap which is high and which is low.

- To cause the motor to stop immediately, set both switches low.

NOTE Always disable the current flow before changing the state of the switches to ensure that a momentary short cannot be created as the switches flip.

First, you should devise the functions that safely execute the previously described motions. Create a new Arduino sketch and start by writing your new functions:

```
//Motor goes forward at given rate (from 0-255)
void forward (int rate)
{
    digitalWrite(EN, LOW);
    digitalWrite(MC1, HIGH);
    digitalWrite(MC2, LOW);
    analogWrite(EN, rate);
}

//Motor goes backward at given rate (from 0-255)
void reverse (int rate)
{
    digitalWrite(EN, LOW);
    digitalWrite(MC1, LOW);
    digitalWrite(MC2, HIGH);
    analogWrite(EN, rate);
```

```
}

//Stops motor
void brake ()
{
    digitalWrite(EN, LOW);
    digitalWrite(MC1, LOW);
    digitalWrite(MC2, LOW);
    digitalWrite(EN, HIGH);
}
```

Note that at the beginning of each function the *EN* pin is always set low, and then the *MC1* and *MC2* pins (Motor Control pins) are adjusted. When that is done, the current flow can be reenabled. To vary the speed, just use the same technique you did before. By using PWM, you can change the duty with which the *EN* pin is toggled, thus controlling the speed. The *rate* variable must be between 0 and 255. The main loop takes care of making the right *rate* from the input potentiometer data.

Next, consider the main program loop:

```
void loop()
{
    val = analogRead(POT);

    //go forward
    if (val > 562)
    {
        velocity = map(val, 563, 1023, 0, 255);
        forward(velocity);
    }

    //go backward
    else if (val < 462)
    {
        velocity = map(val, 461, 0, 0, 255);
        reverse(velocity);
    }

    //brake
    else
    {
        brake();
    }
}
```

In the main loop, the potentiometer value is read, and the appropriate function can be called based on the potentiometer value. Recall that analog inputs are converted to digital values between 0 and 1023. Refer to Figure 4-8 to better understand the control scheme and compare that with the preceding loop code.

| Motor Action | Increasing Reverse Speed | Stopped | Increasing Forward Speed |

Digital Value   0   462 512 562   1023
                                  512-50   512 + 50

Figure 4-8: Motor control plan.

When the potentiometer is within the 100 units surrounding the midpoint, the `brake` function is called. As the potentiometer value increases from `562` to `1023`, the speed forward increases. Similarly, the speed increases in the reverse direction between potentiometer values of `462` and `0`. The `map` function should look familiar to you from the previous chapter. Here, when determining the reverse speed, note the order of the variables: `461` is mapped to `0`, and `0` is mapped to `255`; the `map` function can invert the mapping when the variables are passed in descending order. Putting the loop together with the functions, and the `setup`, you get a completed program that looks like the one shown in Listing 4-3. Ensure that your program matches the one here and load it onto your Arduino.

Listing 4-3: H-Bridge Potentiometer Motor Control—hbridge.ino

```
//Hbridge Motor Control
const int EN=9;    //Half Bridge 1 Enable
const int MC1=3;   //Motor Control 1
const int MC2=2;   //Motor Control 2
const int POT=0;   //POT on Analog Pin 0

int val = 0;       //for storing the reading from the POT
int velocity = 0; //For storing the desired velocity (from 0-255)

void setup()
{
    pinMode(EN, OUTPUT);
    pinMode(MC1, OUTPUT);
    pinMode(MC2, OUTPUT);
    brake(); //Initialize with motor stopped
}

void loop()
{
    val = analogRead(POT);

    //go forward
    if (val > 562)
    {
```

```
        velocity = map(val, 563, 1023, 0, 255);
        forward(velocity);
    }

    //go backward
    else if (val < 462)
    {
        velocity = map(val, 461, 0, 0, 255);
        reverse(velocity);
    }

    //brake
    else
    {
        brake();
    }
}

//Motor goes forward at given rate (from 0-255)
void forward (int rate)
{
    digitalWrite(EN, LOW);
    digitalWrite(MC1, HIGH);
    digitalWrite(MC2, LOW);
    analogWrite(EN, rate);
}

//Motor goes backward at given rate (from 0-255)
void reverse (int rate)
{
    digitalWrite(EN, LOW);
    digitalWrite(MC1, LOW);
    digitalWrite(MC2, HIGH);
    analogWrite(EN, rate);
}

//Stops motor
void brake ()
{
    digitalWrite(EN, LOW);
    digitalWrite(MC1, LOW);
    digitalWrite(MC2, LOW);
    digitalWrite(EN, HIGH);
}
```

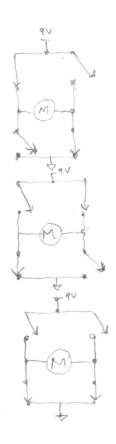

Does everything work as expected? If not, make sure that you wired up your circuit correctly. As an additional challenge, grab a second DC motor and hook it up to the other half of the H-bridge chip. You should be able to drive two motors simultaneously with minimal effort.

Driving Servo Motors

DC motors serve as excellent drive motors, but they are not as ideal for precision work because no feedback occurs. In other words, without using an external encoder of some kind, you will never know the absolute position of a DC motor. Servo motors, or servos, in contrast, are unique in that you command them to rotate to a particular angular position and they stay there until you tell them to move to a new position. This is important for when you need to move your system to a known position. Examples include actuating door locks, moving armatures to specific rotations, and precisely controlling the opening of an aperture. In this section, you learn about servo motors and how to control them from your Arduino.

Understanding the Difference Between Continuous Rotation and Standard Servos

You can buy both standard and continuous rotation servos. Unmodified servos always have a fixed range (usually from 0 to 180 degrees) because there is a potentiometer in line with the drive shaft, which is used for reporting the present position. Servo control is achieved by sending a pulse of a particular length. The length of the pulse, in the case of a standard rotation servo, determines the absolute position that the servo will rotate to. If you remove the potentiometer, however, the servo is free to rotate continuously, and the pulse length sets the speed of the motor instead.

In this book, you use standard servos that rotate to an absolute position. You can experiment with continuous rotation servos either by opening a standard servo and carefully removing the potentiometer, or by buying premodified servos configured for continuous rotation.

Understanding Servo Control

Unlike their DC motor counterparts, servo motors have three pins: power (usually red), ground (usually brown or black), and signal (usually white or orange). These wires are color-coded, typically in the same order, and generally look like the ones shown in Figure 4-9. Some manufactures may use non-standard ordering, so always be sure to check the datasheet to ensure you are wiring the servo correctly.

The coloring might vary slightly between servos, but the color schemes listed previously are the most common. (Check the servo's documentation if you're unsure.) Like DC motors, servos can draw quite a bit of a current (usually more than the Arduino can supply). Although you can sometimes run one or two servos directly from the Arduino's 5V supply, you learn here how to use a separate power supply for the servos so that you have the option to add more if you need to.

WHITE/ORANGE - CONTROL

RED - POWER

BLACK/BROWN - GROUND

Figure 4-9: Servo motors

Servos have a dedicated control pin, unlike DC motors, that instructs them what position to turn to. The power and ground lines of a servo should always be connected to a steady power source.

Servos are controlled using adjustable pulse widths on the signal line. For a standard servo, sending a 1ms 5V pulse turns the motor to 0 degrees, and sending a 2ms 5V pulse turns the motor to 180 degrees, with pulse lengths in the middle scaling linearly. A 1.5ms pulse, for example, turns the motor to 90 degrees. Once a pulse has been sent, the servo turns to that position and stays there until another pulse instruction is received. However, if you want a servo to "hold" its position (resist being pushed on and try to maintain the exact position), you just resend the command once every 20ms. The Arduino servo commands that you will later employ take care of this for you. To better understand how servo control works, study the timing diagram shown in Figure 4-10.

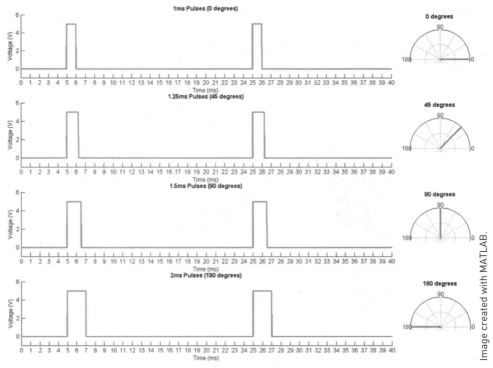

Figure 4-10: Servo motor timing diagram

Note that in each of the examples in Figure 4-10 the pulse is sent every 20ms. As the pulse length increases from 1ms to 2ms, the angle of rotation of the motor (shown to the right of the pulse graph) increases from 0 to 180 degrees.

As mentioned before, servos can draw more current than your Arduino may be able to provide. However, most servos are designed to run at 5V, not 9V or 12V like a DC motor. Even though the voltage is the same as that of an Arduino, you want to use a separate power source that can supply more current.

To do this, you learn here how to use a 9V battery and a linear regulator to generate a 5V supply from your 9V battery. A linear regulator is an extremely simple device that generally has three pins: input voltage, output voltage, and ground. The ground pin is connected to both the ground of the input supply and to the ground of the output. In the case of linear-voltage regulators, the input voltage always must be higher than the output voltage, and the output voltage is set at a fixed value depending on the regulator you use.

The voltage drop between the input and the output is burned off as heat, and the regulator takes care of ensuring that the output always remains the same, even as the voltage of the input drops (in the case of a battery discharging over time). For these experiments, you use an L4940V5 5V voltage regulator. It's capable of supplying up to 1.5 amps at 5V. Figure 4-11 shows a schematic of how to hook up the regulator.

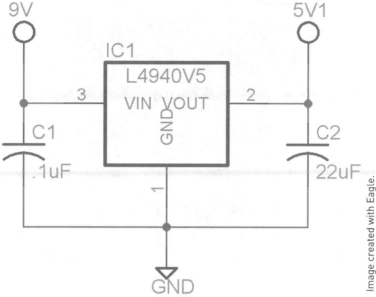

Figure 4-11: 5V Linear regulator schematic

Note the capacitors on each side of the regulator. These are called *decoupling capacitors*; they are used to smooth out the voltage signal from each supply voltage by charging and discharging to oppose ripples in the voltage. Most linear regulator datasheets include a suggested circuit that includes ideal values and types for these capacitors based on your use case scenario. Also keep in mind that the 5V rail created by this regulator should be kept separate from the 5V power rail of the Arduino. Their grounds, however, should be tied together.

Using all this information, it's time to wire up a servo. Referencing Figure 4-12, wire the servo, the 5V regulator, and the potentiometer. Leave the potentiometer connected to analog pin 0, connect the servo control pin to pin 9, and ensure that the 5V regulator supplies the servo's power.

While wiring, keep in mind a few important things. First, ensure that you have the orientation of the regulator correct. With the metal tab on the side farthest from you, connect the battery to the leftmost pin, the ground to the center pin, and the servo's power line to the right pin. Second, if using polarized electrolytic capacitors (as in Figure 4-12), make sure to put them in the correct direction. The stripe indicates the negative terminal and should be connected to the common ground. Make sure that the pins don't touch; otherwise, it could cause a short. After you're all wired up, move on to the next section to learn how to program the servo controller.

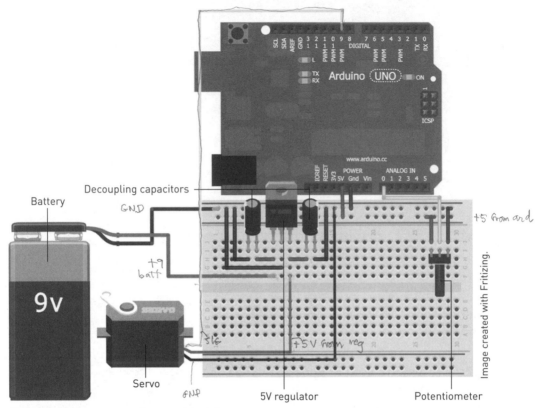

Figure 4-12: Servo experiment wiring diagram

UNDERSTANDING LINEAR REGULATORS AND THE LIMITS OF ARDUINO POWER SUPPLIES

Why is it necessary to use an external power supply when certain items require more current? There are few reasons. The I/O pins cannot supply more than 40 milliamps (mA) each. Because a DC or servo motor can consume hundreds of milliamps, the I/O pins are not capable of driving them directly. Even if they were, you wouldn't want to because of the damage that can be caused by inductive voltage spikes.

It makes sense that you need to use an external supply with a DC motor because you need the higher voltage, but why does a servo need an external supply if it is at the same voltage as the Arduino? The Arduino generates the 5V used for the logic either directly from the USB or by using a built-in linear regulator with the DC barrel jack as the supply voltage. When you use USB, a maximum of 500mA is available to the Arduino and all its peripherals, because that is what the USB specification allows. When you use an external supply of sufficient current, the built-in regulator can supply up to 1 amp to the components on the 5V rail.

Servos have a tendency to consume current in bursts as they turn. They generally consume little current while stationary, and they consume several hundred milliamps for a few milliseconds when they are actuated. These current spikes can ripple on the 5V line, and can even be seen in other components, like LEDs. By keeping the supply for the servo on a separate rail, you ensure that this does not happen.

Insufficient current for a servo might also cause it to behave erratically. When you finish the final project for this chapter, try hooking the servo supply pin up to the built-in 5V rail. (Don't worry; this won't damage anything.) When the servo is powered over USB, you may see the servo doing all kinds of unexpected motions due to an insufficient current supply. Naturally, the degree of this behavior depends on the specification of your particular servo.

Controlling a Servo

The Arduino IDE includes a built-in library that makes controlling servos a breeze. A software library is a collection of code that is useful, but not always needed in sketches. The Arduino IDE contains a number of libraries for common tasks. The servo library abstracts the timing routines you would need to write out on your own for pulsing the servo pin. All you have to do is attach a servo "object" to a particular pin and give it an angle to rotate to. The library takes care of the rest, even setting the pin as an output. The simplest way to test out the functionality of your servo is to map the potentiometer directly to servo positions. Turning the potentiometer to 0 moves the servo to 0 degrees, and moving it to 1023 moves the servo to 180 degrees. Create a new sketch with the code from Listing 4-4 and load it onto your Arduino to see this functionality in action.

Listing 4-4: Servo Potentiometer Control—servo.ino

```
//Servo Potentiometer Control

#include <Servo.h>

const int SERVO=9; //Servo on Pin 9
const int POT=0;   //POT on Analog Pin 0

Servo myServo;
int val = 0;      //for storing the reading from the POT

void setup()
{
    myServo.attach(SERVO);
```

```
}

void loop()
{
    val = analogRead(POT);            //Read Pot
    val = map(val, 0, 1023, 0, 179); //scale it to servo range
    myServo.write(val);               //sets the servo
    delay(15);                        //waits for the servo
}
```

The `include` statement at the top of the program adds the functionality of the servo library to your sketch. `Servo myServo` makes a servo object called `myServo`. In your code, whenever you want to tell the servo what to do, you'll refer to `myServo`. In `setup()`, attaching the servo initializes everything necessary to control the servo. You can add multiple servos by calling the objects different things and attaching a different pin to each one. In `loop()`, the pot is read, scaled to an appropriate value for the servo control, and is then "written" to the servo by pulsing the appropriate pin. The 15ms delay ensures that the servo reaches its destination before you try to send it another command.

Building a Sweeping Distance Sensor

To wrap up this chapter, you apply your knowledge from the past few chapters to build a light-up sweeping distance sensor. The system consists of an infrared (IR) distance sensor mounted on a servo motor and four LEDs. As the servo motor cycles, it pans the distance sensor around the room, allowing you to roughly determine where objects are close and where they are far. The four LEDs correspond to four quadrants of the sweep and change brightness depending on how close an object is in that quadrant.

Because IR light is a part of the electromagnetic spectrum that humans cannot see, a system like this can be implemented to create "night vision." The IR distance sensor works by shining an IR LED and using some fairly complex circuitry to calculate the angle at which that IR light returns to a photo sensor mounted next to the IR LED. Using analog voltages created by the IR photo sensor readings, the distance is calculated and converted to an analog voltage signal that you can read into the microcontroller. Even if the room is dark and you cannot see how close an object is, this sensor can because it is using a wavelength of light that the human eye cannot detect.

Different models of IR rangefinders may have different interfaces. If you're using a rangefinder that is different than the one used in this example, check the datasheet to make sure it sends out a variable voltage as an output.

NOTE You can watch a demo video of the sweeping distance sensor online: www.exploringarduino.com/content/ch4. You can also find this video on the Wiley website shown at the beginning of this chapter.

Start by hot-gluing your distance sensor to the top of a servo motor, as shown in Figure 4-13. I like to use hot glue because it holds well and is fairly easy to remove if you need to. However, you could also use super glue, putty, or tape to get the job done.

Figure 4-13: IR distance sensor mounted to the servo

Next, hook your servo up to your Arduino, using the 5V regulator to power it, just as you did before. The IR distance sensor replaces the potentiometer and plugs into analog pin 0. Four LEDs plug into pins 3, 5, 6, and 11 through 1kΩ resistors. The Arduino Uno has six total PWM pins, but pins 9 and 10 cannot create PWM signals (using analogWrite) when you are using the servo library. This is because the servo library uses the same hardware timer as the one used to control PWM on those two pins. Hence, the other four PWM pins were chosen. (If you want to do this project with more LEDs, either use the Arduino Mega or implement a software PWM solution, something this book does not cover.) Follow the wiring diagram in Figure 4-14 to confirm that you have everything wired up correctly. I chose to use blue LEDs, but you can use any color you want. After you have it all wired up, consider taping it down, as shown in Figure 4-13.

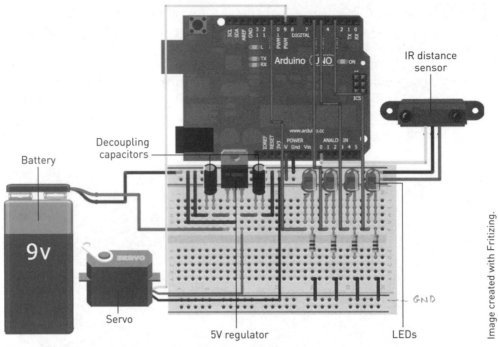

Figure 4-14: Sweeping distance sensor wiring diagram

The last step is to program the sensor. The system works in the following manner: Rotate to a given position, measure the distance, convert it to a value that can be used for the LED, change that LED's brightness, move to the next position, and so on, and so forth. Listing 4-5 shows the code to accomplish this. Copy it into a new sketch and upload it to your Arduino.

Listing 4-5: Sweeping Distance Sensor—sweep.ino

```
//Sweeping Distance Sensor
#include <Servo.h>

const int SERVO   =9;     //Servo on Pin 9
const int IR      =0;     //IR Distance Sensor on Analog Pin 0
const int LED1    =3;     //LED Output 1
const int LED2    =5;     //LED Output 2
const int LED3    =6;     //LED Output 3
const int LED4    =11;    //LED Output 4

Servo myServo;        //Servo Object
int dist1 = 0;        //Quadrant 1 Distance
int dist2 = 0;        //Quadrant 2 Distance
int dist3 = 0;        //Quadrant 3 Distance
```

```
int dist4 = 0;        //Quadrant 4 Distance

void setup()
{
    myServo.attach(SERVO); //Attach the Servo
    pinMode(LED1, OUTPUT); //Set LED to Output
    pinMode(LED2, OUTPUT); //Set LED to Output
    pinMode(LED3, OUTPUT); //Set LED to Output
    pinMode(LED4, OUTPUT); //Set LED to Output
}

void loop()
{
    //Sweep the Servo into 4 regions and change the LEDs
    dist1 = readDistance(15);      //Measure IR Distance at 15 degrees
    analogWrite(LED1, dist1);      //Adjust LED Brightness
    delay(300);                    //delay before next measurement

    dist2 = readDistance(65);      //Measure IR Distance at 65 degrees
    analogWrite(LED2, dist2);      //Adjust LED Brightness
    delay(300);                    //delay before next measurement

    dist3 = readDistance(115);     //Measure IR Distance at 115 degrees
    analogWrite(LED3, dist3);      //Adjust LED Brightness
    delay(300);                    //delay before next measurement

    dist4 = readDistance(165);     //Measure IR Distance at 165 degrees
    analogWrite(LED4, dist4);      //Adjust LED Brightness
    delay(300);                    //delay before next measurement
}

int readDistance(int pos)
{
    myServo.write(pos);                       //Move to given position
    delay(600);                               //Wait for Servo to move
    int dist = analogRead(IR);                //Read IR Sensor
    dist = map(dist, 50, 500, 0, 255);        //scale it to LED range
    dist = constrain(dist, 0, 255);           //Constrain it
    return dist;                              //Return scaled distance
}
```

The program employs a simple function that rotates the servo to the requested degree, takes the distance measurement, scales it, and then returns it to the loop(). Which map you choose for the LED range depends on the setup of your system. I found that the closest object I wanted to detect registered around 500, and the farthest object was around 50, so the map() was set accordingly. loop() executes this function for each of the four LEDs, then repeats. When complete, your system should function similarly to the one shown in the demo video listed at the beginning of this section.

Summary

In this chapter you learned about the following:

- DC motors use electromagnetic induction to create mechanical action from changes in current.
- Motors are inductive loads that must utilize proper protection and power circuitry to interface safely with your Arduino.
- DC motor speed and direction can be controlled with PWM and an H-bridge.
- Servo motors enable precise positioning and can be controlled using the Arduino Servo library.
- A linear regulator can be used to create a secondary 5V supply from a 9V battery.
- IR distance sensors return analog values representing distances detected by bouncing infrared light off objects.
- Code commenting is critical for easing debugging and sharing.

CHAPTER 5

Making Sounds

Parts You'll Need for This Chapter

Arduino Uno

USB cable

Pushbuttons (×5)

10kΩ resistors (×5)

150Ω resistor

Jumper wires

Breadboard

10KΩ potentiometer

8Ω loudspeaker

CODE AND DIGITAL CONTENT FOR THIS CHAPTER

Code downloads, video, and other digital content for this chapter can be found at
www.exploringarduino.com/content/ch5.

The wiley.com code downloads for this chapter are found at www.wiley.com/
go/exploringarduino on the Download Code tab. The code is in the chapter 05
download and individually named according to the names throughout the chapter.

Humans have five senses. As you might have guessed, you won't be interfacing your sense of taste with too many electronics; licking your Arduino is a poor idea. Similarly, smell won't generally come into play. In fact, if you can smell your electronics, something is probably burning (and you should stop what you're doing). That just leaves the senses of touch, sight, and sound. You've already interfaced with potentiometers and buttons that take advantage of your sense of touch, and you've hooked up LEDs that interface with you sense of sight. Now, what about your auditory senses? This chapter focuses on using the Arduino to make sounds so that you can more easily gather feedback from your projects.

You can generate sound with an Arduino in a number of ways. The simplest method is to use the `tone()` function, which this chapter focuses on most heavily. However, you can also use various shields that add more complex, music-playing capabilities to Arduino with the help of some external processing. (Shields are add-on boards that attach to the top of your Arduino to add specific functionality. You won't use any in this chapter, but you'll be using assorted shields in some of the later chapters.) If you own the Arduino Due, you can use its true digital-to-analog converter (DAC) to produce sounds.

Understanding How Speakers Work

Before you can make sounds with your Arduino, you need to understand what sounds are and how humans perceive them. In this first section, you learn about how sound waves are generated, their properties, and how manipulation of those properties can produce music, voices, and so on.

The Properties of Sound

Sound is transmitted through the air as a pressure wave. As an object such as a speaker, a drum, or a bell vibrates, that object also vibrates the air around it. As the air particles vibrate, they transfer energy to the particles around them, vibrating these particles as well. In this fashion, a pressure wave is transferred from the source to your eardrum, by creating a chain reaction of vibrating particles. So, why do you need to know this to understand how to make sounds with your Arduino?

You can control two properties of these vibrating particles with your Arduino: frequency and amplitude. The *frequency* represents how quickly the air particles vibrate back and forth, and the *amplitude* represents the magnitude of their vibrations. In the physical sense, higher amplitude sounds are louder, and lower amplitude sounds are quieter. High-frequency sounds are a higher pitch (like a soprano), and low-frequency sounds are a lower pitch (like bass). Consider the diagram in Figure 5-1, which shows sinusoidal representations of sound waves of various amplitudes and frequencies.

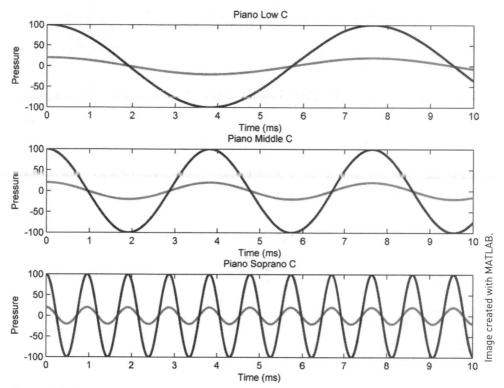

Figure 5-1: Sound waves of varying frequencies and amplitudes

Figure 5-1 shows three piano notes: low, middle, and soprano C. Each one shows the given frequencies at both low and high amplitudes. As an example, to understand frequency and amplitude, focus on middle C. Middle C has a frequency of 261.63 Hertz (Hz). In other words, a speaker, a guitar string, or a piano string would complete 261.63 oscillations per second. By taking the reciprocal of that value, you can find the period of the wave, which is easy to see in Figure 5-1. 1/261.63 equals 3.822 milliseconds, which is the width of one complete oscillation in the graph. Using the Arduino, you can set that period for a square wave and thus adjust the tone of the note.

Importantly, the Arduino (excluding the Due's true DAC) cannot actually make a sinusoidal wave that you might observe in the real world. A square wave is a digital periodic wave—it also oscillates between a high and a low value, but it switches instantaneously, instead of slowly like a sine wave. This still creates a pressure wave that results in sound, but it isn't quite as "pretty" sounding as a sinusoidal wave.

As for the amplitude, you can control that by changing the amount of the current permitted to flow through the speaker. Using a potentiometer in-line with the speaker, you can dynamically adjust the volume level of the speaker.

How a Speaker Produces Sound

Speakers, much like the motors that you learned about in the preceding chapter, take advantage of electromagnetic forces to turn electricity into motion. Try holding a piece of metal up to the rear of your speaker. Did you notice anything interesting? The metal probably sticks to the rear of your speaker, because all speakers have a sizeable permanent magnet mounted to the back. Figure 5-2 shows a cross section of a common speaker.

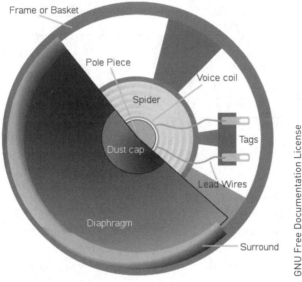

Figure 5-2: Speaker cross section

The permanent magnet is mounted behind the voice coil and pole piece shown in the image. As you send a sinusoidal voltage signal (or a square wave in the case of the Arduino) into the leads of the coil, the changing current induces a magnetic field that causes the pole piece and diaphragm to vibrate up and down as the permanent magnet is attracted to and then repulsed by the magnetic field that you have generated. This back-and-forth vibration, in turn, vibrates the air in front of the speaker, effectively creating a sound wave that can travel to your eardrum.

Using tone() to Make Sounds

The Arduino IDE includes a built-in function for easily making sounds of arbitrary frequencies. The `tone()` function generates a square wave of the selected frequency on the output pin of your choice. The `tone()` function accepts three arguments, though the last one is optional:

- The first argument sets the pin to generate the tone on.
- The second argument sets the frequency of the tone.
- The third (optional) argument sets the duration of the tone. If the third argument is not set, the tone continues playing until you call `noTone()`.

Because `tone()` uses one of the ATMega's hardware timers, you can start a tone and do other things with your Arduino while it continues to play sound in the background.

In the following sections, you learn how to play arbitrary sound sequences. Once you've gotten that working, you can use `tone()` as a response to various inputs (buttons, distance sensors, accelerometers, etc.). At the end of the chapter, you build a simple five-button piano that you can play.

Including a Definition File

When it comes to playing music, a definition file that maps frequencies to note names proves useful. This makes it more intuitive to play simple musical clips. For those familiar with reading sheet music, you know that notes are denoted with letters representing their pitch. The Arduino IDE includes a header file that correlates each of these notes with its respective frequency. Instead of digging through the Arduino install directory to find it, just visit the Exploring Arduino Chapter 5 webpage, and download the pitch file to your desktop (www.exploringarduino.com/content/ch5). You'll place it in your sketch directory after you've created it.

Next, open your Arduino IDE and save the blank sketch that is automatically created when you open the IDE. As you've probably already noticed, when you save a sketch, it actually saves a folder with that name and places an .ino file inside of that folder. By adding other files to that folder, you can include them in your program, all while keeping your code better organized. Copy the pitches.h file you saved to the desktop into the folder created by the IDE; then close the Arduino IDE. Open your .ino file in the Arduino IDE and notice the two tabs that now appear (see Figure 5-3).

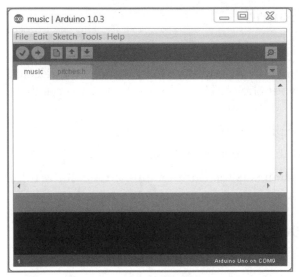

Figure 5-3: Arduino IDE with a secondary header file

Click the pitches.h tab to see the contents of the file. Notice that it's just a list of definition statements, which map human-readable names to given frequency values. Simply having the header file in the IDE does not suffice, though. To ensure that the compiler actually uses those definitions when compiling your program for the Arduino, you need to tell the compiler to look for that file. Doing so is easy. Just add this line of code to the top of your .ino file:

```
#include "pitches.h" //Header file with pitch definitions
```

To the compiler, this is essentially the same thing as copying and pasting the contents of the header file into the top of your main file. However, this keeps the file neater and easier for you to read. In the next sections, you write the code for the rest of this file so that you can actually use the pitch definitions that you have just imported.

Wiring the Speaker

Now that you have your pitches header file included, you're ready to build a test circuit and to write a simple program that can play some music. The electrical setup is fairly simple and just involves hooking up a speaker to an output pin of your Arduino. However, remember what you've learned in previous chapters about current-limiting resistors.

Just as with LEDs, you want to put a current-limiting resistor in series with the speaker to ensure that you don't try to draw too much current from one of the Arduino's I/O pins. As you learned previously, each I/O pin can supply only a max of 40mA, so pick a resistor that prevents you from exceeding that. The

speaker that comes with this book's kit has an internal resistance of 8Ω (as do
most loudspeakers that you can buy); this resistance comes from the windings
of wire that make up the electromagnet. Recall that Ohm's law states that V =
IR. In this scenario, the I/O pin is outputting 5V, and you don't want to exceed
40mA. Solving for R, you find that the minimum resistance must be: R = 5V /
40mA = 125Ω. 8Ω is already accounted for by the speaker, so your in-line resistor
must be at least 125Ω – 8Ω = 117Ω. The nearest common resistor is 150Ω, so you
can use that. By adjusting that resistor value, you can change the volume of the
speaker. To make this as easy as possible, you can use a potentiometer in-line
with the 150Ω resistor, as shown in Figure 5-4. In the schematic, R1 is the 150Ω
resistor, and R2 is the potentiometer.

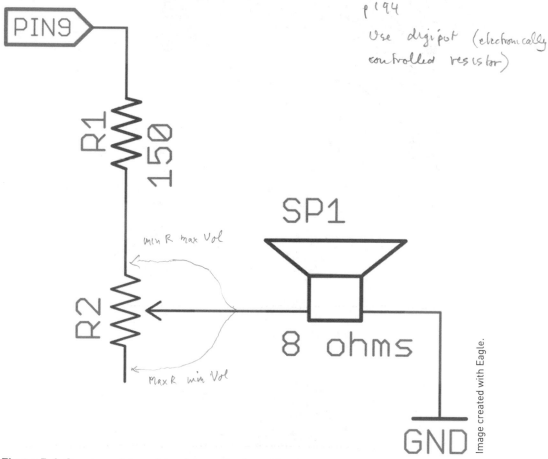

Figure 5-4: Speaker wiring with volume adjustment knob

Note that unlike in your previous usages of potentiometers this configuration
uses only two pins: the middle (or wiper) pin goes to the speaker, and either one

of the end pins connects to the 150Ω resistor. When the knob is turned all the way toward the unconnected terminal, the entire resistance of the potentiometer is added to the series resistance of the 150Ω resistor, and the volume lowers. When the knob is turned all the way toward the connected end terminal, it adds no resistance to the series, and the speaker is at max volume. Referencing the schematic in Figure 5-4, wire your speaker to the Arduino. Then, confirm your wiring using the diagram in Figure 5-5.

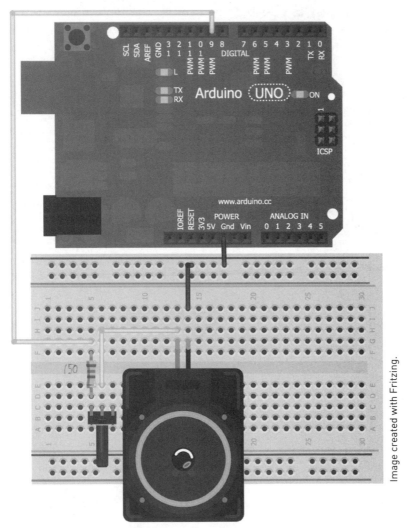

Image created with Fritzing.

Figure 5-5: Speaker wiring diagram

Speakers do not have a polarity; you can connect them in either direction. After wiring your speaker successfully, you're ready to make music!

Making Sound Sequences

To play back some songs, you first learn about using arrays to store multiple values easily. You then implement a simple loop to iterate through the arrays of notes and play them back on the speaker.

Using Arrays

An array is a sequence of values that are related in some way. By grouping them together, it is an ideal format to iterate through. You can think of an array as a numbered list. Each position has an index that indicates its location in the list, and each index has a value that you want to store. You use an array here to store the list of notes that you want to play, in the order that you want to play them.

To ensure that the Arduino's memory is properly managed, you need to declare arrays with a known length. You can do this either by explicitly specifying the number of items or by simply populating the array with all the values you are interested in. For example, if you want to make an array that contains four integer values, you could create it like this:

```
int numbers[4];
```

You can optionally initialize the values when you declare it. If you initialize the values, specifying the length in the brackets is optional. If unspecified, the length is assumed to equal the number elements that you initialized:

```
//Both of these are acceptable
int numbers[4] = {-7, 0, 6, 234};
int numbers[] = {-7, 0, 6, 234};
```

Note that arrays are zero indexed. In other words, the first number is at position 0, the second is at position 1, and so forth. You can access the elements in an array at any given index by putting the index of the relevant value in a square bracket after the variable name. If you want to set the brightness of an LED connected to pin 9 to the third entry in an array, for example, you can do so like this:

```
analogWrite(9,numbers[2]);
```

Note that because numbering starts at zero, the index of 2 represents the third value in the array. If you want to change one of the values of the array, you can do so in a similar fashion:

```
numbers[2] = 10;
```

Next, you will use arrays (as shown in these examples) to create a structure that can hold the sequence of notes that you want to play on your speaker.

Making Note and Duration Arrays

To store the info about the song you want to play, you can use two arrays of the same length. The first contains the list of pitches, and the second contains the list of durations for which each note should play in milliseconds. You can then iterate through the indices of these arrays and play back your tune.

Using the meager musical skills that I've maintained from my music classes back in high school, I've assembled a short and catchy tune:

```
//Note Array
int notes[] = {
 NOTE_A4, NOTE_E3, NOTE_A4, 0,
 NOTE_A4, NOTE_E3, NOTE_A4, 0,
 NOTE_E4, NOTE_D4, NOTE_C4, NOTE_B4, NOTE_A4, NOTE_B4, NOTE_C4, NOTE_D4,
 NOTE_E4, NOTE_E3, NOTE_A4, 0
};

//The Duration of each note (in ms)
int times[] = {
 250, 250, 250, 250,
 250, 250, 250, 250,
 125, 125, 125, 125, 125, 125, 125, 125,
 250, 250, 250, 250
};
```

Note that both arrays are the same length: 20 items. Notice that some of the notes are specified as 0. These are musical rests (unplayed beats). Each note pairs with a duration from the second array. For those familiar with music theory, note that I've made quarter notes 250ms and eighth notes 125ms. The song is in "four-four" time, in musical terms.

Try out this given note sequence, first; then try to create your own!

NOTE Listen to a recording of this tune, played by an Arduino: www.exploringarduino.com/content/ch5. You can also find this recording on the Wiley website shown at the beginning of this chapter.

Completing the Program

The last step is to actually add playback functionality to the sketch. This can be accomplished with a simple `for` loop that goes through each index in the array, and plays the given note for the given duration. Since you presumably don't want to listen to this over and over again, you can put the playback functionality in the `setup()` function so that it only happens once. You can restart playback by hitting the Reset button. Listing 5-1 shows the complete playback program.

Listing 5-1: Arduino Music Player—music.ino

```
//Plays a song on a speaker

#include "pitches.h" //Header file with pitch definitions        95-96

const int SPEAKER=9;   //Speaker Pin

//Note Array
int notes[] = {
 NOTE_A4, NOTE_E3, NOTE_A4, 0,
 NOTE_A4, NOTE_E3, NOTE_A4, 0,
 NOTE_E4, NOTE_D4, NOTE_C4, NOTE_B4, NOTE_A4, NOTE_B4, NOTE_C4, NOTE_D4,
 NOTE_E4, NOTE_E3, NOTE_A4, 0
};

//The Duration of each note (in ms)
int times[] = {
 250, 250, 250, 250,
 250, 250, 250, 250,
 125, 125, 125, 125, 125, 125, 125, 125,
 250, 250, 250, 250
};


void setup()
{
 //Play each note for the right duration
 for (int i = 0; i < 20; i++)
 {
  tone(SPEAKER, notes[i], times[i]);
  delay(times[i]);                        @ 102
 }
}

void loop()
{
 //Press the Reset button to play again.
}
```

If you want to make your own music, make sure that the arrays remain of an equal length and that you change the upper bound on the `for()` loop. Because the `tone()` function can run in the background, it's important to use the `delay()` function. By delaying the code for an amount of time equal to the duration of the note, you ensure that the Arduino doesn't play the next note until the previous not has finished playing for the time you specified.

Understanding the Limitations of the tone() Function

The `tone()` function does have a few limitations to be aware of. Like the servo library, `tone()` relies on a hardware timer that is also used by the board's pulse-width modulation (PWM) functionality. If you use `tone()`, PWM does not work right on pins 3 and 11 (on boards other than the Mega).

Also remember that the Arduino I/O pins are not digital-to-analog converters (DACs). Hence, they output only a square wave at the provided frequency, not a sine wave. Although this suffices for making tones with a speaker, you'll find it undesirable for playing back music. If you want to play back wave files, your options include using a music-playing shield (such as the adafruit Wave Shield or the SparkFun MP3 shield), implementing a DAC converter, or using the built-in DAC available on the Arduino Due using the Due-only Audio library.

The last limitation is that you can use the `tone()` function on only one pin at a time, so it isn't ideal for driving multiple speakers. If you want to drive multiple speakers at the same time from a standard Arduino, you have to use manual timer interrupt control, something you learn more about in Chapter 12, "Hardware and Timer Interrupts."

> **NOTE** To read a tutorial on advanced multispeaker control with an Arduino, visit www.jeremyblum.com/2010/09/05/driving-5-speakers-simultaneously-with-an-arduino/. You can also find this tutorial on the Wiley website shown at the beginning of this chapter.

Building a Micro Piano

Playing back sequences of notes is great for adding audio feedback to projects you've already created. For example, consider replacing or augmenting a green confirmation LED with a confirmation sound. But, what if you want to dynamically control the sound? To wrap up this chapter, you build a simple pentatonic piano. The pentatonic scale consists of just five notes per octave rather than the usual seven. Interestingly, the notes of a pentatonic scale have minimal dissonance between pitches, meaning they always sound good together. So, it makes a lot of sense to use pentatonic notes to make a simple piano.

NOTE The SudoGlove, among others things, is a control glove that can synthesize music using the pentatonic scale. You can learn more about it at www.sudoglove.com.

To make your Arduino piano, you use this pentatonic scale: C, D, E, G, A. You can choose what octave to use based on your preference. I chose to use the fourth octave from the header file.

First, wire five buttons up to your Arduino. As with the buttons in Chapter 2, "Digital Inputs, Outputs, and Pulse-Width Modulation" you use 10kΩ pull-down resistors with the buttons. In this scenario, you do not need to debounce the buttons because the note will be played only while the desired button is held down. Wire the buttons as shown in Figure 5-6 and keep the speaker wired as you had it previously.

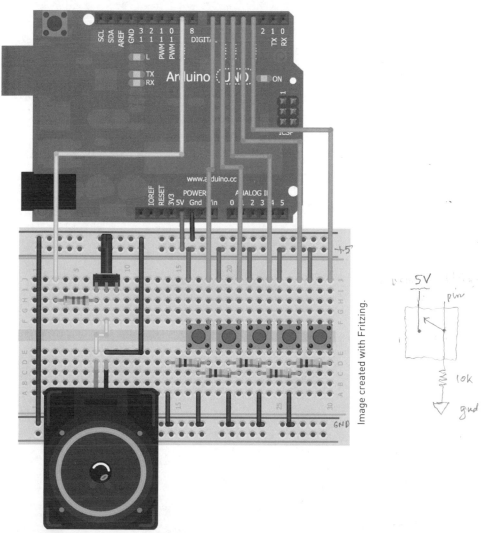

Image created with Fritzing.

Figure 5-6: Micro piano wiring diagram

The code for the piano is actually very simple. In each iteration through the loop, each button is checked. So long as a button is pressed, a note is played. Here, tone() is used without a duration because the note will play as long as the button is held. Instead, noTone() is called at the end of loop() to ensure that the speaker stops making noise when all the buttons have been released. Because only a few notes are needed, you can copy the values from the header file that you care about directly into the main program file. In a new sketch, load up the code shown in Listing 5-2 and upload it to your Arduino. Then, jam away on your piano!

Listing 5-2: Pentatonic Micro Piano—piano.ino

```
//Pentatonic Piano
//C D E G A

#define NOTE_C  262 //Hz
#define NOTE_D  294 //Hz
#define NOTE_E  330 //Hz
#define NOTE_G  392 //Hz
#define NOTE_A  440 //Hz

const int SPEAKER=9;  //Speaker on pin 9

const int BUTTON_C=7;  //Button pin
const int BUTTON_D=6;  //Button pin
const int BUTTON_E=5;  //Button pin
const int BUTTON_G=4;  //Button pin
const int BUTTON_A=3;  //Button pin


void setup()
{
 //No setup needed
 //Tone function sets outputs
}

void loop()
{
 while (digitalRead(BUTTON_C))
  tone(SPEAKER, NOTE_C);
 while(digitalRead(BUTTON_D))
  tone(SPEAKER, NOTE_D);
 while(digitalRead(BUTTON_E))
  tone(SPEAKER, NOTE_E);
 while(digitalRead(BUTTON_G))
  tone(SPEAKER, NOTE_G);
 while(digitalRead(BUTTON_A))
  tone(SPEAKER, NOTE_A);

 //Stop playing if all buttons have been released
 noTone(SPEAKER);
}
```

Each while() loop will continuously call the tone() function at the appropriate frequency for as long as the button is held down. The button can be read within the while() loop evaluation to avoid having to first save the reading to a temporary value. digitalRead() returns a Boolean "true" whenever a button input goes high; the value can be evaluated directly by the while() loop. To keep your code neater, you don't need to use brackets for the contents of a loop if the contents are only one line, as in this example. If you have multiple lines, you must use curly brackets as you have in previous examples.

NOTE To watch a demo video of the micro piano, visit www.exploringarduino.com/content/ch5. You can also find this video on the Wiley website shown at the beginning of this chapter.

Summary

In this chapter you learned about the following:

- Speakers create a pressure wave that travels through the air and is perceived as sound by your ears.
- Changing electric current induces a magnetic field that can be used to create sound from a speaker.
- The tone() function can be used to generate sounds of arbitrary frequencies and durations.
- The Arduino programming language supports the use of arrays for iterating through sequences of data.
- Speaker volume can be adjusted using a potentiometer in series with a speaker.

USB and Serial Communication

Parts You'll Need for This Chapter

Arduino Uno

Arduino Leonardo

USB cable (A to B for Uno)

USB cable (A to Micro B for Leonardo)

LED

RGB LED (common cathode)

150Ω resistor

220Ω resistor (×3)

10kΩ resistor (×2)

Pushbutton

Photoresistor

TMP36 temperature sensor

Two-axis joystick (SparkFun, Parallax, or adafruit suggested)

Jumper wires

Breadboard

Potentiometer

CODE AND DIGITAL CONTENT FOR THIS CHAPTER

Code downloads, video, and other digital content for this chapter can be found at www.exploringarduino.com/content/ch6.

In addition, all code can be found at www.wiley.com/go/exploringarduino on the Download Code tab. The code is in the chapter 06 download and individually named according to the names throughout the chapter.

Perhaps the most important part of any Arduino is its capability to be programmed directly via a USB serial port. This feature enables you to program the Arduino without any special hardware, such as an AVR ISP MKII. Ordinarily, microcontrollers rely on a dedicated piece of external hardware (such as the MKII) to serve as a *programmer* that connects between your computer and the microcontroller you are trying to program. In the case of the Arduino, this programmer is essentially built into the board, instead of being a piece of external hardware. What's more, this gives you a direct connection to the ATMega's integrated Universal Synchronous/Asynchronous Receiver and Transmitter (USART). Using this interface, you can send information between your host computer and the Arduino, or between the Arduino and other serial-enabled components (including other Arduinos).

This chapter covers just about everything you could want to know about connecting an Arduino to your computer via USB and transmitting data between the two. Different Arduinos have different serial capabilities, so this chapter covers each of them, and you build sample projects with each serial communication technology to get yourself acquainted with how to take advantage of them as best as possible. Note that, as a result of this, the parts list includes several types of Arduinos. Depending on which Arduino you are trying to learn about, you can pick and choose which sections to read, which examples to explore, and which parts from the parts list you actually need for your Arduino explorations.

Understanding the Arduino's Serial Communication Capabilities

As already alluded to in the introduction to this chapter, the different Arduino boards offer lots of different serial implementations, both in terms of how the hardware implements the USB-to-serial adapters and in terms of the software support for various features. First, in this section, you learn about the various serial communication hardware interfaces offered on different Arduino boards.

NOTE To learn all about serial communication, check out this tutorial: www.jeremyblum.com/2011/02/07/arduino-tutorial-6-serial-communication-and-processing/. You can also find this tutorial on the Wiley website shown at the beginning of this chapter.

To begin, you need to understand the differences between serial and USB. Depending on how old you are, you might not even remember serial (or technically, RS-232) ports, because they have been primarily replaced by USB. Figure 6-1 shows what a standard serial port looks like.

DB-9 serial connector

Figure 6-1: Serial port

The original Arduino boards came equipped with a serial port that you connected to your computer with a 9-pin serial cable. Nowadays, few computers still have these ports, although you can use adapters to make DB-9 (the type of 9-pin connector) serial ports from USB ports. Microcontrollers like the ATMega328P that you find on the Arduino Uno have one hardware serial port. It includes a transmit (TX) and receive (RX) pin that can be accessed on digital pins 0 and 1. As explained in the sidebar in Chapter 1, "Getting Up and Blinking with the Arduino," the Arduino is equipped with a bootloader that allows you to program it over this serial interface. To facilitate this, those pins are "multiplexed" (meaning that they are connected to more than one function); they connect, indirectly, to the transmit and receive lines of your USB cable. However, serial and USB are not directly compatible, so one of two methods is used to bridge the two. Option one is to use a secondary integrated circuit (IC) to facilitate the conversion between the two (either on or off the Arduino board). This is the type of interface present on an Uno, where an intermediary IC facilitates USB-to-serial communication. Option two is to opt for a microcontroller that has a USB controller built in (such as the Arduino Leonardo's 32U4 MCU).

Arduino Boards with an Internal or External FTDI USB-to-Serial Converter

As just explained, many Arduino boards (and Arduino clones) use a secondary integrated circuit to facilitate the USB-to-serial conversion. The "FTDI" chip is a popular chip that has just one function: convert between serial and USB. When your computer connects to an FTDI chip, it shows up in your computer as a "Virtual Serial Port" that you can access as if it was a DB9 port wired right into your computer. Figure 6-2 shows the bottom of an Arduino Nano, which utilizes an integrated FTDI chip.

FTDI chip

Figure 6-2: Arduino Nano with integrated FTDI chip shown

NOTE For your computer to communicate with a FTDI serial-to-USB adapter, you need to install drivers. You can find the most recent versions for Windows, OS X, and Linux at www.ftdichip.com/Drivers/VCP.htm. This is also linked from the Chapter 6 page on the Exploring Arduino website.

On some boards, usually to reduce board size, the FTDI chip is external to the main board, with a standardized 6-pin "FTDI connector" left for connecting to either an FTDI cable (A USB cable with an FTDI chip built in to the end of the cable) or a small FTDI breakout board. Figures 6-3 and 6-4 show these options.

Credit: adafruit Industries, www.adafruit.com.

Figure 6-3: FTDI cable

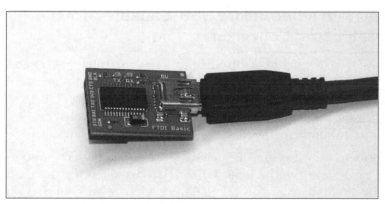

Figure 6-4: SparkFun FTDI adapter board

Using a board with a removable FTDI programmer is great if you are designing a project that will not need to be connected to a computer via USB to run. This will reduce cost if you are making several devices, and will reduce overall size of the finished product.

Following is a list of Arduino boards that use an onboard FTDI chip. Note, new Arduino boards no longer use an FTDI chip, so most of these have been discontinued. However, there are still many clones of these boards available for purchase, so they are listed here for completeness:

use
on board
FTDI chip

- Arduino Nano
- Arduino Extreme
- Arduino NG
- Arduino Diecimila
- Arduino Duemilanove
- Arduino Mega (original)

need
external
FTDI
programmer

Following is a list of Arduino boards that use an external FTDI programmer:

- Arduino Pro
- Arduino Pro Mini
- LilyPad Arduino
- Arduino Fio
- Arduino Mini
- Arduino Ethernet

Arduino Boards with a Secondary USB-Capable ATMega MCU Emulating a Serial Converter

The Arduino Uno was the first board to introduce the use of an integrated circuit other than the FTDI chip to handle USB-to-serial conversion. Functionally, it works exactly the same way, with a few minor technical differences. Figure 6-5 shows the Uno's 8U2 serial converter (now a 16U2 on newer revisions).

Following is a brief list of the differences:

- First, in Windows, boards with this new USB-to-serial conversion solution require a custom driver to be installed. This driver comes bundled with the Arduino IDE when you download it. (Drivers are not needed for OS X or Linux.)

■ Second, the use of this second microcontroller unit (MCU) for the conversion allowed a custom Arduino vendor ID and product ID to be reported to the host computer when the board is connected. When an FTDI-based board was connected to a computer, it just showed up as generic USB-serial device. When an Arduino using a non-FTDI converter IC (an ATMega 8U2 in the case of early Arduino Unos, now a 16U2) is connected, it is identified to the computer as an Arduino.

Atmel 8U2
or 16U2 chip

Figure 6-5: View of the Arduino Uno's 8U2 serial converter chip

■ Lastly, because the secondary MCU is fully programmable (it's running a firmware stack called LUFA that emulates a USB-to-serial converter), you can change its firmware to make the Arduino show up as something different from a virtual serial port, such as a joystick, keyboard, or MIDI device. If you were to make this sort of change, the USB-to-serial LUFA firmware would not be loaded, and you would have to program the Arduino directly using the in-circuit serial programmer with a device like the AVR ISP MKII.

Following is a list of Arduino boards that use an onboard secondary MCU to handle USB-to-serial conversion:

- Arduino Uno
- Arduino Mega 2560
- Arduino Mega ADK (based on 2560)
- Arduino Due (can also be programmed directly)

Arduino Boards with a Single USB-Capable MCU

The Arduino Leonardo was the first board to have only one chip that acts both as the user-programmable MCU and as the USB interface. The Leonardo (and similar Arduino boards) employs the ATMega 32U4 microcontroller, a chip that has direct USB communication built in. This feature results in several new features and improvements.

First, board cost is reduced because fewer parts are required, and because one less factory programming step is needed to produce the boards. Second, the board can more easily be used to emulate USB devices other than a serial port (such as a keyboard, mouse, or joystick). Third, the single ordinary USART port on the ATMega does not have be multiplexed with the USB programmer, so communication with the host computer and a secondary serial device (such as a GPS unit) can happen simultaneously.

Following is a list of Arduino boards that use a single USB-capable MCU:

- Arduino Due (can also be programmed via secondary MCU)
- LilyPad Arduino USB
- Arduino Esplora
- Arduino Leonardo
- Arduino Micro

Arduino Boards with USB-Host Capabilities

Some Arduino boards can connect to USB devices as a host, enabling you to connect traditional USB devices (keyboards, mice, Android phones) to an Arduino. Naturally, there must be appropriate drivers to support the device you are connecting to. For example, you cannot just connect a webcam to an Arduino Due and expect to be able to snap photos with no additional work. The Due presently supports a USB host class that enables you to plug a keyboard or mouse into the Due's on-the-go USB port to control it. The Arduino Mega ADK uses the Android Open Accessory Protocol (AOA) to facilitate communication between the Arduino and an Android device. This is primarily used for controlling Arduino I/O from an application running on the Android device.

Two Arduino boards that have USB-host capabilities are the Arduino Due and the Arduino Mega ADK (based on Mega 2560).

Listening to the Arduino

The most basic serial function that you can do with an Arduino is to print to the computer's serial terminal. You've already done this in several of the previous chapters. In this section, you explore the functionality in more depth, and later in the chapter you build some desktop apps that respond to the data you send instead of just printing it to the terminal. This process is the same for all Arduinos.

Using print Statements

To print data to the terminal, you only need to utilize three functions:

- `Serial.begin(baud_rate)`
- `Serial.print("Message")`
- `Serial.println("Message")`

where `baud_rate` and `"Message"` are variables that you specify.

As you've already learned, `Serial.begin()` must be called once at the start of the program in `setup()` to prepare the serial port for communication. After you've done this, you can freely use `Serial.print()` and `Serial.println()` functions to write data to the serial port. The only difference between the two is that `Serial.println()` adds a carriage return at the end of the line (so that the next thing printed will appear on the following line). To experiment with this functionality, wire up a simple circuit with a potentiometer connected to pin A0 on the Arduino, as shown in Figure 6-6.

Arduino writes to serial end of serial ⟷ usb chip/adapter; computer gets info via usb side

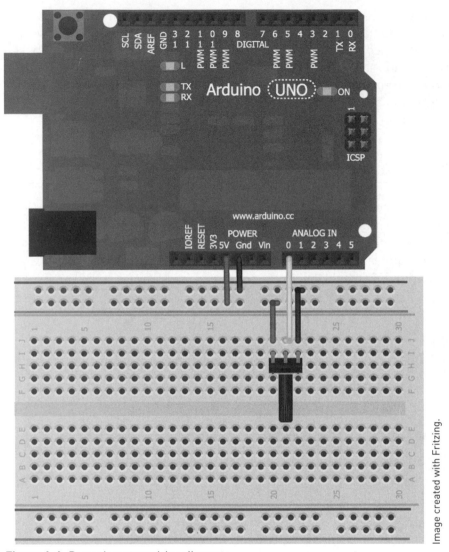

Figure 6-6: Potentiometer wiring diagram

After wiring your potentiometer, load on the simple program shown in Listing 6-1 that will read the value of the potentiometer and print it as both a raw value and a percentage value.

Listing 6-1: Potentiometer Serial Print Test Program—pot.ino

```
//Simple Serial Printing Test with a Potentiometer

const int POT=0;   //Pot on analog pin 0

void setup()
{
  Serial.begin(9600); //Start serial port with baud = 9600
}

void loop()
{
  int val = analogRead(POT);              //Read potentiometer
  int per = map(val, 0, 1023, 0, 100); //Convert to percentage
  Serial.print("Analog Reading: ");
  Serial.print(val);                      //Print raw analog value
  Serial.print("  Percentage: ");
  Serial.print(per);                      //Print percentage analog value
  Serial.println("%");                    //Print % sign and newline
  delay(1000);                            //Wait 1 second, then repeat
}
```

Using a combination of `Serial.print()` and `Serial.println()` statements, this code prints both the raw and percentage values once per second. Note that by our using `Serial.println()` only on the last line, each previous transmission stays on the same line.

Open the serial monitor from the Arduino IDE and ensure that your baud rate is set to 9600 to match the value set in the Arduino sketch. You should see the values printing out once per second as you turn the potentiometer.

Using Special Characters

You can also transmit a variety of "special characters" over serial, which allow you to change the formatting of the serial data you are printing. You indicate these special characters with a slash escape character (\) followed by a command character. There are a variety of these special characters, but the two of greatest interest are the tab and newline characters. To insert a tab character, add a \t to the string. To insert a newline character, add a \n to the string. This proves particularly useful if you want a newline to be inserted at the beginning of a string, instead of at the end as the `Serial.println()` function does. If, for some reason, you actually want to print \n or \t in the string, you can do so by printing \\n or \\t, respectively. Listing 6-2 is a modification of the previous code to use these special characters to show data in a tabular format.

Listing 6-2: Tabular Printing using Special Characters—pot_tabular.ino

```
//Tabular serial printing test with a potentiometer

const int POT=0;   //Pot on analog pin 0

void setup()
{
  Serial.begin(9600); //Start Serial Port with Baud = 9600
}

void loop()
{
  Serial.println("\nAnalog Pin\tRaw Value\tPercentage");
  Serial.println("----------------------------------------");
  for (int i = 0; i < 10; i++)
  {
    int val = analogRead(POT);            //Read potentiometer
    int per = map(val, 0, 1023, 0, 100); //Convert to percentage

    Serial.print("A0\t\t");
    Serial.print(val);
    Serial.print("\t\t");
    Serial.print(per);             //Print percentage analog value
    Serial.println("%");           //Print % sign and newline
    delay(1000);                   //Wait 1 second, then repeat
  }
}
```

As you turn the potentiometer, the output from this program should look something like the results shown in Figure 6-7.

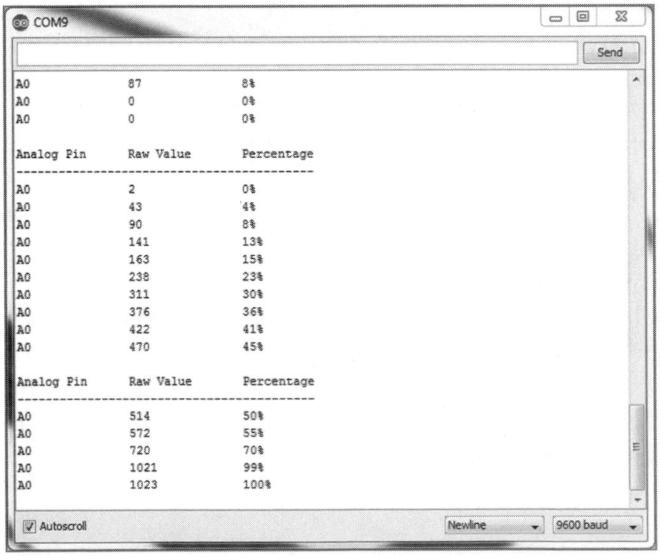

Figure 6-7: Screenshot of serial terminal with tabular data

Changing Data Type Representations

The Serial.print() and Serial.println() functions are fairly intelligent when it comes to printing out data in the format you are expecting. However, you have options for outputting data in various formats, including hexadecimal, octal, and binary. Decimal-coded ASCII is the default format. The Serial.print() and Serial.println() functions have an optional second argument that specifies the print format. Table 6-1 includes examples of how you would print the same data in various formats and how it would appear in your serial terminal.

Table 6-1: Serial Data Type Options

DATA TYPE	EXAMPLE CODE	SERIAL OUTPUT
Decimal	Serial.println(23);	23
Hexadecimal	Serial.println(23, HEX);	17
Octal	Serial.println(23, OCT)	27
Binary	Serial.println(23, BIN)	00010111

Talking to the Arduino

What good is a conversation with your Arduino if it's only going in one direction? Now that you understand how the Arduino sends data to your computer, let's spend some time discussing how to send commands from your computer to the Arduino. You've probably already noticed that the Arduino IDE serial monitor has a text entry field at the top, and a drop-down menu at the bottom. Figure 6-8 highlights both.

Figure 6-8: Screenshot of serial terminal highlighting text entry field and Line Ending Options drop-down menu

First, make sure that the drop-down is set to Newline. The drop-down menu determines what, if anything, is appended to end of your commands when you send them to the Arduino. The examples in the following sections assume that you have Newline selected, which just appends a \n to the end of anything that you send from the text entry field at the top of the serial monitor window.

Unlike with some other terminal programs, the Arduino IDE serial monitor sends your whole command string at one time (at the baud rate you specify) when you press the Enter key or the Send button. This is in contrast to other serial terminals like PuTTy (linked from this chapter's digital content page at www.exploringarduino.com) that send characters as you type them.

Reading Information from a Computer or Other Serial Device

You start by using the Arduino IDE serial monitor to send commands manually to the Arduino. Once that's working, you'll learn how to send multiple command values at once and how to build a simple graphical interface for sending commands.

It's important to recall that the Arduino's serial port has a buffer. In other words, you can send several bytes of data at once and the Arduino will queue them up and process them in order based on the content of your sketch. You do not need to worry about sending data faster than your loop time, but you do need to worry about sending so much data that it overflows the buffer and information is lost.

Telling the Arduino to Echo Incoming Data

The simplest thing you can do is to have the Arduino echo back everything that you send it. To accomplish this, the Arduino basically just needs to monitor its serial input buffer and print any character that it receives. To do this, you need to implement two new commands from the Serial object:

- Serial.available() returns the number of characters (or bytes) that are currently stored in the Arduino's incoming serial buffer. Whenever it's more than zero, you will read the characters and echo them back to the computer.

- Serial.read() reads and returns the next character that is available in the buffer.

Note that each call to Serial.read() will only return 1 byte, so you need to run it for as long as Serial.available() is returning a value greater than zero. Each time Serial.read() grabs a byte, that byte is removed from the buffer, as well, so the next byte is ready to be read. With this knowledge, you can now write and load the echo program in Listing 6-3 on to your Arduino.

Listing 6-3: Arduino Serial Echo Test—echo.ino

```
//Echo every character

char data; //Holds incoming character          ⓑ

void setup()
{
  Serial.begin(9600); //Serial Port at 9600 baud
}
                        # echo what user sends via serial terminal, p 119
void loop()
{
  //Only print when data is received
  if (Serial.available() > 0)
  {
    data = Serial.read(); //Read byte of data
    Serial.print(data);   //Print byte of data   ⓐ        ... a new line as per p 119
  }
}
```

Launch the serial monitor and type anything you want into the text entry field. As soon as you press Send, whatever you typed is echoed back and displayed in the serial monitor. You have already selected to append a "newline" ⓐ to the end of each command, which will ensure that each response is on a new line. That is why `Serial.print()` is used instead of `Serial.println()` in the preceding sketch.

Understanding the Differences Between Chars and Ints

When you send an alphanumeric character via the serial monitor, you aren't actually passing a "5", or an "A". You're sending a byte that the computer interprets as a character. In the case of serial communication, the ASCII character set is used to represent all the letters, number, symbols, and special commands that you might want to send. The base ASCII character set, shown in Figure 6-9, is a 7-bit set and contains a total of 128 unique characters or commands.

When reading a value that you've sent from the computer, as you did in Listing 6-3, the data must be read as a `char` type. Even if you are only expecting ⓑ to send numbers from the serial terminal, you need to read values as a character first, and then convert as necessary. For example, if you were to modify the code to declare `data` as type `int`, sending a value of 5 would return 53 to the serial monitor because the decimal representation of the character 5 is the number 53. You can confirm this by looking at the ASCII reference table in Figure 6-9.

Hex	Dec	Char		Hex	Dec	Char	Hex	Dec	Char	Hex	Dec	Char
0x00	0	NULL	null	0x20	32	Space	0x40	64	@	0x60	96	`
0x01	1	SOH	Start of heading	0x21	33	!	0x41	65	A	0x61	97	a
0x02	2	STX	Start of text	0x22	34	"	0x42	66	B	0x62	98	b
0x03	3	ETX	End of text	0x23	35	#	0x43	67	C	0x63	99	c
0x04	4	EOT	End of transmission	0x24	36	$	0x44	68	D	0x64	100	d
0x05	5	ENQ	Enquiry	0x25	37	%	0x45	69	E	0x65	101	e
0x06	6	ACK	Acknowledge	0x26	38	&	0x46	70	F	0x66	102	f
0x07	7	BELL	Bell	0x27	39	'	0x47	71	G	0x67	103	g
0x08	8	BS	Backspace	0x28	40	(	0x48	72	H	0x68	104	h
0x09	9	TAB	Horizontal tab	0x29	41	)	0x49	73	I	0x69	105	i
0x0A	10	LF	New line	0x2A	42	*	0x4A	74	J	0x6A	106	j
0x0B	11	VT	Vertical tab	0x2B	43	+	0x4B	75	K	0x6B	107	k
0x0C	12	FF	Form Feed	0x2C	44	,	0x4C	76	L	0x6C	108	l
0x0D	13	CR	Carriage return	0x2D	45	-	0x4D	77	M	0x6D	109	m
0x0E	14	SO	Shift out	0x2E	46	.	0x4E	78	N	0x6E	110	n
0x0F	15	SI	Shift in	0x2F	47	/	0x4F	79	O	0x6F	111	o
0x10	16	DLE	Data link escape	0x30	48	0	0x50	80	P	0x70	112	p
0x11	17	DC1	Device control 1	0x31	49	1	0x51	81	Q	0x71	113	q
0x12	18	DC2	Device control 2	0x32	50	2	0x52	82	R	0x72	114	r
0x13	19	DC3	Device control 3	0x33	51	3	0x53	83	S	0x73	115	s
0x14	20	DC4	Device control 4	0x34	52	4	0x54	84	T	0x74	116	t
0x15	21	NAK	Negative ack	0x35	53	5	0x55	85	U	0x75	117	u
0x16	22	SYN	Synchronous idle	0x36	54	6	0x56	86	V	0x76	118	v
0x17	23	ETB	End transmission block	0x37	55	7	0x57	87	W	0x77	119	w
0x18	24	CAN	Cancel	0x38	56	8	0x58	88	X	0x78	120	x
0x19	25	EM	End of medium	0x39	57	9	0x59	89	Y	0x79	121	y
0x1A	26	SUB	Substitute	0x3A	58	:	0x5A	90	Z	0x7A	122	z
0x1B	27	FSC	Escape	0x3B	59	;	0x5B	91	[	0x7B	123	{
0x1C	28	FS	File separator	0x3C	60	<	0x5C	92	\	0x7C	124	|
0x1D	29	GS	Group separator	0x3D	61	=	0x5D	93	]	0x7D	125	}
0x1E	30	RS	Record separator	0x3E	62	>	0x5E	94	^	0x7E	126	~
0x1F	31	US	Unit separator	0x3F	63	?	0x5F	95	_	0x7F	127	DEL

Figure 6-9: ASCII table

Credit: Ben Borowiec, www.benborowiec.com.

However, you'll often want to send numeric values to the Arduino. So how do you do that? You can do so in a few ways. First, you can simply compare the characters directly. If you want to turn an LED on when you send a 1, you can compare the character values like this: if (Serial.read() == '1'). Note that the single quotes around the '1' indicate that it should be treated like a character.

A second option is to convert each incoming byte to an integer by subtracting the zero-valued character, like this: int val = Serial.read() - '0'. However, this doesn't work very well if you intend to send numbers that are greater than 9, because they will be multiple digits. To deal with this, the Arduino IDE includes a handy function called parseInt() that attempts to extract integers from a serial data stream. The examples that follow elaborate on these techniques.

Sending Single Characters to Control an LED

Before your dive into parsing larger strings of multiple-digit numbers, start by writing a sketch that uses a simple character comparison to control an LED.

You'll send a 1 to turn an LED on, and a 0 to turn it off. Wire an LED up to pin 9 of your Arduino as shown in Figure 6-10.

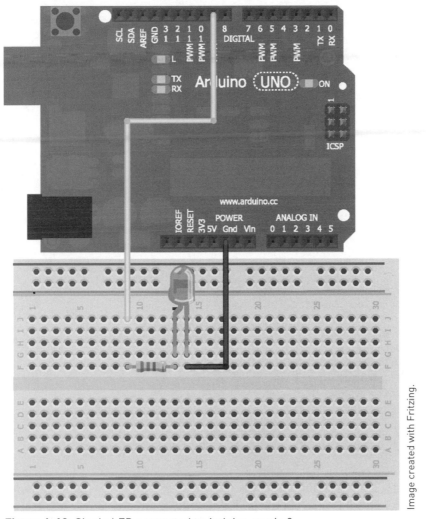

Figure 6-10: Single LED connected to Arduino on pin 9

Image created with Fritzing.

As explained in the previous section, when only sending a single character, the easier thing to do is to do a simple character comparison in an if statement. Each time a character is added to the buffer, it is compared to a '0' or a '1', and the appropriate action is taken. Load up the code in Listing 6-4 and experiment with sending a 0 or a 1 from the serial terminal.

Listing 6-4: Single LED Control using Characters—single_char_control.ino

```
//Single Character Control of an LED

const int LED=9;

char data; //Holds incoming character

void setup()
{
  Serial.begin(9600); //Serial Port at 9600 baud
  pinMode(LED, OUTPUT);
}

void loop()                    // From serial terminal send 0 or 1
{
  //Only act when data is available in the buffer
  if (Serial.available() > 0)     // reads the trailing '\n' also
  {
    data = Serial.read(); //Read byte of data
    //Turn LED on
    if (data == '1')
    {
      digitalWrite(LED, HIGH);
      Serial.println("LED ON");
    }
    //Turn LED off
@   else if (data == '0')
    {
      digitalWrite(LED, LOW);
      Serial.println("LED OFF");
    }
  }

}
```

Note that an `else if` statement is used instead of a simple `else` statement. Because your terminal is also set to send a newline character with each transmission, it's critical to clear these from the buffer. `Serial.read()` will read in the newline character, see that is not equivalent to a `'0'` or a `'1'`, and it will be overwritten the next time `Serial.read()` is called. If just an `else` statement were used, both `'0'` and `'\n'` would trigger turning the LED off. Even when sending a `'1'`, the LED would immediately turn off again when the `'\n'` was received!

Sending Lists of Values to Control an RGB LED

Sending a single command character is fine for controlling a single digital pin, but what if you want to accomplish some more complex control schemes? This section explores sending multiple comma-separate values to simultaneously command multiple devices. To facilitate testing this, wire up a common cathode RGB LED as shown in Figure 6-11.

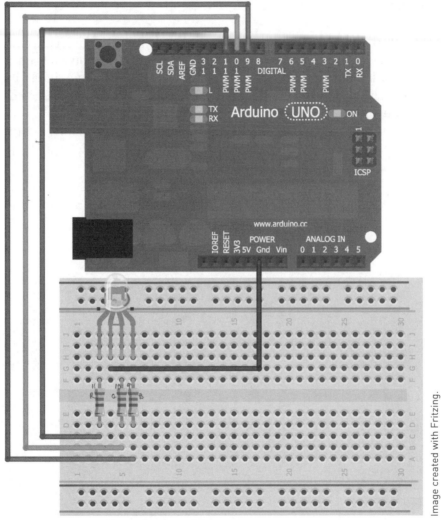

Figure 6-11: RGB LED connected to Arduino

To control this RGB LED, you send three separate 8-bit values (0–255) to set the brightness of each LED color. For example, to set all the colors to full brightness, you send `"255,255,255"`. This presents a few challenges:

- You need to differentiate between numbers and commas.
- You need to turn this sequence of characters into integers that you can pass to `analogWrite()` functions.
- You need to be able to handle the fact that values could be one, two, or three digits.

Thankfully, the Arduino IDE implements a very handy function for identifying and extracting integers: `Serial.parseInt()`. Each call to this function waits until a non-numeric value enters the serial buffer, and converts the previous digits into an integer. The first two values are read when the commas are detected, and the last value is read when the newline is detected.

To test this function for yourself, load the program shown in Listing 6-5 on to your Arduino.

Listing 6-5: RGB LED Control via Serial—list_control.ino

```
//Sending Multiple Variables at Once

//Define LED pins
const int RED   =11;
const int GREEN =10;
const int BLUE  =9;

//Variables for RGB levels
int rval = 0;
int gval = 0;
int bval = 0;

void setup()
{
  Serial.begin(9600); //Serial Port at 9600 baud

  //Set pins as outputs
  pinMode(RED, OUTPUT);
  pinMode(GREEN, OUTPUT);
  pinMode(BLUE, OUTPUT);
}

void loop()
{
  //Keep working as long as data is in the buffer
  while (Serial.available() > 0)
```

```
{
  rval = Serial.parseInt();  //First valid integer
  gval = Serial.parseInt();  //Second valid integer
  bval = Serial.parseInt();  //Third valid integer

  if (Serial.read() == '\n') //Done transmitting
  {
    //set LED
    analogWrite(RED, rval);
    analogWrite(GREEN, gval);
    analogWrite(BLUE, bval);
  }
}
}
```

(handwritten annotations) // read the '\n' in buffer

(handwritten annotations) # : Send ddd, ddd, ddd (\n), where each ddd is in [0, 255] range

The program keeps looking for the three integer values until a newline is detected. Once this happens, the values that were read are used to set the brightness of the LEDs. To use this, open the serial monitor and enter three values between 0 and 255 separated by a comma, like "200,30,180". Try mixing all kinds of pretty colors!

Talking to a Desktop App

Eventually, you're bound to get bored of doing all your serial communication through the Arduino serial monitor. Conveniently, just about any desktop programming language you can think of has libraries that allow it to interface with the serial ports in your computer. You can use your favorite desktop programming language to write programs that send serial commands to your Arduino and that react to serial data being transmitted from the Arduino to the computer.

In this book, Processing is the desktop programming language of choice because it is very similar to the Arduino language that you have already become familiar with. In fact, the Arduino programming language is based on Processing! Other popular desktop languages (that have well-documented serial communication libraries) include Python, PHP, Visual Basic, C, and more. First, you'll learn how to read transmitted serial data in Processing, and then you'll learn how you can use Processing to create a simple graphical user interface (GUI) to send commands to your Arduino.

Talking to Processing

Processing has a fairly simple programming interface, and it's similar to the one you've already been using for the Arduino. In this section, you install Processing, and then write a simple graphical interface to generate a graphical output based on serial data transmitted from your Arduino. Once that's working, you implement communication in the opposite direction to control your Arduino from a GUI on your computer.

Installing Processing

First things first, you need to install Processing on your machine. This is the same process that you followed in the first chapter to get the Arduino IDE installed. Visit `http://processing.org/download/` (or find the download link on the digital content page for this chapter on `www.exploringarduino.com`) and download the compressed package for your operating system. Simply unzip it to your preferred location and you are ready to go! Run the Processing application, and you should see an IDE that looks like the one shown in Figure 6-12.

Figure 6-12: The Processing IDE. Does it look familiar?

Controlling a Processing Sketch from Your Arduino

For your first experiment with Processing, you use a potentiometer connected to your Arduino to control the color of a window on your computer. Wire up your Arduino with a potentiometer, referencing Figure 6-6 again. You already know the Arduino code necessary to send the analog values from the potentiometer to your computer. The fact that you are now feeding the serial data into Processing does not have any impact on the way you transmit it.

116

Reference the code in Listing 6-6 and load it on to your Arduino. It sends an updated value of the potentiometer to the computer's serial port every 50 milliseconds. The 50ms is important; if you were to send it as fast as possible, the Processing sketch wouldn't be able to handle it as quickly as you are sending it, and you would eventually overflow the serial input buffer on your computer.

below

Listing 6-6: Arduino Code to send Data to the Computer—pot_to_processing/arduino_read_pot

240 w, XBee

```
//Sending POT value to the computer

const int POT=0; //Pot on analog pin 0

int val; //For holding mapped pot value

void setup()
{
  Serial.begin(9600); //Start Serial
}

void loop()
{
  val = map(analogRead(POT), 0, 1023, 0, 255); //Read and map POT
  Serial.println(val);                          //Send value
  delay(50);                                    //Delay so we don't flood
                                                //the computer
}
```

Now comes the interesting part: writing a Processing sketch to do something interesting with this incoming data. The sketch in Listing 6-7 reads the data in the serial buffer and adjusts the brightness of a color on the screen of your computer based on the value it receives. First, copy the code from Listing 6-7 into a new Processing sketch. You need to change just one important part. The Processing sketch needs to know which serial port to expect data to arrive on. This is the same port that you've been programming the Arduino from. In the following listing, replace `"COM3"` with your serial port number. Remember that on Linux and Mac it will look like `/dev/ttyUSB0`, for example. You can copy the exact name from within the Arduino IDE if you are unsure.

```
port = new Serial(this, "COM3", 9600); //setup serial
```

Listing 6-7: Processing Code to Read Data and Change Color on the Screen—pot_to_ processing/processing_display_color

```
//Processing Sketch to Read Value and Change Color on the Screen

//Import and initialize serial port library
import processing.serial.*;
Serial port;

float brightness = 0; //For holding value from pot

void setup()
{
  size(500,500);                              //Window size
  port = new Serial(this, "COM3", 9600); //Set up serial
  port.bufferUntil('\n');                     //Set up port to read until    ⓐ
                                              //newline
}

void draw()                    0,0,0   black
{                            / 0,0,255  blue
  background(0,0,brightness); //Updates the window
}

void serialEvent (Serial port)    // Called when bufferUntil ( )  condition @ is met
{
  brightness = float(port.readStringUntil('\n')); //Gets val
}
```

After you've loaded the code into your Processing IDE and set the serial port properly, make sure that the Arduino serial monitor isn't open. Only one program on your computer can have access to the serial port at a time. Click the Run button in the Processing IDE (the button in the top left of the window with a triangle); when you do so, a small window will pop up (see Figure 6-13). As you turn the potentiometer, you should see the color of the window change from black to blue.

Now that you've seen it working, let's walk through the code to gain a better understanding of how the Processing sketch is working. Unlike in Arduino, the serial library is not imported automatically. By calling `import processing .serial.*;` and `Serial port;` you are importing the serial library and making a serial object called `port`.

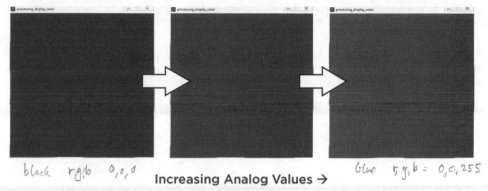

black rgb 0,0,0   **Increasing Analog Values →**   *Blue r,g,b = 0,0,255*

Figure 6-13: Example windows from Processing sketch

Like the Arduino, Processing has a `setup()` function that runs once at the beginning of the sketch. In this sketch, it sets up the serial port and creates a window of size 500×500 pixels with the command `size(500,500)`. The command `port = new Serial(this, "COM3", 9600)` tells Processing everything it needs to know about creating the serial port. The instance (referred to as "port") will run in this sketch and communicate on COM3 (or whatever your serial port is) at 9600 baud. The Arduino and the program on your computer must agree on the speed at which they communicate; otherwise, you'll get garbage characters. `port.bufferUntil('\n')` tells Processing to buffer the serial input and not do anything with the information until it sees a newline character.

Instead of `loop()`, Processing defines other special functions. This program uses `draw()` and `serialEvent()`. The `draw()` function is similar to Arduino's `loop()`; it runs continuously and updates the display. The `background()` function sets the color of the window by setting red, green, and blue values (the three arguments of the function). In this case, the value from the potentiometer is controlling the blue intensity, and red and green are set to `0`. You can change what color your pot is adjusting simply by swapping which argument `brightness` is filling in. RGB color values are 8-bit values ranging from `0` to `255`, which is why the potentiometer is mapped to those values before being transmitted.

`serialEvent()` is called whenever the `bufferUntil()` condition that you specified in the `setup()` is met. Whenever a newline character is received, the `serialEvent()` function is triggered. The incoming serial information is read as a string with `port.readStringUntil('\n')`. You can think of a string as an array of text. To use the string as a number, you must convert it to a floating-point number with `float()`. This sets the brightness variable, changing the background color of the application window.

To stop the application and close the serial port, click the Stop button in the Processing IDE; it's the square located next to the Run button.

buffer Until ()   gets ccc \n   into buffer
port.read String Until ()   extracts ccc as string , discarding \n

---

SUDOGLOVE PROCESSING DEBUGGER

The SudoGlove is a control glove that drives RC cars and controls other hardware. I developed a Processing debugging display that graphically shows the values of various sensors. You can learn more about it here: `www.sudoglove.com`.

Download the source code for the Processing display here: `www.jeremyblum.com/2011/03/25/processing-based-sudoglove-visual-debugger/`. You can also find this source code on the Wiley website shown at the beginning of this chapter.

Sending Data from Processing to Your Arduino

The obvious next step is to do the opposite. Wire up an RGB LED to your Arduino as shown in Figure 6-11 and load on the same program from earlier that you used to receive a string of three comma-separated values for setting the red, green, and blue intensities (Listing 6-5). Now, instead of sending a string of three values from the serial monitor, you select a color using a color picker.

Load and run the code in Listing 6-8 in Processing, remembering to adjust the serial port number accordingly as you did with the previous sketch. Processing sketches automatically load collateral files from a folder called "data" in the sketch folder. The hsv.jpg file is included in the code download for this chapter. Download it and place it in a folder named "data" in the same directory as your sketch. Processing defaults to saving sketches in your Documents folder. The structure will look similar to the one shown in Figure 6-14.

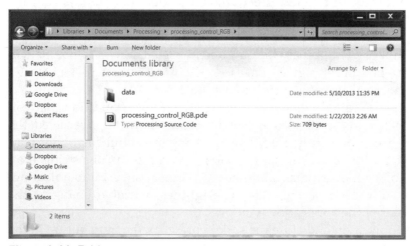

Figure 6-14: Folder structure

The image in the data folder will serve as the color selector.

Listing 6-8: Processing Sketch to Set Arduino RGB Colors— processing_control_RGB/ processing_control_RGB

```
import processing.serial.*; //Import serial library
PImage img;                 //Image object
Serial port;                //Serial port object

void setup()
{
  size(640,256);                           //Size of HSV image
  img = loadImage("hsv.jpg");              //Load in background image    (from data folder in
  port = new Serial(this, "COM9", 9600); //Open serial port                    sketch dir)
}

void draw()
{
  background(0);    //Black background
  image(img,0,0);   //Overlay image
}

void mousePressed()
{
  color c = get(mouseX, mouseY); //Get the RGB color where mouse was       (@134
pressed
  String colors = int(red(c))+","+int(green(c))+","+int(blue(c))+"\n"; //
extract
values from color
  print(colors);       //Print colors for debugging
  port.write(colors); //Send values to Arduino
}
```

When you execute the program, you should see a screen like the one shown in Figure 6-15 pop up. Click different colors and the RGB values will be transmitted to the Arduino to control the RGB LED's color. Note that the serial console also displays the commands being sent to assist you in any debugging.

After you've finished staring at all the pretty colors, look back at the code and consider how it's working. As before, the serial library is imported and a serial object called `port` is created. A `PImage` object call `img` is also created. This will hold the background image. In the `setup()`, the serial port is initialized, the display window is set to the size of the image, and image is imported into the image object by calling `img = loadImage("hsv.jpg")`.

In the `draw()` function, the image is loaded in the window with `image(img,0,0)`. `img` is the image you want to draw in the window, and `0, 0` are coordinates where the image will start to be drawn. `0,0` is the top left of the application window.

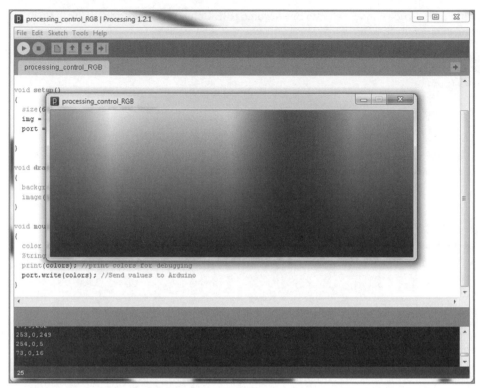

Figure 6-15: Processing color selection screen

@133   Every time the mouse button is pressed, the mousePressed() function is called. The color of the pixel where you clicked is saved to a color object named c. The get() method tells the application where to get the color from (in this case, the location of the mouse's X and Y position in the sketch). The sketch converts the object c into a string that can be sent to the Arduino by converting to integers representing red, green, and blue. These values are also printed to the Processing console so that you can see what is being sent.

126   Ensure that the Arduino is connected and programmed with the code from Listing 6-5. Run the processing sketch (with the correct serial port specified) and click around the color map to adjust the color of the LED connected to your Arduino.

Learning Special Tricks with the Arduino Leonardo (and Other 32U4-Based Arduinos)

The Leonardo, in addition to other Arduinos that implement MCUs that connect directly to USB, has the unique ability to emulate nonserial devices such as a keyboard or mouse. In this section you learn about using a Leonardo to emulate these devices. You need to be extremely careful to implement these functions in a way that does not make reprogramming difficult. For example, if you write a sketch that emulates a mouse and continuously moves your pointer around the screen, you might have trouble clicking on the Upload button in the Arduino IDE! In this section, you learn a few tricks that you can use to avoid these circumstances.

> **TIP** If you get stuck with a board that's too hard to program due to its keyboard or mouse input, hold down the Reset button and release it while pressing the Upload button in the Arduino IDE to reprogram it.

When you first connect a Leonardo to a Windows computer, you need to install drivers, just as you did with the Arduino Uno in the first chapter. Follow the same directions at `http://arduino.cc/en/Guide/ArduinoLeonardoMicro#toc8` for Leonardo-specific instructions. (These instructions are also linked from the digital content page for this chapter from `www.exploringarduino.com`.)

Emulating a Keyboard

Using the Leonardo's unique capability to emulate USB devices, you can easily turn your Arduino into a keyboard. Emulating a keyboard allows you to easily send key-combination commands to your computer or type data directly into a file that is open on your computer.

Typing Data into the Computer

The Leonardo can emulate a USB keyboard, sending keystrokes and key combinations. This section explores how to use both concepts. First, you write a simple program that records data from a few analog sensors into a comma-separated-value (.csv) format that you can later open up with Excel or Google spreadsheets to generate a graph of the values.

Start by opening the text editor of your choice and saving a blank document with a .csv extension. To do this, you can generally choose the file type in the Save dialog, select "All Files," and manually type the file name with the extension, such as "data.csv." The demo video also shows how to create a .csv file.

Next, create a simple circuit like the one shown in Figure 6-16. It will monitor both light and temperature levels using analog sensors that you have already seen in Chapter 3, "Reading Analog Sensors." In addition to the sensors, the circuit includes a button for turning the logging functionality on and off, and an LED that will indicate whether it is currently logging data.

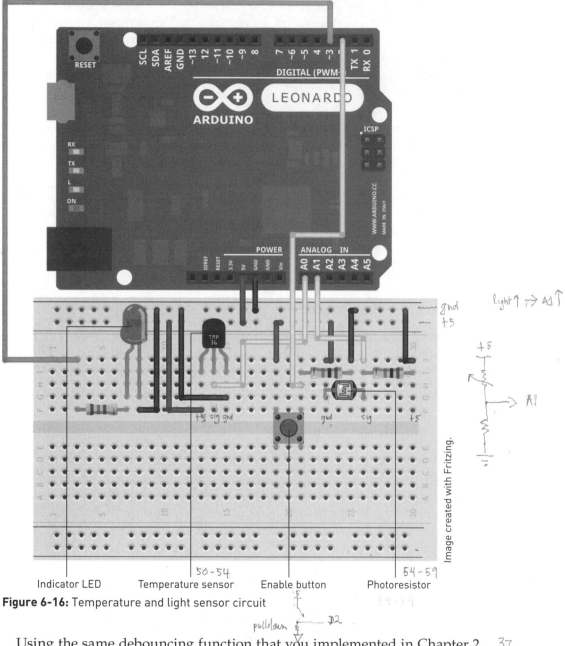

Figure 6-16: Temperature and light sensor circuit

Indicator LED   Temperature sensor   Enable button   Photoresistor

Using the same debouncing function that you implemented in Chapter 2, "Digital Inputs, Outputs, and Pulse-Width Modulation," you use the pushbutton to toggle the logging mode on and off. While in logging mode, the Arduino polls the sensors and "types" those values into your computer in a comma-separated format once every second. An indicator LED remains illuminated while you are logging data. Because you want the Arduino to be constantly polling the state of the button, you cannot use a `delay()` function to wait 1000ms between each update. Instead, you use the `millis()` function, which returns the number of milliseconds since the Arduino was last reset. You can make the Arduino send data every time the `millis()` function returns a multiple of 1000ms, effectively creating a nonblocking 1-second delay between transmissions. To do this, you can use the modulo operator (`%`). Modulo returns the remainder of a division. If, for example, you executed `1000%1000`, you would find that the result is 0 because 1000/1000=1, with a remainder of 0. `1500%1000`, on the other hand, would return 500 because 1500/1000 is equal to 1, with a remainder of 500. If you take the modulus of `millis()` with `1000`, the result is zero every time `millis()` reaches a value that is a multiple of 1000. By checking this with an `if()` statement, you can execute code once every second.

Examine the code in Listing 6-9 and load it onto your Arduino Leonardo. Ensure that you've selected "Arduino Leonardo" from the Tools > Board menu in the Arduino IDE.

Listing 6-9: Temperature and Light Data Logger—csv_logger.ino

```
//Light and Temp Logger

const int TEMP   =0;        //Temp sensor on analog pin 0
const int LIGHT  =1;        //Light sensor on analog pin 1
const int LED    =3;        //Red LED on pin 13
const int BUTTON =2;        //The button is connected to pin 2

boolean lastButton = LOW;     //Last button state
boolean currentButton = LOW;  //Current button state
boolean running = false;      //Not running by default
int counter = 1;              //An index for logged data entries

void setup()
{
  pinMode (LED, OUTPUT);    //Set blue LED as output
  Keyboard.begin();         //Start keyboard emulation
}

void loop()
{
  currentButton = debounce(lastButton);            //Read debounced state

  if (lastButton == LOW && currentButton == HIGH) //If it was pressed…
    running = !running;                            //Toggle running state

  lastButton = currentButton;                      //Reset button value

  if (running)                          //If logger is running
```

```
  {
    digitalWrite(LED, HIGH);                //Turn the LED on
    if (millis() % 1000 == 0)               //If time is multiple
                                            //of 1000ms
    {
      int temperature = analogRead(TEMP); //Read the temperature
      int brightness = analogRead(LIGHT); //Read the light level
      Keyboard.print(counter);              //Print the index number
      Keyboard.print(",");                  //Print a comma
      Keyboard.print(temperature);          //Print the temperature
      Keyboard.print(",");                  //Print a comma
      Keyboard.println(brightness);         //Print brightness, newline
      counter++;                            //Increment the counter
    }
  }
  else
  {
    digitalWrite(LED, LOW);  //If logger not running, turn LED off
  }
}


/*
 * Debouncing Function
 * Pass it the previous button state,
 * and get back the current debounced button state.
 */
boolean debounce(boolean last)
{
  boolean current = digitalRead(BUTTON);    //Read the button state
  if (last != current)                      //If it's different…
  {
    delay(5);                               //Wait 5ms
    current = digitalRead(BUTTON);          //Read it again
  }
  return current;                           //Return the current
                                            //value
}
```

Before you test the data logger, let's highlight some of the new functionality that has been implemented in this sketch. Similarly to how you initialized the serial communication, the keyboard communication is initialized by putting Keyboard.begin() in the setup().

Each time through loop(), the Arduino checks the state of the button and runs the debouncing function that you are already familiar with. When the button is pressed, the value of the *running* variable is inverted. This is accomplished by setting it to its opposite with the ! operator.

While the Arduino is in *running* mode, the logging step is executed only every 1000ms using the logic described previously. The keyboard functions work very similarly to the serial functions. Keyboard.print() "types" the given string into your computer. After reading the two analog sensors, the Arduino sends the values to your computer as keystrokes. When you use `Keyboard.println()`, the Arduino emulates pressing the Enter or Return key on your keyboard after sending the given string. An incrementing counter and both analog values are entered in a comma-separated format.

Follow the demo video from this chapter's web page to see this sketch in action. Make sure that your cursor is actively positioned in a text document, and then press the button to start logging. You should see the document begin to populate with data. Hold your hand over the light sensor to change the value or squeeze the temperature sensor to see the value increase. When you have finished, press the button again to stop logging. After you save your file, you can import it into the spreadsheet application of your choice and graph it over time. This is shown in the demo video.

How, using google spreadsheet

NOTE To watch a demo video of the live temperature and light logger, visit www.exploringarduino.com/content/ch6. You can also find this video on the Wiley website shown at the beginning of this chapter.

Commanding Your Computer to Do Your Bidding

In addition to typing like a keyboard, you can also use the Leonardo to emulate key combinations. On Windows computers, pressing the Windows+L keys locks the computer screen (On Linux, you can use Control+Alt+L). Using that knowledge paired with a light sensor, you can have your computer lock automatically when you turn the lights off. OS X uses the Control+Shift+Eject, or Control+Shift+Power keys to lock the machine, which can't be emulated by the Leonardo because it cannot send an Eject or Power simulated button press. In this example, you learn how to lock a Windows computer. You can continue to use the same circuit shown in Figure 6-16, though only the light sensor will be used in this example.

Run the previous sketch at a few different light levels and see how the light sensor reading changes. Using this information, you should pick a threshold value below which you will want your computer to lock. (In my room, I found that with the lights off the value was about 300, and it was about 700 with the lights on. So, I chose a threshold value of 500.) When the light sensor value drops below that value, the lock command will be sent to the computer. You might want to adjust this value for your environment.

Load the sketch in Listing 6-10 on to your Arduino. Just make sure you have your threshold set to a reasonable value first, by testing what light levels in your room correspond to various analog levels. If you pick a poorly calibrated value, it might lock your computer as soon as you upload it!

Listing 6-10: Light-Based Computer Lock—lock_computer.ino

```
//Locks your computer when you turn off the lights

const int LIGHT     =1;    //Light sensor on analog pin 1
const int THRESHOLD =500;  //Brightness must drop below this level
                           //to lock computer

void setup()
{
  Keyboard.begin();
}

void loop()
{
  int brightness = analogRead(LIGHT);    //Read the light level

  if (brightness < THRESHOLD)
  {
    Keyboard.press(KEY_LEFT_GUI);    // Windows · key
    Keyboard.press('l');             // L key
    delay(100);                      // hold em down ...
    Keyboard.releaseAll();           // now release
  }
}
```

After loading the program, try flipping the lights off. Your computer should lock immediately. The following video demo shows this in action. This sketch implements two new keyboard functions: Keyboard.press() and Keyboard.releaseAll(). Running Keyboard.press() is equivalent to starting to hold a key down. So, if you want to hold the Windows key and the L key down at the same time, you run Keyboard.press() on each. Then, you delay for a short period of time and run the Keyboard.releaseAll() function to let go of, or release, the keys. Special keys are defined on the Arduino website: http://arduino.cc/en/Reference/KeyboardModifiers. (This definition table is also linked from the content page for this chapter at www.exploringarduino.com/content/ch6.)

NOTE To watch a demo video of the light-activated computer lock, visit www.exploringarduino.com/content/ch6. You can also find this video on the Wiley website shown at the beginning of this chapter.

Emulating a Mouse

Using a two-axis joystick and some pushbuttons, you can use an Arduino Leonardo to make your own mouse! The joystick will control the mouse location, and the buttons will control the left, middle, and right buttons of the mouse.

Just like with the keyboard functionality, the Arduino language has some great functions built in that make it easy to control mouse functionality.

First things first, get your circuit set up with a joystick and some buttons as shown in Figure 6-17. Don't forget that your buttons need to have pull-down resistors! The joystick will connect to analog pins 0 and 1. (Joysticks are actually just two potentiometers hooked up to a knob.) When you move the joystick all the way in the x direction, it maxes out the x potentiometer, and the same goes for the y direction.

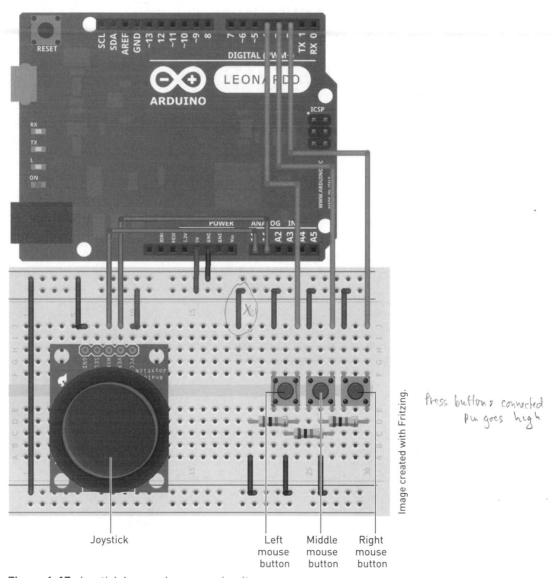

Press button : connected pin goes high

Figure 6-17: Joystick Leonardo mouse circuit

The diagram shows a SparkFun joystick, but any will do. (In the video described after the listing, I used a Parallax joystick.) Depending on the orientation of the joystick, you might need to adjust the bounds of the map function or swap the x/y in the code below.

After you've wired the circuit, it's time to load some code onto the Leonardo. Load up the code in Listing 6-11 and play with the joystick and buttons; the pointer on your screen should respond accordingly.

Listing 6-11: Mouse Control Code for the Leonardo—mouse.ino

```
// Make a Mouse!

const int LEFT_BUTTON   =4;   //Input pin for the left button
const int MIDDLE_BUTTON =3;   //Input pin for the middle button
const int RIGHT_BUTTON  =2;   //Input pin for the right button
const int X_AXIS        =0;   //Joystick x-axis analog pin
const int Y_AXIS        =1;   //Joystick y-axis analog pin

void setup()
{
  Mouse.begin();
}

void loop()
{
  int xVal = readJoystick(X_AXIS);        //Get x-axis movement
  int yVal = readJoystick(Y_AXIS);        //Get y-axis movement

  Mouse.move(xVal, yVal, 0);              //Move the mouse

  readButton(LEFT_BUTTON, MOUSE_LEFT);    //Control left button
  readButton(MIDDLE_BUTTON, MOUSE_MIDDLE); //Control middle button
  readButton(RIGHT_BUTTON, MOUSE_RIGHT);  //Control right button

  delay(5);                               //This controls responsiveness
}

//Reads joystick value, scales it, and adds dead range in middle
int readJoystick(int axis)
{
  int val = analogRead(axis);             //Read analog value
  val = map(val, 0, 1023, -10, 10);       //Map the reading

  if (val <= 2 && val >= -2)              //Create dead zone to stop mouse
drift
    return 0;

  else                                    //Return scaled value
    return val;
```

↳ movement of scroll wheel

```
}

//Read a button and issue a mouse command
void readButton(int pin, char mouseCommand)
{
  //If button is depressed, click if it hasn't already been clicked
  if (digitalRead(pin) == HTGH)          // User has pressed button
  {
    if (!Mouse.isPressed(mouseCommand))   // If the virtual mouse button is not pressed
    {
      Mouse.press(mouseCommand);          // press it ... !
    }
  }
  //Release the mouse if it has been clicked.
  else                                    (else)
  {
    if (Mouse.isPressed(mouseCommand))    // If the virtual button is pressed
    {
      Mouse.release(mouseCommand);        // release it
    }
  }
}
```

This is definitely one of the more complicated sketches that have been covered so far, so it's worth stepping through it to both understand the newly introduced functions and the program flow used to make the joystick mouse.

Each of the button and joystick pins are defined at the top of the sketch, and the mouse library is started in the setup. Each time through the loop, the joystick values are read and mapped to movement values for the mouse. The mouse buttons are also monitored and the button presses are transmitted if necessary.

A readJoystick() function was created to read the joystick values and map them. Each joystick axis has a range of 1024 values when read into the analog-to-digital converter (ADC). However, mouse motions are relative. In other words, passing a value of 0 to Mouse.move() for each axis will result in no movement on that axis. Passing a positive value for the x-axis will move the mouse to the right, and a negative value will move it to the left. The larger the value, the more the mouse will move. Hence, in the readJoystick() function, a value of 0 to 1023 is mapped to a value of –10 to 10. A small buffer value around 0 is added where the mouse will not move. This is because even while the joystick is in the middle position, the actual value may fluctuate around 512. By setting the desired distance back to 0 after being mapped within a certain range, you guarantee that the mouse will not move on its own while the joystick is not being actuated. Once the values are ascertained, Mouse.move() is given the x and y values to move the mouse. A third argument for Mouse.move() determines the movement of the scroll wheel.

To detect mouse clicks, the `readButton()` function was created so that it can be repeated for each of the three buttons to detect. The function detects the current state of the mouse with the `Mouse.isPressed()` command and controls the mouse accordingly using the `Mouse.press()` and `Mouse.release()` functions.

NOTE To watch a demo video of the joystick mouse controlling a computer pointer, check out www.exploringarduino.com/content/ch6. You can also find this video on the Wiley website shown at the beginning of this chapter.

Summary

In this chapter you learned about the following:

- Arduinos connect to your computer via a USB-to-serial converter.
- Different Arduinos facilitate a USB-to-serial conversion using either dedicated ICs or built-in USB functionality.
- Your Arduino can print data to your computer via your USB serial connection.
- You can use special serial characters to format your serial printing with newlines and tabs.
- All serial data is transmitted as character that can be converted to integers in a variety of ways.
- You can send comma-separated integer lists and use integrated functions to parse them into commands for your sketch.
- You can send data from your Arduino to a Processing desktop application.
- You can receive data from a Processing application on your desktop to control peripherals connected to your Arduino.
- An Arduino Leonardo can be used to emulate a keyboard or mouse.

CHAPTER 7

Shift Registers

Parts You'll Need for This Chapter

Arduino Uno

USB cable (A to B for Uno)

Red LEDs (×8)

Yellow LEDs (×3)

Green LEDs (×5)

220Ω resistors (×8)

SN74HC595N shift register DIP IC

Sharp GP2Y0A41SK0F IR distance sensor with cable

Jumper wires

Breadboard

CODE AND DIGITAL CONTENT FOR THIS CHAPTER

Code downloads, videos, and other digital content for this chapter can be found at www.exploringarduino.com/content/ch7.

In addition, all code can be found at www.wiley.com/go/exploringarduino on the Download Code tab. The code is in the chapter 07 download and individually named according to the names throughout the chapter.

As you chug away building exciting new projects with your Arduino, you might already be thinking: "What happens when I run out of pins?" Indeed, one of the most common projects with the Arduino is using the platform to put an enormous number of blinking LEDs on just about anything. Light up your room! Light up your computer! Light up your dog! Okay, maybe not that last one.

But there's a problem. What happens when you want to start blinking 50 LEDs (or controlling other digital outputs) but you've used up all of your I/O pins? That's where shift registers can come in handy. With shift registers, you can expand the I/O capabilities of your Arduino without having to pay a whole lot more for a more expensive microcontroller with additional I/O pins. In this chapter, you'll learn how shift registers work, and you'll implement both the software and hardware necessary to interface your Arduino with shift registers for the purpose of expanding digital output capabilities of your Arduino. Completing the exercises in this chapter will familiarize you with shift registers, and will help you to make a more informed design decision when you are developing a project with a large number of digital outputs.

CHOOSING THE RIGHT ARDUINO FOR THE JOB

This chapter, like most of the earlier chapters, uses the Arduino Uno as the development platform. Any other Arduino will work just as well to complete the exercises in this chapter, but it's worth considering why you might want to use one Arduino over another for a particular project you may be pursuing. For example, you might already be wondering why you wouldn't just use an Arduino with more I/O pins, such as the Mega2560 or the Due. Of course, that is a completely reasonable way to complete projects that require more outputs. However, as an engineer, you should always be mindful of other considerations when designing a new project. If you only need the processing power of an Uno, but you need more digital outputs, for example, adding a few shift registers will be considerably cheaper than upgrading your entire platform, and will also be more compact. As a tradeoff, it will also require you to write slightly more complex code, and it might necessitate more debugging time to get it working right.

Understanding Shift Registers

A *shift register* is a device that accepts a stream of serial bits and simultaneously outputs the values of those bits onto parallel I/O pins. Most often, these are used for controlling large numbers of LEDs, such as the configurations found in seven-segment displays or LED matrices. Before you dive into using a shift register with your Arduino, consider the diagram in Figure 7-1, which shows the inputs and outputs to a serial-to-parallel shift register. Variations to this diagram throughout the chapter illustrate how various inputs affect the outputs.

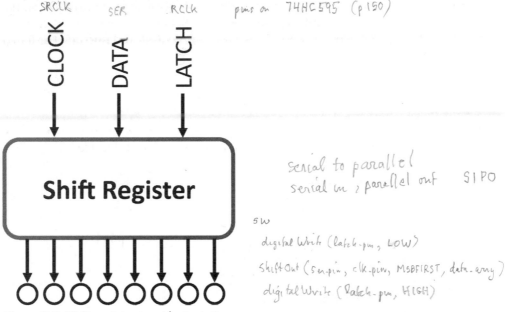

Figure 7-1: Shift register input/output diagram

The eight circles represent LEDs connected to the eight outputs of the shift register. The three inputs are the serial communication lines that connect the shift register to the Arduino.

Sending Parallel and Serial Data

There are essentially two ways to send multiple bits of data. Recall that the Arduino, like all microcontrollers, is digital; it only understands 1s and 0s. So, if you want sufficient data to control eight LEDs digitally (each one on or off), you need to find a way to transmit 8 total bits of information. In previous chapters, you did this in a parallel fashion by using the digitalWrite() and analogWrite() commands to exert control over multiple I/O pins. For an example of parallel information transmission, suppose that you were to turn on eight LEDs with eight digital outputs; all the bits would be transmitted on independent I/O pins at roughly the same time. In Chapter 6, "USB and Serial

Communication," you learned about serial transmission, which transmits 1 bit of data at time. Shift registers allow you to easily convert between serial and parallel data transmission techniques. This chapter focuses on serial-to-parallel shift registers, sometimes called serial in, parallel out (SIPO) shift registers. With these handy devices, you can "clock in" multiple bytes of data serially, and output them from the shift register in a parallel fashion. You can also chain together shift registers, and thus control hundreds of digital outputs from just three Arduino I/O pins.

Working with the 74HC595 Shift Register

The particular shift register you'll be using is the 74HC595 shift register. Take a look at the pin-out diagram from the datasheet shown in Figure 7-2.

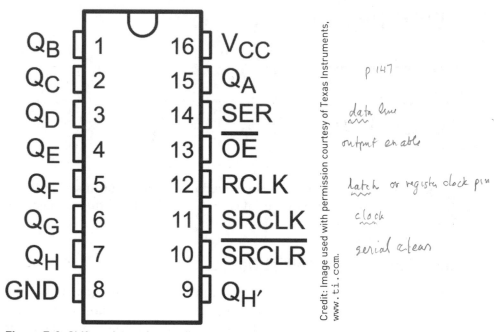

Credit: Image used with permission courtesy of Texas Instruments, www.ti.com.

p 147

data line

output enable

latch or register clock pin

clock

serial clear

Figure 7-2: Shift register pin-out diagram

Understanding the Shift Register Pin Functions

Following is a breakdown of the shift register pin functions:

- Pins Q_A through Q_H represent the eight parallel outputs from the shift register (connected to the circles shown in Figure 7-1).

- VCC will connect to 5V.
- GND will connect to a shared ground with the Arduino.
- The SER pin is represented by the DATA input in Figure 7-1. This is the pin where you will feed in 8 sequential bit values to set the values of the parallel outputs.
- The SRCLK pin is represented by the CLOCK pin in Figure 7-1. Every time this pin goes high, the values in the shift register shift by 1 bit. It will be pulsed eight times to pull in all the data that you are sending on the data pin.
- The RCLK pin is represented by the LATCH pin in Figure 7-1. Also known as the *register clock pin*, the latch pin is used to "commit" your recently shifted serial values to the parallel outputs all at once. This pin allows you to sequentially shift data into the chip and have all the values show up on the parallel outputs at the same time.   *"latch out" all at once, that data that was shifted in 1 bit at a time*

You will not be using the $\overline{\text{SRCLR}}$ or $\overline{\text{OE}}$ pins in these examples, but you might want to use them for your project, so it's worth understanding what they do. $\overline{\text{OE}}$ stands for output enable. The bar over the pin name indicates that it is active low. In other words, when the pin is held low, the output will be enabled. When it is held high, the output will be disabled. In these examples, this pin will be connected directly to ground, so that the parallel outputs are always enabled. You could alternatively connect this to an I/O pin of the Arduino to simultaneously turn all the LEDs on or off. The $\overline{\text{SRCLR}}$ pin is the serial clear pin. When pulled low, it empties the contents of the shift register. For your purposes in this chapter, you tie it directly to 5V to prevent the shift register values from being cleared.

Understanding How the Shift Register Works

The shift register is a synchronous device; it only acts on the rising edge of the clock signal. Every time the clock signal transitions from low to high, all the values currently stored in the eight output registers are shifted over one position. (The last one is either discarded or output on the Q_H' pin if you are cascading registers.) Simultaneously, the value currently on the DATA input is shifted into the first position. By doing this eight times, the present values are shifted out and the new values are shifted into the register. The LATCH pin is set high at the end of this cycle to make the newly shifted values appear on the outputs. The flowchart shown in Figure 7-3 further illustrates this program flow. Suppose, for example, that you want to set every other LED to the ON state (Q_A, Q_C, Q_E, Q_G). Represented in binary, you want the output of the parallel pins on the shift register to look like this: 10101010.

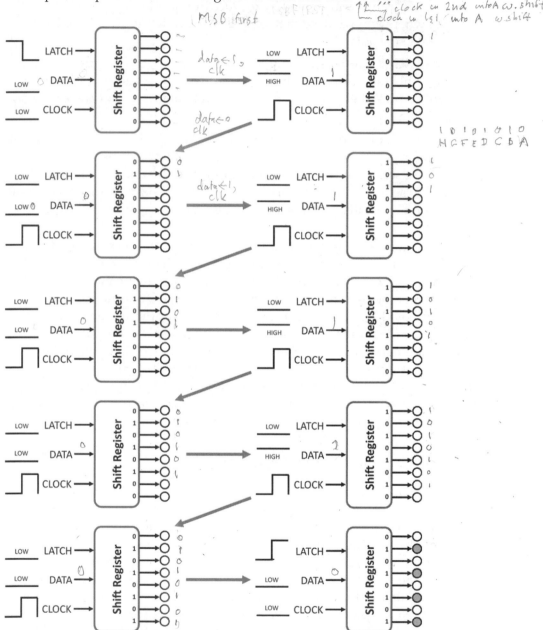

Figure 7-3: Shifting a value into a shift register

Now, follow the steps for writing to the shift register above. First, the LATCH pin is set low so that the current LED states are not changed while new values are shifted in. Then, the LED states are shifted into the registers in order on the CLOCK edge from the DATA line. After all the values have been shifted in, the LATCH pin is set high again, and the values are outputted from the shift register.

Shifting Serial Data from the Arduino

Now that you understand what's happening behind the scenes, you can write the Arduino code to control the shift register in this fashion. As with all your previous experiments, you use a convenient function that's built in to the Arduino IDE to shift data into the register IC. You can use the shiftOut() function to easily shift out 8 bits of data onto an arbitrary I/O pin. It accepts four parameters:

- The data pin number
- The clock pin number
- The bit order
- The value to shift out

If, for example, you want to shift out the alternating pattern described in the previous section, you could use the shiftOut() function as follows:

```
shiftOut(DATA, CLOCK, MSBFIRST, B10101010);
```

The DATA and CLOCK constants are set to the pin numbers for those lines. MSBFIRST indicates that the most significant bit will be sent first (the leftmost bit when looking at the binary number to send). You could alternatively send the data with the LSBFIRST setting, which would start by transmitting the bits from the right side of the binary data. The final parameter is the number to be sent. By putting a capital B before the number, you are telling the Arduino IDE to interpret the following numbers as a binary value rather than as a decimal integer.

Next, you build a physical version of the system that you just learned about in the previous sections. First, you need to get the shift register wired up to your Arduino:

- The DATA pin will connect to pin 8.
- The LATCH pin will connect to pin 9.
- The CLOCK pin will connect to pin 10.

Don't forget to use current limiting resistors with your LEDs. Reference the diagram shown in Figure 7-4 to set up the circuit.

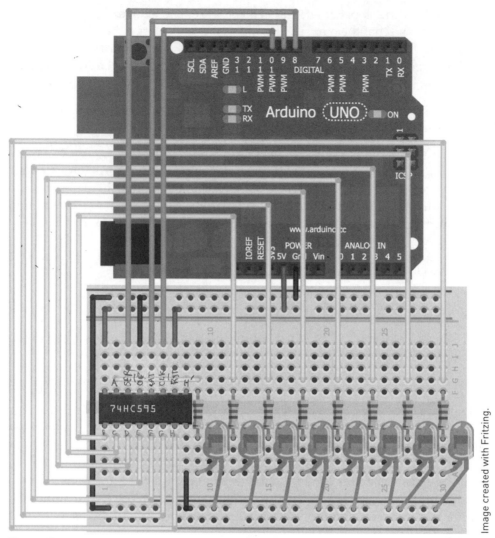

Figure 7-4: Eight LED shift register circuit diagram

Now, using your understanding of how shift registers work, and your understanding of the shiftOut() function, you can use the code in Listing 7-1 to write the alternating LED pattern to the attached LEDs.

Listing 7-1: Alternating LED Pattern on a Shift Register—alternate.ino

```
const int SER    =8;      //Serial output to shift register
const int LATCH  =9;      //Shift register latch pin
const int CLK    =10;     //Shift register clock pin

void setup()
```

```
{
  //Set pins as outputs
  pinMode(SER, OUTPUT);
  pinMode(LATCH, OUTPUT);
  pinMode(CLK, OUTPUT);

  digitalWrite(LATCH, LOW);                    //Latch low
  shiftOut(SER, CLK, MSBFIRST, B10101010);     //Shift most sig. bit first
  digitalWrite(LATCH, HIGH);                   //Latch high - show pattern
}

void loop()
{
  //Do nothing
}
```

Because the shift register will latch the values, you need to send them only one time in the setup; they then stay at those values until you change them to something else. This program follows the same steps that were shown graphically in Figure 7-3. The LATCH pin is set low, the 8 bits of data shifted in using the shiftOut() function, and then the LATCH pin is set high again so that the shifted values are output on the parallel output pins of the shift register IC.

DAISY CHAINING SHIFT REGISTERS

Getting eight digital outputs from three I/O pins is a pretty good tradeoff, but what if you could get even more? You can! By daisy chaining multiple shift registers together, you could theoretically add hundreds of digital outputs to your Arduino using just three pins. If you do this, you'll probably want to use a beefier power supply than just USB. The current requirements of a few dozen LEDs can add up very quickly.

Recall from the pin-out in Figure 7-2 that there is an unused pin called Q_H'. When the oldest value is shifted out of the shift register, it isn't discarded; it's actually sent out on that pin. By connecting the Q_H' to the DATA pin of another shift register, and sharing the LATCH and CLOCK pins with the first shift register, you can create a 16-bit shift register that controls twice as many pins.

You can keep adding more and more shift registers, each connected to the last one, to add a crazy of number outputs to your Arduino. You can try this out by hooking up another shift register as described and simply executing the shiftOut() function in your code twice. (Each call to shiftOut() can handle only 8 bits of information.)

Converting Between Binary and Decimal Formats

In Listing 7-1, the LED state information was written as a binary string of digits. This string helps you visualize which LEDs will be turned on and off. However, you can also write the pattern as a decimal value by converting between base2 (binary) and base10 (decimal) systems. Each bit in a binary number (starting from the rightmost, or least significant, bit) represents an increasing power of 2. Converting binary representations to decimal representations is very straightforward. Consider the binary number from earlier displayed in Figure 7-5 with the appropriate decimal conversion steps.

$$1 \quad 0 \quad 1 \quad 0 \quad 1 \quad 0 \quad 1 \quad 0$$

$$2^7 \quad 2^6 \quad 2^5 \quad 2^4 \quad 2^3 \quad 2^2 \quad 2^1 \quad 2^0$$

$$1{\times}128 + 0{\times}64 + 1{\times}32 + 0{\times}16 + 1{\times}8 + 0{\times}4 + 1{\times}2 + 0{\times}1 = 170$$

Figure 7-5: Binary to decimal conversion

The binary value of each bit represents an incrementing power of 2. In the case of this number, bits 7, 5, 3, and 1 are high. So, to find the decimal equivalent, you add 2^7, 2^5, 2^3, and 2^1. The resulting decimal value is 170. You can prove to yourself that this value is equivalent by substituting it into the code listed earlier. Replace the shiftOut() line with this version:

```
shiftOut(SER, CLK, MSBFIRST, 170);
```

You should see the same result as when you used the binary notation.

Controlling Light Animations with a Shift Register

In the previous example, you built a static display with a shift register. However, you'll probably want to display more dynamic information on your LEDs. In the next two examples, you use a shift register to control a lighting effect and a physical bar graph.

Building a "Light Rider"

The light rider is a neat effect that makes it looks like the LEDs are chasing each other back and forth. Continue to use the same circuit that you used previously. The shiftOut() function is very fast, and you can use it to update the shift register several thousand times per second. Because of this, you can quickly update the shift register outputs to make dynamic lighting animations. Here, you light up each LED in turn from left to right, then from right to left. Watch the demo video linked at the end of this section to see this finished circuit in action.

You first want to figure out each animation state so that you can easily cycle through them. For each time step, the LED currently illuminated turns off, and the next light turns on. When the lights reach the end, the same thing happens in reverse. The timing diagram in Figure 7-6 shows how the lights will look for each time step and the decimal value required to turn that specific LED on.

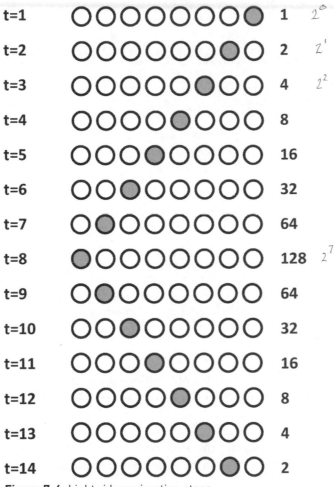

t=1	○○○○○○○●	1 2^0
t=2	○○○○○○●○	2 2^1
t=3	○○○○○●○○	4 2^2
t=4	○○○○●○○○	8
t=5	○○○●○○○○	16
t=6	○○●○○○○○	32
t=7	○●○○○○○○	64
t=8	●○○○○○○○	128 2^7
t=9	○●○○○○○○	64
t=10	○○●○○○○○	32
t=11	○○○●○○○○	16
t=12	○○○○●○○○	8
t=13	○○○○○●○○	4
t=14	○○○○○○●○	2

Figure 7-6: Light rider animation steps

Recalling what you learned earlier in the chapter, convert the binary values for each light step to decimal values that can easily be cycled through. Using a `for` loop, you can cycle through an array of each of these values and shift them out to the shift register one at the time. The code in Listing 7-2 does just that.

Listing 7-2: Light Rider Sequence Code—lightrider.ino

```
//Make a light rider animation

const int SER   =8;     //Serial output to shift register
const int LATCH =9;     //Shift register latch pin
const int CLK   =10;    //Shift register clock pin

//Sequence of LEDs
int seq[14] = {1,2,4,8,16,32,64,128,64,32,16,8,4,2};

void setup()
{
  //Set pins as outputs
  pinMode(SER, OUTPUT);
  pinMode(LATCH, OUTPUT);
  pinMode(CLK, OUTPUT);
}

void loop()
{
  for (int i = 0; i < 14; i++)
  {
    digitalWrite(LATCH, LOW);             //Latch low - start sending
    shiftOut(SER, CLK, MSBFIRST, seq[i]); //Shift most sig. bit first
    digitalWrite(LATCH, HIGH);            //Latch high - stop sending
    delay(100);                           //Animation speed
  }
}
```

Handwritten annotations under the seq array: 2^0 2^1 2^2 2^3 2^4 2^5 2^6 2^7 2^6 ... 2^0

By adjusting the value within the `delay` function, you can change the speed of the animation. Try changing the values of the `seq` array to make different pattern sequences.

> **NOTE** To watch a demo video of the light rider, check out www.exploringarduino .com/content/ch7. You can also find this video on the Wiley website shown at the beginning of this chapter.

Responding to Inputs with an LED Bar Graph

Using the same circuit but adding an IR distance sensor, you can make a bar graph that responds to how close you get. To mix it up a bit more, try using multiple LED colors. The circuit diagram in Figure 7-7 shows the circuit modified with different colored LEDs and an IR distance sensor.

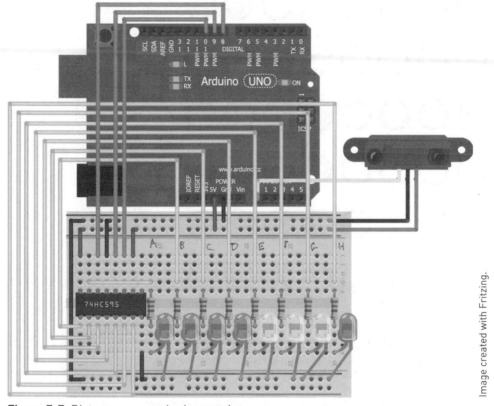

Figure 7-7: Distance-responsive bar graph

Image created with Fritzing.

Using the knowledge you already have from working with analog sensors and the shift register, you should be able to make thresholds and set the LEDs accordingly based on the distance reading. Figure 7-8 shows the decimal values that correspond to each binary representation of LEDs.

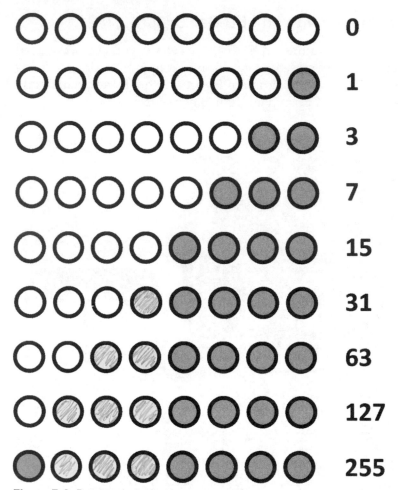

Figure 7-8: Bar graph decimal representations

As you discovered in Chapter 3, "Reading Analog Sensors," the range of usable values for the IR distance sensor is not the full 10-bit range. (I found that a max value of around 500 worked for me, but your setup will probably differ.) Your minimum might not be 0 either. It's best to test the range of your sensor and fill in appropriate values. You can place all the bar graph decimal representations in an array of nine values. By mapping the IR distance sensor (and constraining it) from 0 to 500 down to 0 to 8, you can quickly and easily assign distances to bar graph configurations. The code in Listing 7-3 shows this method in action.

Listing 7-3: Bar Graph Distance Control—bargraph.ino

```
//A bar graph that responds to how close you are

const int SER   =8;     //Serial output to shift register
const int LATCH =9;     //Shift register latch pin
const int CLK   =10;    //Shift register clock pin
const int DIST  =0;     //Distance sensor on analog pin 0

//Possible LED settings
int vals[9] = {0,1,3,7,15,31,63,127,255};

//Maximum value provided by sensor
int maxVal = 500;

//Minimum value provided by sensor
int minVal = 0;

void setup()
{                                          ( <  Serial.begin (9600);   )
  //Set pins as outputs
  pinMode(SER, OUTPUT);
  pinMode(LATCH, OUTPUT);
  pinMode(CLK, OUTPUT);
}

void loop()
{                                          ( ← Serial. println (distance);  )
  int distance = analogRead(DIST);
  distance = map(distance, minVal, maxVal, 0, 8);
  distance = constrain(distance,0,8);

  digitalWrite(LATCH, LOW);                      //Latch low - start sending
  shiftOut(SER, CLK, MSBFIRST, vals[distance]); //Send data, MSB first
  digitalWrite(LATCH, HIGH);                     //Latch high - stop sending
  delay(10);                                     //Animation speed
}
```

Load the above program on to your Arduino, and move your hand back and forth in front of the distance sensor—you should see the bar graph respond by going up and down in parallel with your hand. If you find that the graph hovers too much at "all on" or "all off", try adjusting the maxVal and minVal values to better fit the readings from your distance sensor. To test the values you are getting at various distances, you can initialize a serial connection in the setup() and call Serial.println(distance); right after you perform the ＊ analogRead(DIST); step.

NOTE To watch a demo video of the distance responsive bar graph, visit www.exploringarduino.com/content/ch7. You can also find this video on the Wiley website shown at the beginning of this chapter.

Summary

In this chapter you learned about the following:

- How a shift register works
- The differences between serial and parallel data transmission
- The differences between decimal and binary data representations
- How to create animations using a shift register

Communication Interfaces

In This Part

The I²C Bus

Parts You'll Need for This Chapter

Arduino Uno

USB cable (A to B for Uno)

Red LED

Yellow LEDs (×3)

Green LEDs (×4)

220Ω resistors (×8)

4.7kΩ resistors (×2)

SN74HC595N shift register DIP IC

TC74A0-5.0VAT I2C temperature sensor

Jumper wires

Breadboard

CODE AND DIGITAL CONTENT FOR THIS CHAPTER

Code downloads, video, and other digital content for this chapter can be found at www.exploringarduino.com/content/ch8.

In addition, all code can be found at www.wiley.com/go/exploringarduino on the Download Code tab. The code is in the chapter 08 download and individually named according to the names throughout the chapter.

You've already learned how to connect both analog and digital inputs/outputs, but what about more complicated devices? The Arduino can expand its capabilities by interfacing with a variety of external components. Many integrated circuits implement standardized digital communication protocols to facilitate communication between your microcontroller and a wide array of possible modules. This chapter explores the I²C bus (pronounced "eye squared see" or "eye two see").

The I²C bus enables robust, high-speed, two-way communication between devices while using a minimal number of I/O pins to facilitate communication. An I²C bus is controlled by a master device (usually a microcontroller), and contains one or more slave devices that receive information from the master. In this chapter, you learn about the I²C protocol, and you implement it to communicate with a digital I²C temperature sensor capable of returning measurements as degree values rather than as arbitrary analog values. You build upon knowledge from previous chapters by combining what you learn in this chapter to expand earlier projects.

> **NOTE** Follow the steps of this chapter with this tutorial video: www.jeremyblum .com/2011/02/13/arduino-tutorial-7-i2c-and-processing/. You can also find this video on the Wiley website shown at the beginning of this chapter.

History of the I²C Bus

When it comes to communication protocols, understanding how the protocol evolved over time makes it a lot easier to understand why it works the way it does. The I²C protocol was invented by Phillips in the early 1980s to allow for relatively low-speed communication between various ICs. The protocol was standardized by the 1990s, and other companies quickly began to adopt the protocol, releasing their own compatible chips. Generically, the protocol is known as the "two-wire" protocol because two lines are used for communication, a clock and data line. Although not all two-wire protocol devices have paid the license fee to be called I²C devices, they are commonly all referred to as I²C. This is similar to how Kleenex® is often used to refer to all tissues, even those that aren't manufactured by Kleenex®. If you find a device that says it uses the "two-wire" communication protocol, you can be fairly certain that it will work in the ways described in this chapter.

I²C Hardware Design

Figure 8-1 shows a common reference setup for an I²C communication system. Unlike previous digital communication that you've seen in this book, I²C is unique in that multiple devices all share the same communication lines: a clock signal (SCL) and a bidirectional data line used for sending information back and forth between the master and the slaves (SDA). Notice, as well, that the I²C bus requires pull-up resistors on both data lines.

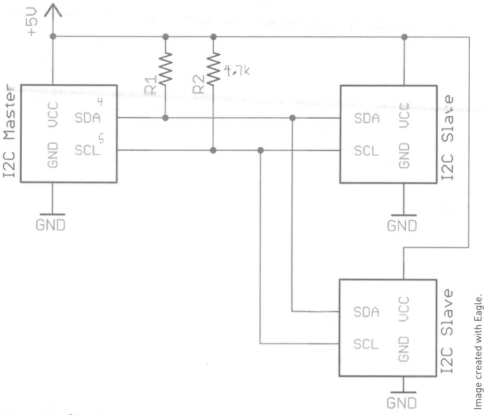

Figure 8-1: I²C reference hardware configuration

Communication Scheme and ID Numbers

The I²C bus allows multiple slave devices to share communication lines with a single master device. In this chapter, the Arduino acts as the master device. The bus master is responsible for initiating all communications. Slave devices cannot initiate communications; they can only respond to requests that are sent by the master device. Because multiple slave devices share the same communication lines, it's very important that only the master device can initiate communication. Otherwise, multiple devices may try to talk at the same time and the data would get garbled.

All commands and requests sent from the master are received by all devices on the bus. Each I²C slave device has a unique 7-bit address, or ID number. When communication is initiated by the master device, a device ID is transmitted. I²C slave devices react to data on the bus only when it is directed at their ID number. Because all the devices are receiving all the messages, each device on the I²C bus must have a unique address. Some I²C devices have selectable addresses, whereas others come from the manufacturer with a fixed address. If you want to have multiple numbers of the same device on one bus, you need to identify components that are available with different IDs.

Temperature sensors, for example, are commonly available with various pre-programmed I²C addresses because it is common to want more than one on a single I²C bus. In this chapter, you use the TC74 temperature sensor. A peek at the TC74 datasheet reveals that it is available with a variety of different addresses. Figure 8-2 shows an excerpt of the datasheet. In this chapter, you use TC74A0-5.0VAT, which is the 5V, T0-220 version of the IC with an address of 1001000.

TC74   A0   5.0   V   AT   = 0X 48   = 72

PART NO.	XX	-XX	X	XX
Device	Address Options	Supply Voltage	Operating Temperature	Package

Device: TC74: Serial Digital Thermal Sensor

Address Options: A0 = 1001 000 ≠ 72
                   A1 = 1001 001
                   A2 = 1001 010
                   A3 = 1001 011
                   A4 = 1001 100
                   A5 = 1001 101 *
                   A6 = 1001 110
                   A7 = 1001 111

                   * Default Address

Output Voltage: 3.3 = Accuracy optimized for 3.3V
                   5.0 = Accuracy optimized for 5.0V

Operating Temperature: V = -40°C ≤ T_A ≤ +125°C

Package: AT = TO-220-5

Examples:

a) TC74A0-3.3VAT: TO-220 Serial Digital Thermal Sensor
b) TC74A1-3.3VAT: TO-220 Serial Digital Thermal Sensor
c) TC74A2-3.3VAT: TO-220 Serial Digital Thermal Sensor
d) TC74A3-3.3VAT: TO-220 Serial Digital Thermal Sensor
e) TC74A4-3.3VAT: TO-220 Serial Digital Thermal Sensor
f) TC74A5-3.3VAT: TO-220 Serial Digital Thermal Sensor *
g) TC74A6-3.3VAT: TO-220 Serial Digital Thermal Sensor
h) TC74A7-3.3VAT: TO-220 Serial Digital Thermal Sensor

a) TC74A0-5.0VAT: TO-220 Serial Digital Thermal Sensor
b) TC74A1-5.0VAT: TO-220 Serial Digital Thermal Sensor
c) TC74A2-5.0VAT: TO-220 Serial Digital Thermal Sensor
d) TC74A3-5.0VAT: TO-220 Serial Digital Thermal Sensor
e) TC74A4-5.0VAT: TO-220 Serial Digital Thermal Sensor
f) TC74A5-5.0VAT: TO-220 Serial Digital Thermal Sensor *
g) TC74A6-5.0VAT: TO-220 Serial Digital Thermal Sensor
h) TC74A7-5.0VAT: TO-220 Serial Digital Thermal Sensor

* Default Address

Credit: © 2013 Microchip Technology, Inc.

Figure 8-2: TC74 address options

You can purchase this particular IC with eight different ID numbers; hence, you could put up to eight of them on one I²C bus and read each of them independently. While you're writing programs to interface with this temperature sensor later in this chapter, make sure to be aware of the ID of the device you ordered so that you send the right commands!

Other I²C chips, such as the AD7414 and AD7415, have address select (AS) pins that allow you to configure the I²C address of the device. Take a look at the excerpt from the AD7414 datasheet in Figure 8-3.

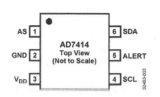

Figure 3. AD7414 Pin Configuration (SOT-23)

Figure 8-3: AD7414 addressing

Table 4. I²C Address Selection

Part Number	AS Pin	I²C Address
AD7414-0	Float	1001 000
AD7414-0	GND	1001 001
AD7414-0	V_DD	1001 010
AD7414-1	Float	1001 100
AD7414-1	GND	1001 101
AD7414-1	V_DD	1001 110
AD7414-2	N/A	1001 011
AD7414-3	N/A	1001 111

handwritten annotations: set AS pin to F, G, V to configure addr; version 0,1,2, or 3; 72 73 74 75 76 77 78 79; 64 8

Credit: Analog Devices, Inc., www.ana_og.com.

As shown in Figure 8-3, the AD7414 is available in four versions, two with an AS pin and two without. The versions with AS pins can each have three possible ID numbers depending on whether the AS pin is left disconnected, is tied to VCC, or is tied to GND.

Hardware Requirements and Pull-Up Resistors

You may have noticed in Figure 8-1 that the standard I²C bus configuration requires pull-up resistors on both the clock and data lines. The value for these resistors depends on the slave devices and how many of them are attached. In this chapter, you use 4.7kΩ resistors for both pull-ups; this is a fairly standard value that will be specified by many datasheets.

handwritten: yell - video - red ; 4.7 k Ω

Communicating with an I²C Temperature Probe

The steps for communicating with different I²C devices vary based on the requirements of the specific device. Thankfully, you can use the Arduino I²C library to abstract away most of the difficult timing work. In this section of the chapter, you talk to the I²C temperature sensor described earlier. You learn how to interpret the datasheet information as you progress so that you can apply these concepts to other I²C devices with relative ease.

The basic steps for controlling any I²C device are as follows:

1. Master sends a start bit. *est start cond*

2. Master sends 7-bit slave address of device it wants to talk to.

3. Master sends read (1) or write (0) bit depending on whether it wants to write data into an I²C device's register or if it wants to read from one of the I²C device's registers.

4. Slave responds with an "acknowledge" or ACK bit (a logic low). *bit*

5. In write mode, master sends 1 byte of information at a time, and slave responds with ACKs. In read mode, master receives 1 of byte information at a time and sends an ACK to the slave after each byte.

6. When communication has been completed, the master sends a stop bit.

*est
s top
cond*

Setting Up the Hardware

To confirm that your first program works as expected, you can use the serial monitor to print out temperature readings from an I²C temperature sensor to your computer. Because this is a digital sensor, it prints the temperature in degrees. Unlike the temperature sensors that you used in previous chapters, you do not have to worry about converting an analog reading to an actual temperature. How convenient! Now, wire a temperature senor to the Arduino as shown in Figure 8-4.

Unot Use

*A4 for SDA
A5 for SCL*

*A4 SDA
A5 SCL*

TC74

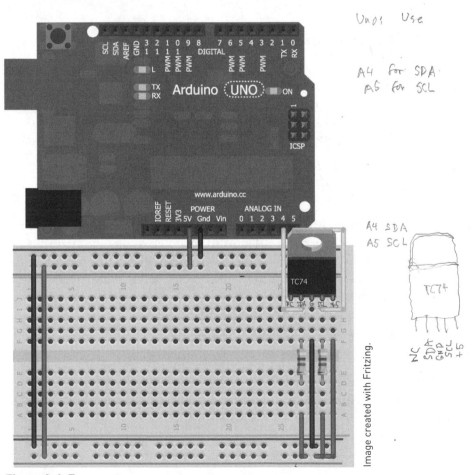

Figure 8-4: Temperature sensor

Note that the SDA and SCL pins are wired to pins A4 and A5, respectively. Recall from earlier in the chapter that the SDA and SCL are the two pins used for communicating with I²C devices—they carry data and clock signals, respectively. You've already learned about multiplexed pins in previous chapters. On the Arduino, pins A4 and A5 are multiplexed between the analog-to-digital converter (ADC) and the hardware I²C interface. When you initialize the Wire library in your code, those pins connect to the ATMega's I²C controller, enabling you to communicate with the `Wire` object to I²C devices via those pins. When using the Wire library, you cannot use pins A4 and A5 as analog inputs because they are reserved for communication with I²C devices.

or Uno's

Referencing the Datasheet

Next up, you need to write the software that instructs the Arduino to request data from the I²C temperature sensor. The Arduino Wire library makes this fairly easy. To use it properly, you need to know how to read the datasheet to determine the communication scheme that this particular chip uses. Let's dissect the communication scheme presented in the datasheet using what you already know about how I²C works. Consider the diagrams from the datasheet shown in Figures 8-5 and 8-6.

@ Swire.beginTransmission (temp_addr)
Wire.write (0)
wire.endTransmission (7

not using this in sketch

Using this in sketch

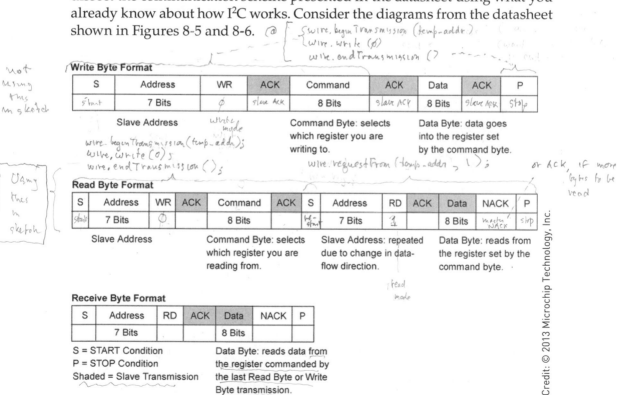

Write Byte Format

S	Address	WR	ACK	Command	ACK	Data	ACK	P
Start	7 Bits	0	slave Ack	8 Bits	slave Ack	8 Bits	slave Ack	Stop

Slave Address — *write mode*

Command Byte: selects which register you are writing to.

Data Byte: data goes into the register set by the command byte.

wire.beginTransmission (temp_addr);
wire.write (0);
wire.endTransmission ();

wire.requestFrom (temp_addr, 1);

or ACK, if more bytes to be read

Read Byte Format

S	Address	WR	ACK	Command	ACK	S	Address	RD	ACK	Data	NACK	P
Start	7 Bits	0		8 Bits		half start	7 Bits	1		8 Bits	master NACK	stop

Slave Address

Command Byte: selects which register you are reading from.

Slave Address: repeated due to change in data-flow direction.

Data Byte: reads from the register set by the command byte.

read mode

Receive Byte Format

S	Address	RD	ACK	Data	NACK	P
	7 Bits			8 Bits		

S = START Condition
P = STOP Condition
Shaded = Slave Transmission

Data Byte: reads data from the register commanded by the last Read Byte or Write Byte transmission.

Figure 8-5: TC74 sensor communication scheme

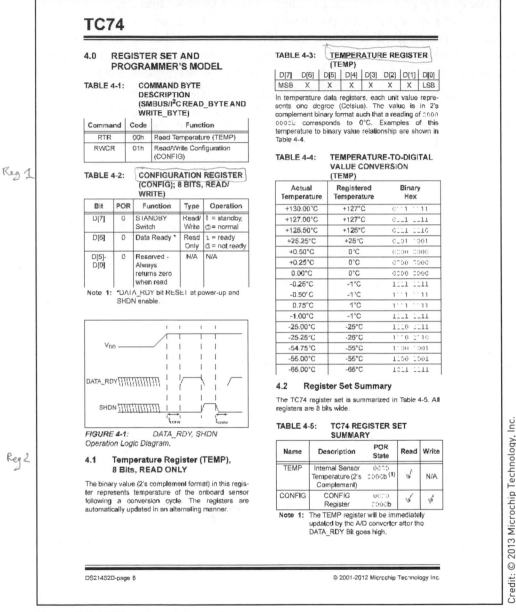

Reg 1

Reg 2

Credit: © 2013 Microchip Technology, Inc.

Figure 8-6: TC74 register information

You can both read from and write to this IC, as shown in the datasheet in Figure 8-5. The TC74 has two registers, one that contains the current temperature in Celsius and one that contains configuration information about the chip (including standby state and data-ready state). Table 4-1 of the datasheet shows this. You don't need to mess with the configuration info; you only want to read the temperature from the device. Tables 4-3 and 4-4 within Figure 8-6 show how the temperature information is stored within the 8-bit data register.

The "Read Byte Format" section of Figure 8-5 outlines the process of reading the temperature from the TC74:

1. Send to the device's address in write mode and write a 0 to indicate that you want to read from the data register.

2. Send to the device's address in read mode and request 8 bits (1 byte) of information from the device.

3. Wait to receive all 8 bits of temperature information. *then send NACK*

Now that you understand the steps necessary to request information from this device, you should be able to better understand how similar I²C devices would also work. When it doubt, search the web for code examples that show how to connect your Arduino to various I²C devices. Next up, you write the code that executes the three steps outlined earlier.

Writing the Software

Arduino's I²C communication library is called the Wire library. After you've included it at the top of your sketch, you can easily write to and read from I²C devices. As a first step for your I²C temperature sensor system, load up the code in Listing 8-1, which takes advantage of the functions built in to the Wire library. See whether you can match up various Wire commands in the following code with the steps outlined in the previous section.

Listing 8-1: I²C Temperature Sensor Printing Code—read_temp.ino

```
//Reads Temp from I2C temperature sensor
//and prints it on the serial port

//Include Wire I2C library
#include <Wire.h>
int temp_address = 72; //1001000 written as decimal number

void setup()
{
  //Start serial communication at 9600 baud
Serial.begin(9600);

  //Create a Wire object
  Wire.begin();
}

void loop()
```

```
{
  //Send a request
  //Start talking to the device at the specified address
  Wire.beginTransmission(temp_address);
  //Send a bit asking for register zero, the data register
  Wire.write(0);
  //Complete Transmission
  Wire.endTransmission();

  //Read the temperature from the device
  //Request 1 Byte from the specified address
  Wire.requestFrom(temp_address, 1);
  //Wait for response
  while(Wire.available() == 0);
  //Get the temp and read it into a variable
  int c = Wire.read();

  //Do some math to convert the Celsius to Fahrenheit
  int f = round(c*9.0/5.0 +32.0);

  //Send the temperature in degrees C and F to the serial monitor
  Serial.print(c);
  Serial.print("C ");
  Serial.print(f);
  Serial.println("F");

  delay(500);
}
```

[Handwritten annotations: "start cond, i'addr, 0 brt..." pointing to beginTransmission line; "byte cmd" / "Set register Ø as reg of interest   write 0 byte" near Wire.write(0); "stop cond" near endTransmission; "start cmd, addr, 1 brt. and then read 1 byte" near requestFrom; "// tight loop" near while loop; "(est. stop cond)" at right; "∿∿" under "round"]

Consider how the commands in this program relate to previously mentioned steps. `Wire.beginTransmission()` starts the communication with a slave device with the given ID. Next, the `Wire.write()` command sends a 0, indicating that you want to be reading from the temperature register. You then send a stop bit with the `Wire.endTransmission()` to indicate that you have finished writing to the device. With the next three steps, the master reads from the slave I²C device. Because you issue a `Wire.requestFrom()` command, the master will expect to receive 1 byte of data back from the slave. The `Wire.available()` command within the `while()` loop will block the program from executing the rest of the code until data is available on the I²C line. This gives the slave device time to respond. Finally, the 8-bit value is read into an integer variable with a `Wire.read()` command.

The program in Listing 8-1 also handles converting the Celsius temperature to Fahrenheit, for those who are not metrically inclined. You can find the formula for this conversion with a simple web search. I've chosen to round the result to a whole number.

Now, run the preceding code on your Arduino and open up the serial monitor on your computer. You should see an output that looks something like that shown in Figure 8-7.

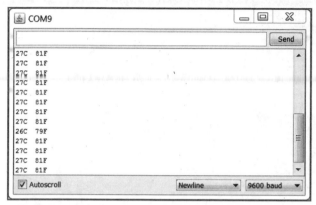

Figure 8-7: I^{2}C temperature sensor serial output

Combining Shift Registers, Serial Communication, and I^{2}C Communications

Now that you have a simple I^{2}C communication scheme set up with serial printing, you can apply some of your knowledge from previous chapters to do something more interesting. You use the shift register graph circuit from Chapter 7, "Shift Registers," along with a Processing desktop sketch to visualize temperature in the real world and on your computer screen.

Building the Hardware for a Temperature Monitoring System

First things first, get the system wired up. You're essentially just combining the shift register circuit from the previous chapter with the I^{2}C circuit from this chapter. Your setup should look like Figure 8-8.

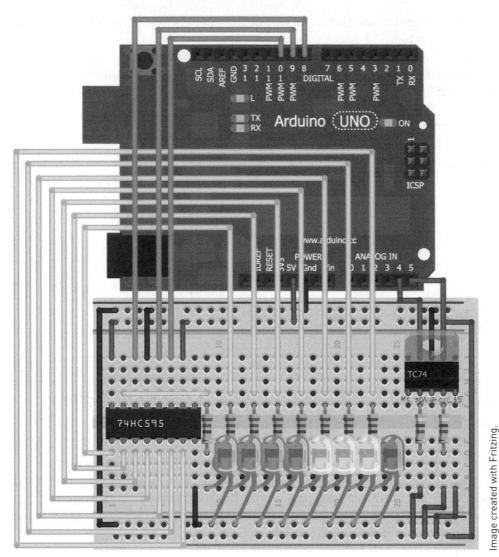

Figure 8-8: I²C temperature sensor with shift register bar graph (part of the TC74 has been made transparent so you can see the wires that connect behind it)

Modifying the Embedded Program

You need to make two adjustments to the previous Arduino program to make serial communication with Processing easier, and to implement the shift register functionality. First, modify the print statements in the program you just wrote to look like this:

```
Serial.print(c);
Serial.print("C,");
```

```
Serial.print(f);
Serial.print("F.");
```

Processing needs to parse the Celsius and Fahrenheit temperature data. By replacing the spaces and carriage returns with commas and periods, you can easily look for these delimiting characters and use them to parse the data.

Next, you need to add the shift register code from the previous chapter, and map the LED levels appropriately to the temperature range that you care about. If you a need a refresher on the shift register code that you previously wrote, take another look at Listing 7-3; much of the code from that program will be reused here, with a few small tweaks. To begin, change the total number of light variables from nine to eight. With this change, you always leave one LED on as an indication that the system is working (the 0 value is eliminated from the array). You need to accommodate for that change in the variable value mapping, and you need to map a range of temperatures to LED states. Check out the complete code sample in Listing 8-2 to see how that is accomplished. I chose to make my range from 24°C to 31°C (75°F to 88°F), but you can choose any range.

Listing 8-2: I²C Temperature Sensors Code with Shift Register LEDs and Serial Communication—temp_unit.ino

```
//Reads temp from I2C temperature sensor
//Show it on the LED bar graph, and show it in Processing

//Include Wire I2C library
#include <Wire.h>

const int SER   =8;   //Serial Output to Shift Register
const int LATCH =9;   //Shift Register Latch Pin
const int CLK   =10;  //Shift Register Clock Pin

int temp_address = 72;

//Possible LED settings
int vals[8] = {1,3,7,15,31,63,127,255};

void setup()
{
  //Instantiate serial communication at 9600 bps
  Serial.begin(9600);

  //Create a Wire Object
  Wire.begin();

  //Set shift register pins as outputs
  pinMode(SER, OUTPUT);
  pinMode(LATCH, OUTPUT);
```

```
    pinMode(CLK, OUTPUT);
}

void loop()
{
  //Send a request
  //Start talking to the device at the specified address
  Wire.beginTransmission(temp_address);
  //Send a bit asking for register zero, the data register
  Wire.write(0);
  //Complete Transmission
  Wire.endTransmission();

  //Read the temperature from the device
  //Request 1 Byte from the specified address
  Wire.requestFrom(temp_address, 1);
  //Wait for response
  while(Wire.available() == 0);
  //Get the temp and read it into a variable
  int c = Wire.read();

  //Map the temperatures to LED settings
  int graph = map(c, 24, 31, 0, 7);
  graph = constrain(graph,0,7);

  digitalWrite(LATCH, LOW);            //Latch low - start sending data
  shiftOut(SER, CLK, MSBFIRST, vals[graph]); //Send data, most
                                       //significant bit first
  digitalWrite(LATCH, HIGH);          //Latch high - stop sending data

  //Do some math to convert the Celsius to Fahrenheit
  int f = round(c*9.0/5.0 +32.0);

  Serial.print(c);
  Serial.print("C,");
  Serial.print(f);
  Serial.print("F.");

  delay(500);
}
```

(handwritten note: ↰ no of bytes to be read (ie, sent by slave))

(handwritten note: cf 149 ff)

(handwritten note: @ 178)

After loading this on to your Arduino, you can see the LEDs changing color with the temperature. Try squeezing the temperature sensor with you finger-tips to make the temperature go up. You should see a response in the LEDs. Next, you write a Processing sketch that displays the temperature value on the computer in an easy-to-read format.

Writing the Processing Sketch

At this point, your Arduino is already transmitting easy-to-parse data to your computer. All you need to do is write a Processing program that can interpret it and display it in an attractive way.

Because you'll be updating text in real time, you need to first learn how to load fonts into Processing. Open Processing to create a new, blank sketch. Save the sketch before continuing. Then, navigate to Tools > Create Font. You'll get a screen that looks like Figure 8-9.

Figure 8-9: Processing font creator

Pick your favorite font and choose a size. (I recommend a size around 200 for this exercise.) After doing so, click OK. The font is then automatically generated and added to the "data" subfolder of your Processing sketch folder. The Processing sketch needs to accomplish a few things:

- Generate a graphical window on your computer showing the temperature in both Celsius and Fahrenheit.

- Read the incoming data from the serial port, parse it, and save the values to local variables that can be displayed on the computer.

- Continually update the display with the new values received over serial.

Copy the code from Listing 8-3 into your Processing sketch and adjust the serial port name to the right value for your computer and the name of the font you created. Then, ensure your Arduino is connected and click the Run icon to watch the magic!

Listing 8-3: Processing Sketch for Displaying Temperature Values—display_temp.pde

```
//Displays the temperature recorded by an I2C temp sensor

import processing.serial.*;
Serial port;
String temp_c = "";
String temp_f = "";
String data = "";
int index = 0;
PFont font;

void setup()
{
  size(400,400);
//Change "COM9" to the name of the serial port on your computer
  port = new Serial(this, "COM9", 9600);
  port.bufferUntil('.');
//Change the font name to reflect the name of the font you created
  font = loadFont("AgencyFB-Bold-200.vlw");
  textFont(font, 200);
}

void draw()
{
  background(0,0,0);
  fill(46, 209, 2);
  text(temp_c, 70, 175);
  fill(0, 102, 153);
  text(temp_f, 70, 370);
}

void serialEvent (Serial port)
{
  data = port.readStringUntil('.');
  data = data.substring(0, data.length() - 1);

  //Look for the comma between Celcius and Farenheit
  index = data.indexOf(",");
  //Fetch the C Temp
  temp_c = data.substring(0, index);
  //Fetch the F temp
  temp_f = data.substring(index+1, data.length());
}
```

Handwritten annotations:

@ 176

← color to fill the text

val , x , y

// called when bufferUntil ( ) event happens

As in previous Processing examples that you've run, the sketch starts by importing the serial library and setting up the serial port. In `setup()`, you are defining the size of the display window, loading the font you just created, and setting up the serial port to buffer until it receives a period. `draw()` fills the background in black and prints out the Celsius and Fahrenheit values in two colors. With the `fill()` command, you are telling Processing to make the next element it adds to the screen that color (in RGB values). `serialEvent()` is called whenever the `bufferUntil()` event is triggered. It reads the buffer into a string, and then breaks it up based on the location of the comma. The two temperature values are stored in variables that get printed out in the application window.

When you execute the program, the output should look like the results shown in Figure 8-10.

Figure 8-10: Processing temperature display

When you squeeze the sensor, the Processing display should update, and the lights on your board should illuminate.

NOTE To watch a demo video of the temperature monitoring hardware and Processing system, check out www.exploringarduino.com/content/ch8. You can also find this video on the Wiley website shown at the beginning of this chapter.

Summary

In this chapter you learned about the following:

- I²C uses two data lines to enable digital communication between the Arduino and multiple slave devices (so long as they have different addresses).
- The Arduino Wire library can be used to facilitate communicate with I²C devices connected to pins A4 and A5.
- I²C communication can be employed alongside shift registers and serial communication to create more complex systems.
- You can create fonts in Processing to generate dynamically-updating on-screen displays.
- Processing can be used to display parsed serial data obtained from I²C devices connected to the Arduino.

CHAPTER 9

The SPI Bus

Parts You'll Need for This Chapter

Arduino Uno

USB cable (A to B for Uno)

Red LED

Yellow LED

Green LED

Blue LED

100Ω resistors (×4)

Speaker

Jumper wires

Breadboard

MCP4231 Digital SPI Potentiometer IC (×2)

CODE AND DIGITAL CONTENT FOR THIS CHAPTER

Code downloads, video, and other digital content for this chapter can be found at www.exploringarduino.com/content/ch9.

In addition, all code can be found at www.wiley.com/go/exploringarduino on the Download Code tab. The code is in the chapter 09 download and individually named according to the names throughout the chapter.

You've already learned about two important digital communication methods available to you on the Arduino: the I²C bus and the serial UART bus. In this chapter, you learn about the third digital communication method supported by the Arduino hardware: The Serial Peripheral Interface bus (or SPI bus for short).

Unlike the I²C bus, the SPI bus uses separate lines for sending and receiving data, and it employs an additional line for selecting which slave device you are talking to. This adds additional wires, but also eliminates the issue of needing different slave device addresses. SPI is generally easier to get running than I²C and can run at a faster speed. In this chapter, you use the Arduino's built-in SPI library and hardware to communicate with a digitally controllable potentiometer. You use the potentiometer to control both LED brightness and speaker volume, allowing you to make a simple audio/visual display.

NOTE Follow the steps of this chapter with this tutorial video, www.jeremyblum .com/2011/02/20/arduino-tutorial-8-spi-interfaces. You can also find this video on the Wiley website shown at the beginning of this chapter.

Overview of the SPI Bus

Originally created by Motorola, the SPI bus is a full-duplex serial communication standard that enables simultaneous bidirectional communication between a master device and one or more slave devices. Because the SPI protocol does not follow a formal standard, it is common to find SPI devices that operate slightly different (the number of transmitted bits may differ, or the slave select line might be omitted, among other things). This chapter focuses on implementing the most commonly accepted SPI commands (which are the ones that are supported by the Arduino IDE).

WARNING Bear in mind that SPI implementations can vary, so reading the datasheet is extremely important.

SPI can act in four main ways, which depend on the requirements of your device. SPI devices are often referred to as *slave devices*. SPI devices are synchronous, meaning that data is transmitted in sync with a shared clock signal (SCLK). Data can be shifted into the slave device on either the rising or falling edge of the clock signal (called the *clock phase*), and the SCLK default state can be set to either high or low (called the *clock polarity*). Because there are two options for each, you can configure the SPI bus in a total of four ways. Table 9-1 shows each of the possibilities and the modes that they correspond to in the Arduino SPI library.

Table 9-1: SPI Communication Modes

SPI MODE	CLOCK POLARITY	CLOCK PHASE
Mode 0	Low at Idle	Data Capture on Clock Rising Edge
Mode 1	Low at Idle	Data Capture on Clock Falling Edge
Mode 2	High at Idle	Data Capture on Clock Falling Edge
Mode 3	High at Idle	Data Capture on Clock Rising Edge

SPI Hardware and Communication Design

The SPI system setup is relatively simple. Three pins are used for communicating between a master and all slave devices:

- Shared/Serial Clock (SCLK)
- Master Out Slave In (MOSI)
- Master In Slave Out (MISO)

Each slave device also requires an additional slave select (SS) pin. Hence, the total number of I/O pins required on the master device will always be $3 + n$, where n is the number of slave devices. Figure 9-1 shows an example SPI system with two slave devices.

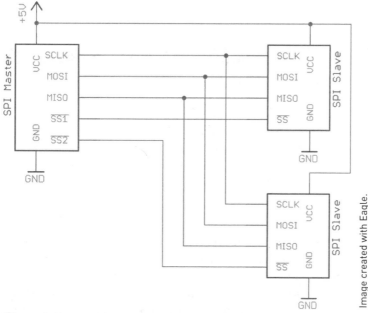

Figure 9-1: SPI reference hardware configuration

Hardware Configuration

Four data lines, at a minimum, are present in any SPI system. Additional SS lines are added for each slave device appended to the network. Before you learn how to actually send and receive data to and from an SPI device, you need to understand what these I/O lines do and how they should be wired. Table 9-2 describes these lines.

Table 9-2: SPI Communication Lines

SPI COMMUNICATION LINE	DESCRIPTION
MOSI	Used for sending serial data from the master device to a slave device.
MISO	Used for sending serial data from a slave device to the master device.
SCLK	The signal by which the serial data is synchronized with the receiving device, so it knows when to read the input.
SS	A line indicating slave device selection. Pulling it low means you are speaking with that slave device.

(handwritten annotations: MOSI — pin 11, MISO — 12, SCLK — 13 "default pins"; SS — "eg: 10")

Unlike with the I²C bus, pull-up resistors are not required, and communication is fully bidirectional. To wire an SPI device to the Arduino, all you have to do is connect the MOSI, MISO, SCLK, and SS pins and you'll be ready to use to the SPI communication library.

NAMING CONVENTIONS

Because SPI is not a universal standard, some devices and manufacturers may use different names for the SPI communication lines. Slave select is sometimes referred to as chip select (CS), serial clock is sometimes just called clock (CLK), MOSI and MISO pins on slave devices are sometimes abbreviated to serial data in (SDI), and serial data out (SDO).

(handwritten: MOSI ~ SDI, MISO ~ SDO)

Communication Scheme

The SPI communication scheme is synced with the clock signal and depends on the state of the SS line. Because all devices on the bus share the MOSI, MISO, and SCLK lines, all commands sent from the master arrive at each slave. The SS pin tells the slave whether it should ignore this data or respond to it. Importantly, this means that you must make sure to only have one SS pin set low (the active mode) at a time in any program that you write.

The basic process for communicating with an SPI device is as follows:

1. Set the SS pin low for the device you want to communicate with.

2. Toggle the clock line up and down at a speed less than or equal to the transmission speed supported by the slave device.

3. For each clock cycle, send 1 bit on the MOSI line, and receive 1 bit on the MISO line.

4. Continue until transmitting or receiving is complete, and stop toggling the clock line.

5. Return the SS pin to high state.

Note that on every clock cycle a bit must be sent and received, but that bit does not necessarily need to mean anything. For example, later in this chapter you will use a digital potentiometer in a scenario in which the Arduino will send data but does not need to receive anything back from the slave. So, it will clock data out on the MOSI pin and will just ignore anything that comes back on the MISO pin.

Comparing SPI to I²C

Many kinds of devices, including accelerometers, digital potentiometers, and displays, are available in both SPI and I²C versions. So how do you decide? Table 9-3 lists some of the trade-offs between I²C and SPI. Ultimately, which one you choose to use will depend on what you believe is easier to implement, and best suited for your situation. Most beginners find that they can get SPI working more easily than I²C.

Table 9-3: SPI and I2C Comparison

SPI ADVANTAGES	I²C ADVANTAGES
Can operate at higher speeds	Requires only two communication lines
Generally easier to work with	Built-in Arduino hardware support
No pull-up resistors needed	
Built-in Arduino hardware support	

Communicating with an SPI Digital Potentiometer

Now that you've got all the basics down, it's time to actually implement what you've learned. You'll start by controlling LED brightness using a digital potentiometer (a DigiPot for short). Specifically, you'll use the Microchip MCP4231 103E Digital Potentiometer IC. (Several versions of this chip are available, each with different potentiometer resistance values.) When looking for an integrated circuit (IC) like this to use on your breadboard, you want to look for the dual in-line package (DIP) version of the chip. Just a like a regular potentiometer, a DigiPot has an adjustable wiper that determines the resistance between the wiper terminal and one of the end terminals. The MCP4231 has two potentiometers on one chip. Each pot has a resolution of 7 bits, resulting in 129 wiper positions, (the extra position results from the chip's direct taps to power or ground) which vary the resistance between 0 and 10kΩ. First, you will use the DigiPot to adjust LED brightness. After you get it working with LEDs, you will use it to control speaker volume. When you finish, you will have a platform that you can use to develop more complicated audio/visual projects.

Gathering Information from the Datasheet

First things first, you always need to consult the datasheet. A quick Google search for "MCP4231" will turn up the datasheet. You can also find a link to the datasheet from the Exploring Arduino website: www.exploringarduino.com/content/ch9. The datasheet answers the following questions:

- What is the pin-out of the IC, and which pins are the control pins?
- What is the resistance of the potentiometer in my chip?
- Which SPI commands must be sent to control the two digital wipers?

To help you reference this information, Figures 9-2 through 9-4 show some of the key parts of this datasheet. First, take a look at the pin-out presented on the first page of the datasheet.

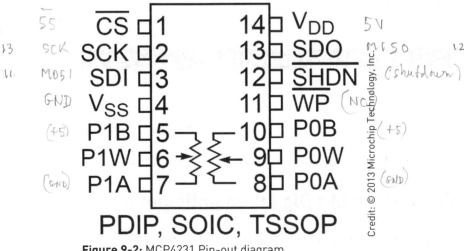

Figure 9-2: MCP4231 Pin-out diagram

The pin-out should usually be your first step when getting ready to work with a new device. Following is a breakdown of all the pins and their functions:

- **Pins P0A, P0W, and P0B:** These are the pins for the first digitally controlled potentiometer.

- **Pins P1A, P1W, and P1B:** These are the pins for the second digitally controlled potentiometer.

- **VDD:** Connects to your 5V supply.

- **VSS:** Connects to ground.

- **CS:** CS is the SS pin for the SPI interface, and the bar above it indicates that it is active low. (0V means the chip is selected, and 5V means it is not selected.)

- **SDI and SDO:** These pins correspond to serial data in and out, respectively (a.k.a. MOSI and MISO).

- **SCK:** This is the SPI clock line that was explained earlier in the chapter.

- **SHDN and WP:** These stand for shut down and write protect, respectively. For this chip, it is revealed later in the datasheet that the WP pin is actually NC (not connected). You can ignore this pin. The SHDN pin is active low, like the CS pin. When held low, the hardware "disconnects" the wiper from the internal resistor network. You always want your potentiometer to be active, so in these examples the SHDN pin is connected directly to 5V.

The next thing worth considering is the resistance of the potentiometer and wiper. Just like an ordinary potentiometer, there is a fixed resistance between the A and B terminals of each digital potentiometer. The wiper itself also has a resistance that you should take into account. Consider the information from the fifth page of the datasheet (see Figure 9-3).

AC/DC CHARACTERISTICS (CONTINUED)

DC Characteristics		Standard Operating Conditions (unless otherwise specified) Operating Temperature −40°C ≤ T_A ≤ +125°C (extended) All parameters apply across the specified operating ranges unless noted. V_{DD} = +2.7V to 5.5V, 5 kΩ, 10 kΩ, 50 kΩ, 100 kΩ devices. Typical specifications represent values for V_{DD} = 5.5V, T_A = +25°C.				
Parameters	**Sym**	**Min**	**Typ**	**Max**	**Units**	**Conditions**
Resistance (± 20%)	R_{AB}	4.0	5	6.0	kΩ	-502 devices (Note 1)
		8.0	10	12.0	kΩ	-103 devices (Note 1)
		40.0	50	60.0	kΩ	-503 devices (Note 1)
		80.0	100	120.0	kΩ	-104 devices (Note 1)
Resolution	N		257		Taps	8-bit	No Missing Codes
			129		Taps	7-bit	No Missing Codes
Step Resistance	R_S	—	R_{AB} / (256)	—	Ω	8-bit	Note 6
		—	R_{AB} / (128)	—	Ω	7-bit	Note 6
Nominal Resistance Match	$|R_{AB0} - R_{AB1}|$ / R_{AB}	—	0.2	1.25	%	**MCP42X1 devices only**
	$|R_{BW0} - R_{BW1}|$ / R_{BW}	—	0.25	1.5	%	**MCP42X2 devices only,** Code = Full-Scale
Wiper Resistance (Note 3, Note 4)	R_W	—	75	160	Ω	V_{DD} = 5.5 V, I_W = 2.0 mA, code = 00h
		—	75	300	Ω	V_{DD} = 2.7 V, I_W = 2.0 mA, code = 00h

Figure 9-3: MCP4231 AC/DC characteristics table

[handwritten annotations: ← Using 103E, R_{AB} ∈ [8k, 12k]; ← R_W ∈ [75, 160]]

First, note the resistance of the potentiometer, denoted by R_{AB}. Four available variants of this chip are available, each with a different resistance value, ranging from 5kΩ to 100kΩ. The devices themselves are marked with their variation. In this chapter, you use the 103 variant, which has a resistance of about 10kΩ. Importantly, DigiPots are generally not very accurate devices. You can see from the datasheet that the actual resistance for your device may vary as much as ±20%! Also worth noting is the wiper resistance. The actual wiper pin has a resistance somewhere between 75 and 160Ω. This can be significant, especially when driving a speaker or an LED.

You also need to understand the SPI commands that you must to issue to the device to control it. In the case of the MCP4231, you issue two commands to the device. The first specifies the register to control (there is one register for each DigiPot), and the second specifies the value to set the potentiometer. Take a look at the SPI communication specification excerpted from the datasheet in Figure 9-4.

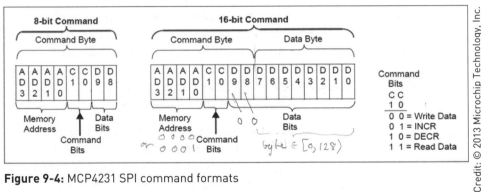

Figure 9-4: MCP4231 SPI command formats

You can see from the diagram that two command types are available: an 8-bit command and a 16-bit command. The 8-bit command allows you to increment the potentiometer with a single byte of communication, whereas the 16-bit command allows you to set the state of the potentiometer arbitrarily. To keep things simple, focus on using the 16-bit command, because it offers more flexibility. Over the SPI bus, you transmit a memory address, a command (read, write, increment, or decrement), and a data value (0–128).

The datasheet also indicates the memory addresses associated with each potentiometer. The value of potentiometer 0 is located in memory address 0, and potentiometer 1 is located in memory address 1. Using this information, you can construct the necessary command bytes for writing to each of the pots. To write to potentiometer 0, you transmit 00000000 in binary, followed by a value from 0 to 128. To write to potentiometer 1, you transmit 00010000 in binary followed by a value from 0 to 128. Referencing Figure 9-4, the first four digits are the memory address, the next two are the command (00 means write), and the next 2 bits are the first 2 data bits, which should always be 0 because the potentiometer can only be as high as 128.   *values 0 to $2^6 + 2^5 +...+ 2^1$ ≅ 127*

This is all the information you need to wire the DigiPot correctly and to send SPI commands to it from your Arduino. Now, you wire it up to control the brightness of some LEDs.

Setting Up the Hardware

To fully flesh out your knowledge of SPI communication, you'll use two MCP44231 DigiPot ICs, for a total of four controllable potentiometer channels. Each one is used to control the brightness of two LEDs by varying the series resistance in-line with the LED. When used in this fashion, you need to use only two terminals of each potentiometer. One end of each potentiometer connects to the 5V rail (through a resistor), and the wiper pin connects to the anode of the LED. Consider the schematic Figure 9-5, which shows this connection scheme.

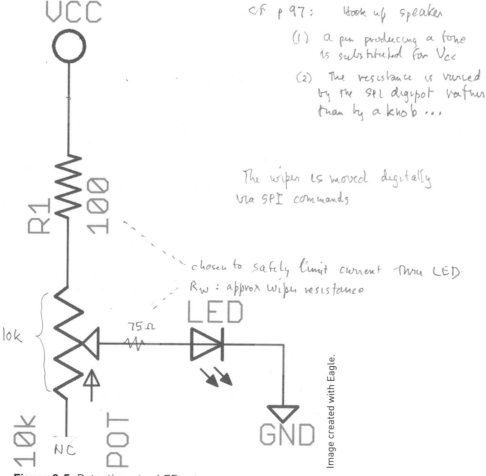

cf p 97:   Hook up speaker

(1) a pin producing a tone is substituted for Vcc

(2) The resistance is varied by the SPI digipot rather than by a knob ...

The wiper is moved digitally via SPI commands

chosen to safely limit current thru LED.

Rw : approx wiper resistance

Image created with Eagle.

Figure 9-5: Potentiometer LED setup

The cathode of the LED is connected to ground. When the wiper for the potentiometer is digitally turned to its maximum value, current flows from the 5V rail, through the 100Ω resistor, through the wiper (which has a resistance of ~75Ω), then through the LED. Alternatively, when the wiper is turned all the way down, current flows through the 100Ω resistor, through the entire resistance of the potentiometer (10kilohms), through the wiper, and then through the LED. Even when the potentiometer is turned all the way, the minimum resistance in series with the LED will be 175Ω (enough to safely current-limit it). As the DigiPots are adjusted, the resistance increases and decreases, changing the current through the LED and, therefore, its brightness. This method of brightness control can prove very useful if you have exhausted all of your pulse-width modulation (PWM)-capable pins.

Now, wire up the two digital potentiometers to the SPI bus and to the LEDs, as shown in the previous schematic using the information from the datasheet about the pin-out. On the Arduino Uno, pin 13 is SCK, pin 12 is MISO, and pin 11 is MOSI. Pin 10 is commonly used for SS, so use that for one of the chips. For the other, use pin 9. After you have wired up everything, it should look something like Figure 9-6. Remember that the SCK, MISO, and MOSI lines are shared between both devices.

Double-check that your wiring matches the wiring diagram, and then move on to the next section, where you write the software that will control the LED brightness.

Writing the Software

To confirm that your wiring is working and that you can successfully use the SPI library, you'll write a simple program to simultaneously adjust the brightness of all four LEDs using the four potentiometers on the two ICs.

As with I²C, a convenient library is built right in to the Arduino IDE that makes SPI communication very easy. All you need to do is import the library and "write" data to the SPI bus using the integrated commands. Of course, you also have to toggle the SS pins for whatever device you are controlling. So, pulling together all the knowledge from earlier in this chapter, here are the steps you need to complete to send a command to change the brightness of an LED on one of the SPI digital potentiometers:

1. Bring the SS pin for the chip low.

2. Send the appropriate register/command byte to choose which potentiometer you are going to write to. (on the 2 on the chip)

3. Send a value between 0 and 128.

4. Bring the SS pin for this chip high.

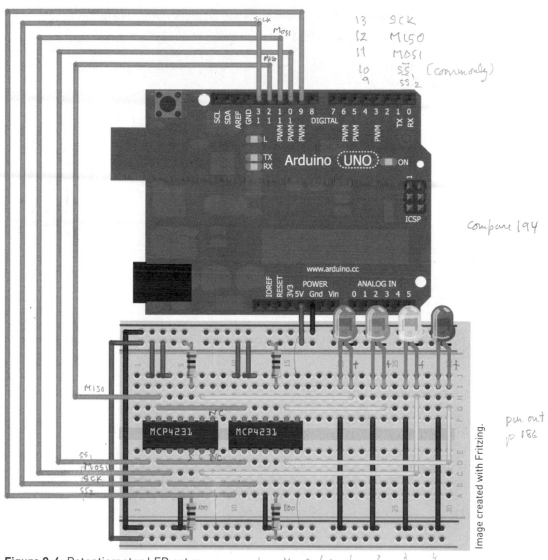

Figure 9-6: Potentiometer LED setup

Handwritten annotations:

UNO:

13 SCK
12 MISO
11 MOSI
10 SS₁ (commonly)
9   SS₂

Compare 194

pin out
p 186

MISO
NC
MCP4231   MCP4231
SS₁
MOSI
SCK
SS₂

100   10   100

Image created with Fritzing.

Note: the 2 chips are
not missing ground connections on the diagram: @ 189

The code in Listing 9-1 executes all these steps and includes a function for
passing the SS pin, register byte, and command to a given chip via SPI. The SPI
.begin() command enables you to initialize the SPI interface on the hardware
SPI pins of the Arduino, and you can use SPI.transfer() to actually send data
over the SPI bus.

Handwritten diagram annotations:

+5   +5
V_DD SDO SHDN WP P0B P0W P0A

+5
100

C̅S̅ SCK SDI V_SS P1B P1W P1A

75

Listing 9-1: SPI Control of Multiple Digital Potentiometers—SPI_led.ino

```
//Changes LED brightness using voltage input instead of PWM

//Include SPI library
#include <SPI.h>

//When using the SPI library, you only have to worry
//about picking your slave selects
//By default, 11 = MOSI, 12 = MISO, 13 = CLK
const int SS1=10; //Slave Select Chip 1
const int SS2=9;  //Slave Select Chip 2

const byte REG0=B00000000; //Register 0 Write command
const byte REG1=B00010000; //Register 1 Write command

void setup()
{
  //Set pin directions for SS
  pinMode(SS1, OUTPUT);
  pinMode(SS2, OUTPUT);

  //Initialize SPI
  SPI.begin();
}

//This will set 1 LED to the specifed level
//Chip 1 (SS 10) Register 0 is Red
//Chip 1 (SS 10) Register 1 is Yellow
//Chip 2 (SS 9) Register 0 is Green
//Chip 2 (SS 9) Register 1 is Blue
void setLed(int SS, int reg, int level)
{
  digitalWrite(SS, LOW); //Set the given SS pin low
  SPI.transfer(reg);   //Choose the register to write to
  SPI.transfer(level); //Set the LED level (0-128)
  digitalWrite(SS, HIGH); //Set the given SS pin high again
}

void loop()
{
  for (int i=0; i<=128; i++)
  {
    setLed(SS1, REG0, i);
    setLed(SS1, REG1, i);
    setLed(SS2, REG0, i);
    setLed(SS2, REG1, i);
    delay(10);
  }
  delay(300);
  for (int i=128; i>=0; i--)
```

(handwritten annotations) ✳

addr W Fixed

// transfer 1 byte

// ramp up brightness of all LED's
// when i = 128 (127?), have wiper at Px1 end (min R)
//   i = 0   have wiper at Px0 end (max R)

// ramp down brightness

```
{
    setLed(SS1, REG0, i);
    setLed(SS1, REG1, i);
    setLed(SS2, REG0, i);
    setLed(SS2, REG1, i);
    delay(10);
}
delay(300);
}
```

In Listing 9-1, SS for chip 1 is connected to pin 10, and SS for chip 2 is connected to pin 9. You can cross reference this with the hardware connections that you made while wiring the system in the previous section. The byte register values at the top of the file are the same binary sequences that you determined from the datasheet earlier in this chapter. When you put a B before a string of 0s and 1s when creating a `byte` variable, you are telling the Arduino compiler that what follows is in binary format, and not the default decimal format that you use elsewhere in your program. The `setLed()` function accepts an SS pin number, a register byte, and potentiometer level value. This function uses the information to transmit the data to the appropriate chip. In `loop()`, all the LEDs are ramped up, then back down again, with short delays so that the transition does not occur so fast that you cannot see it. When you load this onto your Arduino, you should observe all four lights changing intensity in tandem as the potentiometers are all adjusted.

NOTE To watch a demo video of the SPI digital potentiometer color adjuster, visit www.exploringarduino.com/content/ch9. You can also find this video on the Wiley website shown at the beginning of this chapter.

Now that you have this simple example working, you can move on to the next section, where you increase the complexity of the system by turning it into an audiovisual display.

Creating an Audiovisual Display Using SPI Digital Potentiometers

Changing LED brightness is a good test to confirm your understanding of SPI communication, but it is also something that you can do with PWM. Next, you integrate some technology that you cannot replicate with a PWM interface: sound. As you learned in Chapter 5, "Making Sounds," the Arduino IDE has a tone library that allows you to easily produce square waves from any pin on the Arduino to drive a speaker. Although this allows you to easily create a range of frequencies, it does not allow you to change the volume of the audio, because that is a function of the waveform's amplitude. You have already learned how

to put an ordinary potentiometer in series with a speaker to adjust its volume.
Now, you use the SPI DigiPot to adjust speaker volume digitally.

> **NOTE** Intentionally, this project is designed as a jumping-off point; you make
> a simple audiovisual display that you can expand on in software to create much
> more inspired projects. Get this example working first; then, see how you can
> build upon it to make something truly personal. This exercise offers an ideal
> opportunity to get creative with your Arduino.

Setting Up the Hardware

The setup here is similar to what you used to adjust LED brightness. In fact, to
keep things interesting, you keep three of the LEDs in place and replace one of
them with a speaker. However, for the speaker, one end of the digital potentiometer connects through a resistor to an I/O pin of the Arduino that will adjust
the frequency of the speaker. The generated square wave passes through the
DigiPot, which then adds a series resistance, thus dropping the voltage to the
speaker, changing its amplitude. Remove one of the LEDs, put a speaker in its
place, and connect that DigiPot to an I/O pin on the Arduino, as shown in the
wiring diagram in Figure 9-7.

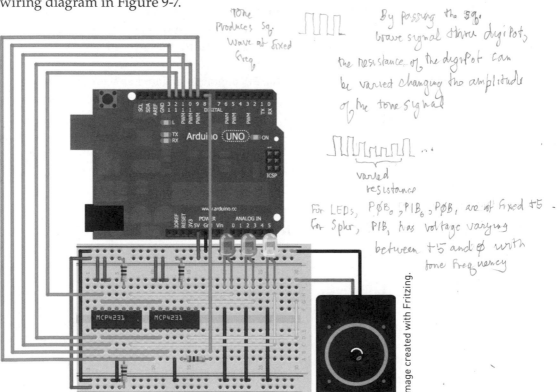

Handwritten annotations:

Tone produces sq. wave at fixed freq.

By passing the sq. wave signal thru digiPot, the resistance of the digiPot can be varied changing the amplitude of the tone signal

varied resistance

For LEDs, $P\emptyset B_0$, PIB_6, $P\emptyset B_1$ are at fixed +5.
For Spkr, PIB_7 has voltage varying between +5 and $\emptyset$ with tone frequency

Image created with Fritzing.

Figure 9-7: Potentiometer LED setup

Compare 191

MCP4231   186

You might also want to consider adding some analog sensors to this later to experiment with using light, movement, and sound to control the output from your audiovisual display system.

Modifying the Software

To get started with this setup, make some simple modifications to your previous program for controlling the LEDs. Add a pin variable for the speaker, as well as a variable to set to the frequency of the speaker. (You'll have it change throughout the program to keep things exciting.) Inside loop(), you can optionally add some iterators that increase the speaker frequency on each run through the loop. You can use the exact same setLed() function as before to set the speaker volume, but the name is now a bit misleading, so you might want to rename the function for clarity. In the complete code shown in Listing 9-2, it has been renamed to setReg().

Listing 9-2: LED and Speaker Volume SPI Digital Potentiometer Control—LED_speaker.ino

```
//Changes LED brightness using voltage input instead of PWM
//Controls speaker volume and tone

//Include SPI library
#include <SPI.h>

const int SPEAKER=8; //Speaker Pin
int freq = 100;

//When using the SPI library, you only have to worry
//about picking your slave selects
//By default, 11 = MOSI, 12 = MISO, 13 = CLK
const int SS1=10; //Slave Select Chip 1
const int SS2=9;  //Slave Select Chip 2

const byte REG0=B00000000; //Register 0 Write command
const byte REG1=B00010000; //Register 1 Write command

void setup()
{
  //Set pin directions for SS
  pinMode(SS1, OUTPUT);
  pinMode(SS2, OUTPUT);

  //Initialize SPI
  SPI.begin();
}

//This will set one pot to the specifed level
//Chip 1 (SS 10) Register 0 is Red
```

```
//Chip 1 (SS 10) Resiter 1 is Yellow
//Chip 2 (SS 9) Register 0 is Green
//Chip 2 (SS 9) Register 1 is the Speaker
void setReg(int SS, int reg, int level)
{
  digitalWrite(SS, LOW);   //Set the given SS pin low
  SPI.transfer(reg);       //Choose the register to write to
  SPI.transfer(level);     //Set the LED level (0-128)
  digitalWrite(SS, HIGH); //Set the given SS pin high again
}

void loop()
{
  tone(SPEAKER, freq); //Set speaker to given frequency
  for (int i=0; i<=128; i++)
  {
    setReg(SS1, REG0, i);
    setReg(SS1, REG1, i);
    setReg(SS2, REG0, i);
    setReg(SS2, REG1, i);
    delay(10);
  }
  delay(300);
  for (int i=128; i>=0; i--)
  {
    setReg(SS1, REG0, i);
    setReg(SS1, REG1, i);
    setReg(SS2, REG0, i);
    setReg(SS2, REG1, i);
    delay(10);
  }
  delay(300);
  freq = freq+100;
  if (freq > 2000) freq = 100;

}
```

// tone/freq ramps up reaching
// 2000 then restarts at 100

// at each tone level, the
// 3 LED's & speaker vol ramp
// up then down

Load this program onto your Arduino, and in addition to the lights changing intensity, the speaker will change volume. On each cycle, the frequency is incremented by 100Hz until it reaches 2000Hz. This is controlled by the `if` statement at the end of `loop()`. The for loops that are controlling LED brightness and volume do not need to change at all from what you wrote in Listing 9-1, because speaker volume is being controlled by the same potentiometer action that is controlling the LEDs.

This is just a starting point. You now have sufficient knowledge to really make this multimedia platform into something exciting. Here are some suggestions:

- Correlate sound frequency and volume with sensor inputs (for example, an infrared [IR] distance sensor can control the frequency of the speaker based on movement in front of the unit).
- Correlate LED intensity with a different metric such as temperature.
- Add a debounced pushbutton to allow you to dynamically choose the volume or frequency of the speaker.
- Program light sequences that match up with simple music.

NOTE To watch a demo video of the audiovisual platform in action: www.exploringarduino.com/content/ch9. You can also find this video on the Wiley website shown at the beginning of this chapter.

Summary

In this chapter you learned about the following:

- The SPI bus uses two data lines, a clock line, and a slave select line. An additional slave select line is added for each slave device, but the other three lines are shared on the bus.
- The Arduino SPI library can be used to facilitate easy communication between the Arduino and slave devices.
- You can talk to multiple SPI devices over the same bus lines by using multiple SS pins.
- You can control SPI potentiometers using the Arduino Library.
- You learned how to dive deeper into understanding and working with datasheets.
- You learned how to simultaneously adjust speaker volume and frequency using the tone library paired with an SPI digital potentiometer.

Interfacing with Liquid Crystal Displays

Parts You'll Need for This Chapter

Arduino Uno

USB cable (A to B for Uno)

Speaker

Pushbuttons (×2)

Small DC fan

16x2 character LCD

4.7kΩ resistors (×2)

10kΩ resistors (×2)

150Ω resistor

10kΩ potentiometer

TC74A0-5.0VAT I2C temperature sensor

Jumper wires

Breadboard

CODE AND DIGITAL CONTENT FOR THIS CHAPTER

Code downloads, video, and other digital content for this chapter can be found at www.exploringarduino.com/content/ch10.

In addition, all code can be found at www.wiley.com/go/exploringarduino on the Download Code tab. The code is in the chapter 10 download and individually named according to the names throughout the chapter.

One of the best things about designing embedded systems is the fact that they can operate independently of a computer. Up until now, you've been tethered to the computer if you want to display any kind of information more complicated than an illuminated LED. By adding a liquid crystal display (LCD) to your Arduino, you can more easily display complex information (sensor values, timing information, settings, progress bars, etc.) directly on your Arduino project without having to interface with the serial monitor through the computer.

In this chapter, you learn how to connect an LCD to your Arduino, and you learn how to use the Arduino LiquidCrystal library to write text and arbitrary custom characters to your LCD. After you have the basics down, you add some components from previous chapters to make a simple thermostat capable of obtaining local temperature data, reporting it to you, and controlling a fan to compensate for heat. An LCD will give you live information, a speaker will alert you when the temperature is getting too hot, and the fan will turn on to automatically cool you down.

> **NOTE** To watch a video tutorial about interfacing to an LCD, check out
> www.jeremyblum.com/2011/07/31/tutorial-13-for-arduino-liquid-
> crystal-displays. You can also find this video on the Wiley website shown at
> the beginning of this chapter.

Setting Up the LCD

To complete the examples in this chapter, you use a parallel LCD screen. These are extremely common and come in all kinds of shapes and sizes. The most common is a 16×2 character display with a single row of 16 pins (14 if it does not have a backlight). In this chapter, you use a 16-pin LCD display that can show a total of 32 characters (16 columns and 2 rows).

If your display didn't come with a 16-pin header already soldered on, you need to solder one on so that you can easily install it in your breadboard. With the header successfully soldered on, your LCD should look like the one shown in Figure 10-1, and you can insert it into your breadboard.

Next, you wire up your LCD to a breadboard and to your Arduino. All of these parallel LCD modules have the same pin-out and can be wired in one of two modes: 4-pin or 8-pin mode. You can accomplish everything you might want to do using just 4 pins for communication; that's how you'll wire it up. There are also pins for enabling the display, setting the display to command mode or character mode, and for setting it to read/write mode. Table 10-1 describes all of these pins.

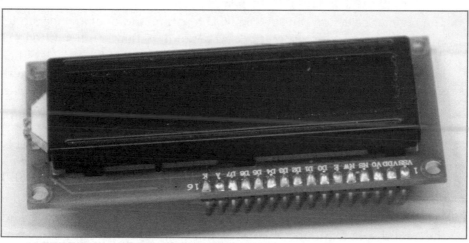

Figure 10-1: LCD with Headers soldered on

Table 10-1: Parallel LCD Pins

PIN NUMBER		PIN NAME		PIN PURPOSE
1		VSS		Ground connection
2		VDD		+5V connection
3		V0		Contrast adjustment (to potentiometer)
4		RS		Register selection (Character vs. Command)
5		RW		Read/write
6		EN		Enable
7		D0		Data line 0 (unused)
8		D1		Data line 1 (unused)
9		D2		Data line 2 (unused)
10		D3		Data line 3 (unused)
11		D4		Data line 4
12		D5		Data line 3
13		D6		Data line 6
14		D7		Data line 7
15		A		Backlight anode
16		K		Backlight cathode

Here's a breakdown of the pin connections:

- The contrast adjustment pin changes how dark the display is. It connects to the center pin of a potentiometer.

- The register selection pin sets the LCD to command or character mode, so it knows how to interpret the next set of data that is transmitted via the data lines. Based on the state of this pin, data sent to the LCD is either interpreted as a command (for example, move the cursor) or characters (for example, the letter *a*).

- The RW pin is always tied to ground in this implementation, meaning that you are only writing to the display and never reading from it.

- The EN pin is used to tell the LCD when data is ready.

- Data pins 4–7 are used for actually transmitting data, and data pins 0–3 are left unconnected.

- You can illuminate the backlight by connecting the anode pin to 5V and the cathode pin to ground if you are using an LCD with a built-in resistor for the backlight. If you are not, you must put a current-limiting resistor in-line with the anode or cathode pin. The datasheet for your device will generally tell you if you need to do this.

You can connect the communication pins of the LCD to any I/O pins on the Arduino. In this chapter, they are connected as shown in Table 10-2.

Table 10-2: Communication Pins Connections

LCD PIN	ARDUINO PIN NUMBER
RS	Pin 2
EN	Pin 3
D4	Pin 4
D5	Pin 5
D6	Pin 6
D7	Pin 7

Reference the wiring diagram shown in Figure 10-2 and hook up your LCD accordingly.

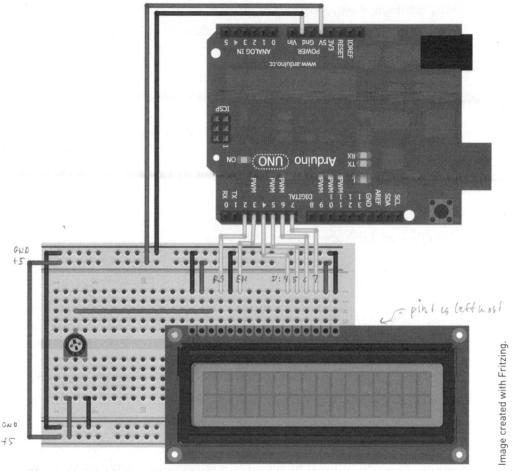

RS EN   D: 4 5 6 7

⟶ pin 1 is leftmost

Image created with Fritzing.

GND
+5

GND
+5

Figure 10-2: LCD wired to breadboard and Arduino

Now your LCD is ready for action! Once you get the code loaded in the next section, you can start displaying text on the screen. The potentiometer will adjust the contrast between the text and the background color of the screen.

Using the LiquidCrystal Library to Write to the LCD

The Arduino IDE includes the LiquidCrystal library, a set of functions that makes it very easy to interface with the parallel LCD that you are using. The LiquidCrystal library has an impressive amount of functionality, including blinking the cursor, automatically scrolling text, creating custom characters, and changing the direction of text printing. This chapter does not cover every function, but instead gives you the tools you need to understand to interface with the display using the most important functions. You can find descriptions of the library functions and examples illustrating their use on the Arduino website: http://arduino.cc/en/Reference/LiquidCrystal (also linked from www.exploringarduino.com/content/ch10).

Adding Text to the Display

In this first example, you add some text and an incrementing number to the display. This exercise demonstrates how to initialize the display, how to write text, and how to move the cursor. First, include the LiquidCrystal library:

```
#include <LiquidCrystal.h>
```

Then, initialize an LCD object, as follows:

```
LiquidCrystal lcd (2,3,4,5,6,7);
```

The arguments for the LCD initialization represent the Arduino pins connected to RS, EN, D4, D5, D6, and D7, in that order. In the setup, you call the library's begin() function to set up the LCD display with the character size. (The one I'm using is a 16×2 display, but you might be using another size, such as a 20×4.) The arguments for this command represent the number of columns and the number of rows, respectively:

```
lcd.begin(16, 2);
```

After doing that, you can call the library's print() and setCursor() commands to print text to a given location on the display. For example, if you want to print my name on the second line, you issue these commands:

```
lcd.setCursor(0,1);
lcd.print("Jeremy Blum");
```

The positions on the screen are indexed starting with (0,0) in the top-left position. The first argument of setCursor() specifies which column number, and the second specifies which row number. By default, the starting location is (0,0). So, if you call print() without first changing the cursor location, the text starts in the top-left corner.

> **WARNING** The library does not check for strings that are too long. So, if you try to print a string starting at position 0 that is longer than the number of characters in the row you are addressing, you might notice strange behavior. Make sure to check that whatever you are printing will fit on the display!

Using this knowledge, you can now write a simple program that displays some text on the first row and that prints a counter that increments once every second on the second row. Listing 10-1 shows the complete program to accomplish this. Load it on to your Arduino and confirm that it works as expected. If you don't see anything, adjust the contrast with the potentiometer.

Listing 10-1: LCD Text with an Incrementing Number—LCD_text.ino

```
//LCD text with incrementing number

//Include the library code:
#include <LiquidCrystal.h>

//Start the time at 0
int time = 0;

//Initialize the library with the numbers of the interface pins
LiquidCrystal lcd(2, 3, 4, 5, 6, 7);

void setup()
{
  //Set up the LCD's number of columns and rows:
  lcd.begin(16, 2);
  //Print a message to the LCD.
  lcd.print("Jeremy's Display");       // based at 0,0 by default
}

void loop()
{
  //Move cursor to second line, first position
  lcd.setCursor(0,1);
  //Print Current Time
  lcd.print(time);
  //Wait 1 second
  delay(1000);
  //Increment the time
  time++;
}
```

This program combines all the steps that you learned about earlier. The library is first included at the top of the program. A `time` variable is initialized to 0, so that it can be incremented once per second during the `loop()`. A `LiquidCrysal` object called `lcd` is created with the proper pins assigned based on the circuit you've already wired up. In the setup, the LCD is configured as having 16 columns and 2 rows, by calling `lcd.begin(16,2)`. Because the first line never changes, it can be written in the setup. This is accomplished with a call to `lcd.print()`. Note that the cursor position does not need to be set first, because you want to the text to be printed to position (0,0), which is already the default starting location. In the loop, the cursor is always set back to position (0,1) so that the number you print every second overwrites the previous number. The display updates once per second with the incremented time value.

Creating Special Characters and Animations

What if you want to display information that cannot be expressed using normal text? Maybe you want to add a Greek letter, a degree sign, or some progress bars. Thankfully, the LiquidCrystal library supports the definition of custom characters that can be written to the display. In the next example, you use this capability to make an animated progress bar that scrolls across the display. After that, you take advantage of custom characters to add a degree sign when measuring and displaying temperature.

Creating a custom character is pretty straightforward. If you take a close look at your LCD, you'll see that each character block is actually made up of a 5×8 grid of pixels. To create a custom character, you simply have to define the value of each of these pixels and send that information to the display. To try this out, you make a series of characters that will fill the second row of the display with an animated progress bar. Because each character space is 5 pixels wide, there will be a total of five custom characters: one with one column filled, one with two columns filled, and so on.

At the top of your sketch where you want to use the custom characters, create a byte array with 1s representing pixels that will be turned on and with 0s representing pixels that will be turned off. The byte array representing the character that fills the first column (or the first 20% of the character) looks like this:

```
byte p20[8] = {
  B10000,
  B10000,
  B10000,
  B10000,
  B10000,
  B10000,
  B10000,
  B10000,
};
```

*block is 5×8 : 5 cols
                    8 rows*

I chose to call this byte array p20, to represent that it is filling 20 percent of one character block (the p stands for percent).

In the setup() function, call the createChar() function to assign your byte array to a custom character ID. Custom character IDs start at 0 and go up to 7, so you can have a total of eight custom characters. To map the 20% character byte array to custom character 0, type the following within your `setup()` function:

```
lcd.createChar(0, p20);
```

When you're ready to write a custom character to the display, place the cursor in the right location and use the library's `write()` function with the ID number:

```
lcd.write((byte)0);
```

In the preceding line, `(byte)` casts, or changes, the 0 to a byte value. This is necessary *only* when writing character ID 0 directly (without a variable that is defined to 0), to prevent the Arduino compiler from throwing an error caused by the variable type being ambiguous. Try removing the "byte cast" and observe the error that the Arduino IDE displays. You can write other character IDs without it, like this:

```
lcd.write(1);
```

Putting this all together, you can add the rest of the characters and put two nested `for()` loops in your program loop to handle updating the progress bar. The completed code looks like the code shown in Listing 10-2.

Listing 10-2: LCD Updating Progress Bar Code—LCD_progress_bar.ino

```
//LCD with Progress Bar

//Include the library code:
#include <LiquidCrystal.h>

//Initialize the library with the numbers of the interface pins
LiquidCrystal lcd(2, 3, 4, 5, 6, 7);

//Create the progress bar characters
byte p20[8] = {
  B10000,
  B10000,
  B10000,
  B10000,
  B10000,
  B10000,
  B10000,
  B10000,
};
```

```
byte p40[8] = {
  B11000,
  B11000,
  B11000,
  B11000,
  B11000,
  B11000,
  B11000,
  B11000,
};
byte p60[8] = {
  B11100,
  B11100,
  B11100,
  B11100,
  B11100,
  B11100,
  B11100,
  B11100,
};
byte p80[8] = {
  B11110,
  B11110,
  B11110,
  B11110,
  B11110,
  B11110,
  B11110,
  B11110,
};
byte p100[8] = {
  B11111,
  B11111,
  B11111,
  B11111,
  B11111,
  B11111,
  B11111,
  B11111,
};

void setup()
{
  //Set up the LCDs number of columns and rows:
  lcd.begin(16, 2);
  // Print a message to the LCD.
  lcd.print("Jeremy's Display");

  //Make progress characters
  lcd.createChar(0, p20);
  lcd.createChar(1, p40);
```

```
  lcd.createChar(2, p60);
  lcd.createChar(3, p80);
  lcd.createChar(4, p100);
}

void loop()
{
  //Move cursor to second line
  lcd.setCursor(0,1);
  //Clear the line each time it reaches the end
  //with 16 " " (spaces)
  lcd.print("                ");

  //Iterate through each character on the second line
  for (int i = 0; i<16; i++)
  {
    //Iterate through each progress value for each character
    for (int j=0; j<5; j++)
    {
      lcd.setCursor(i, 1); //Move the cursor to this location
      lcd.write(j);        //Update progress bar
      delay(100);          //Wait
    }
  }
}
```

Single char Effect | → || → ||| → |||| → |||||
"Rolls" across the 16 chars filling vert bars

At the beginning of each pass through the loop, the 16-character-long string of spaces is written to the display, clearing the progress bar before it starts again. The outer `for()` loop iterates through all 16 positions. At each character position, the inner `for()` loop keeps the cursor there and writes an incrementing progress bar custom character to that location. The byte cast is not required here because the ID 0 is defined by the `j` variable in the `for()` loop.

NOTE To watch a demo video of the updating progress bar, visit www.exploringarduino.com/content/ch10. You can also find this video on the Wiley website shown at the beginning of this chapter.

Building a Personal Thermostat

Now, let's make this display a bit more useful. To do so, you add the temperature sensor from Chapter 8, "The I²C Bus," a fan, and the speaker from Chapter 5, "Making Sounds." The display shows the temperature and the current fan state. When it gets too hot, the speaker makes a noise to alert you, and the fan turns on. When it gets sufficiently cool again, the fan turns off. Using two pushbuttons and the debounce code in Listing 2-5 in Chapter 2, "Digital Inputs, Outputs, and Pulse-Width Modulation," you add the ability to increment or decrement the desired temperature.

172
101

34

Setting Up the Hardware

The hardware setup for this project is a conglomeration of previous projects. If you want the fan to have some oomph, you can drive it with a transistor and an external voltage supply (like the DC motor from Chapter 4, "DC Motors, Transistors, and Servos"). A low-power DC fan hooked directly to a 5V I/O pin will suffice to show that it spins when it should. It will be accelerating slowly enough that you don't need to worry too much about inductive spikes. If you actually want it to make a breeze, use the same schematic that you used for driving a DC motor in Chapter 4 (see Figure 4-1).

To wire the project, leave the LCD and trim potentiometer in the same location they were in for the previous example.

The two buttons have one side connected to power; the other side is connected to ground through 10kΩ pull-down resistors and to the Arduino.

The speaker is connected to an I/O pin through a 150Ω resistor and to ground. The frequency of the sound will be set in the program.

You hook up the I²C temperature sensor exactly as you did in Chapter 8. Placing it in front of the LCD's contrast potentiometer allows you to conserve some breadboard space and to fit everything onto the same half-size breadboard that you've been using so far. The diagram in Figure 10-3 shows the complete wiring setup with everything you need to create this project. The symbol for the TC74 temperature sensor has been made partially transparent so that you can see the potentiometer behind it.

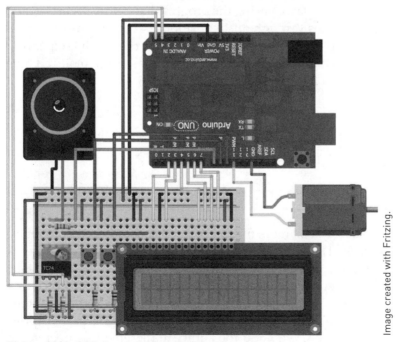

Figure 10-3: LCD thermostat system

Image created with Fritzing.

Displaying Data on the LCD

Having some parameters in place beforehand makes writing information to the LCD screen easier. First, use degrees Celsius for the display, and second, assume that you'll always be showing two digits for the temperature. Once the software is running, the LCD display will look something like Figure 10.4.

Figure 10-4: LCD display

The `"Current:"` and `"Set:"` strings are static; they can be written to the screen once at the beginning and left there. Similarly, because the temperatures are assumed to be two digits, you can statically place both `"°C"` strings into the correct locations. The current reading will be displayed in position `(8,0)` and will be updated on every run through the `loop()`. The desired, or set, temperature will be placed in position `(8,1)` and updated every time a button is used to adjust its value. The fan indicator in the lower right of the display will be at position `(15,1)`. It should update to reflect the fan's state every time it changes.

The degree symbol, fan off indicator, and fan on indicator are not part of the LCD character set. Before using them in your sketch, you need to create them as byte arrays at the beginning of your program, as shown in the following snippet.

```
//Custom degree character
byte degree[8] = {
  B00110,
  B01001,
  B01001,
  B00110,
  B00000,
  B00000,
  B00000,
  B00000,
};
```

```
//Custom "fan on" indicator
byte fan_on[8] = {
  B00100,
  B10101,
  B01110,
  B11111,
  B01110,
  B10101,
  B00100,
  B00000,
};

//Custom "fan off" indicator
byte fan_off[8] = {
  B00100,
  B00100,
  B00100,
  B11111,
  B00100,
  B00100,
  B00100,
  B00000,
};
```

Writing these characters will be done in `setup()`. Move the cursor to the right locations, and with the LCD library's `write()` and `print()` functions, update the screen, as shown in the following snippet.

```
//Make custom characters
lcd.createChar(0, degree);
lcd.createChar(1, fan_off);
lcd.createChar(2, fan_on);

//Print a static message to the LCD
lcd.setCursor(0,0);
lcd.print("Current:");
lcd.setCursor(10,0);
lcd.write((byte)0);
lcd.setCursor(11,0);
lcd.print("C");
lcd.setCursor(0,1);
lcd.print("Set:");
lcd.setCursor(10,1);
lcd.write((byte)0);
lcd.setCursor(11,1);
lcd.print("C");
lcd.setCursor(15,1);
lcd.write(1);
```

You also update the fan indicator and temperature values each time through `loop()`. You need to move the cursor to the right location each time before you update these characters.

Adjusting the Set Point with a Button

In Chapter 2, you used a `debounce()` function. Here, you modify it slightly to use it with multiple buttons. One button will increase the set point, and the other will decrease it. You need to define variables for holding the previous and current button states:

```
//Variables for debouncing
boolean lastDownTempButton = LOW;
boolean currentDownTempButton = LOW;
boolean lastUpTempButton = LOW;
boolean currentUpTempButton = LOW;
```

You can modify the `debounce()` function to support multiple buttons. To accomplish this, add a second argument that specifies which button you want to debounce:

```
//A debouncing function that can be used by both buttons
boolean debounce(boolean last, int pin)
{
  boolean current = digitalRead(pin);
  if (last != current)
  {
    delay(5);
    current = digitalRead(pin);
  }
  return current;
}
```

In `loop()`, you want to check both buttons using the `debounce()` function, change the `set_temp` variable as needed, and update the set value that is displayed on the LCD:

```
//Debounce both buttons
currentDownTempButton = debounce(lastDownTempButton, DOWN_BUTTON);
currentUpTempButton = debounce(lastUpTempButton, UP_BUTTON);

//Turn down the set temp
if (lastDownTempButton == LOW && currentDownTempButton == HIGH)
{
  set_temp--;
}
```

```
//Turn up the set temp
else if (lastUpTempButton == LOW && currentUpTempButton == HIGH)
{
  set_temp++;
}
//Print the set temp
lcd.setCursor(8,1);
lcd.print(set_temp);
//Update the button state with the current
lastDownTempButton = currentDownTempButton;
lastUpTempButton = currentUpTempButton;
```

The preceding code snippet first runs the `debounce()` function for each button, and then adjusts the set temperature variable if one of the buttons has been pressed. Afterward, the temperature displayed on the LCD is updated, as are the button state variables.

Adding an Audible Warning and a Fan

In this section, you add code to control the fan and the speaker. Although the LCD showing you live information is nice, you'll often find it useful to have an additional form of feedback to tell you when something is happening. For example, the speaker beeps when the fan turns on. In this example, you use `tone()` paired with `delay()` and a `notone()` command. You could instead add a duration argument to `tone()` to determine the duration of the sound. You want to make sure that the tone plays only one time so (and does not beep forever when above the set temperature).

Using a state variable, you can detect when the speaker has beeped and thus keep it from beeping again until after the temperature dips below the set temperature and resets the state variable.

When the fan turns on, an indicator changes on the LCD (represented by the custom character you defined at the top of the program). The following code snippet checks the temperature and controls the speaker, the fan indicator on the LCD, and the fan:

```
//If it's too hot!
if (c >= set_temp)
{
  //Check if the speaker has already beeped
  if (!one_time)
  {
    tone(SPEAKER, 400);
    delay(500);
    one_time = true;
  }
```

```
    //Turn off the speaker when it's done
    else
    {
      noTone(SPEAKER);
    }
    //Turn the Fan on and update display
    digitalWrite(FAN, HIGH);
    lcd.setCursor(15,1);
    lcd.write(2);
  }
  //If it's not too hot!
  else
  {
    //Make sure the speaker is off
    //reset the "one beep" variable
    //update the fan state and LCD display
    noTone(SPEAKER);
    one_time = false;
    digitalWrite(FAN, LOW);
    lcd.setCursor(15,1);
    lcd.write(1);
  }
```

The one_time variable is used to make sure that the beep plays only one time instead of continuously. Once the speaker has beeped for 500ms at 400Hz, the variable is set to true and is reset to false only when the temperature drops back below the desired temperature.

Bringing It All Together: The Complete Program

It's time to bring all the parts together into a cohesive whole. You need to make sure that you include the appropriate libraries, define the pins, and initialize the state variables at the top of the sketch. Listing 10-3 shows the complete program. Load it on to your Arduino and compare your results to the demo video showing the system in action.

Listing 10-3: Personal Thermostat Program—LCD_thermostat.ino

```
//Keep yourself cool! This is a thermostat.
//This assumes temperatures are always two digits

//Include Wire I2C library and set the address
#include <Wire.h>
#define TEMP_ADDR 72

//Include the LCD library and initialize:
#include <LiquidCrystal.h>
```

```
LiquidCrystal lcd(2, 3, 4, 5, 6, 7);

//Custom degree character
byte degree[8] = {
  B00110,
  B01001,
  B01001,
  B00110,
  B00000,
  B00000,
  B00000,
  B00000,
};

//Custom "fan on" indicator
byte fan_on[8] = {
  B00100,
  B10101,
  B01110,
  B11111,
  B01110,
  B10101,
  B00100,
  B00000,
};

//Custom "fan off" indicator
byte fan_off[8] = {
  B00100,
  B00100,
  B00100,
  B11111,
  B00100,
  B00100,
  B00100,
  B00000,
};

//Pin Connections
const int SPEAKER      =8;
const int DOWN_BUTTON =9;
const int UP_BUTTON    =10;
const int FAN          =11;

//Variables for debouncing
boolean lastDownTempButton = LOW;
boolean currentDownTempButton = LOW;
boolean lastUpTempButton = LOW;
boolean currentUpTempButton = LOW;

int set_temp = 23;    //The Default desired temperature
boolean one_time = false; //Used for making the speaker beep only 1 time
```

```
void setup()
{
  pinMode(FAN, OUTPUT);

  //Create a wire object for the temp sensor
  Wire.begin();

  //Set up the LCD's number of columns and rows
  lcd.begin(16, 2);

  //Make custom characters
  lcd.createChar(0, degree);
  lcd.createChar(1, fan_off);
  lcd.createChar(2, fan_on);

  //Print a static message to the LCD
  lcd.setCursor(0,0);
  lcd.print("Current:");
  lcd.setCursor(10,0);
  lcd.write((byte)0);
  lcd.setCursor(11,0);
  lcd.print("C");
  lcd.setCursor(0,1);
  lcd.print("Set:");
  lcd.setCursor(10,1);
  lcd.write((byte)0);
  lcd.setCursor(11,1);
  lcd.print("C");
  lcd.setCursor(15,1);
  lcd.write(1);
}

//A debouncing function that can be used by multiple buttons
boolean debounce(boolean last, int pin)
{
  boolean current = digitalRead(pin);
  if (last != current)
  {
    delay(5);
    current = digitalRead(pin);
  }
  return current;
}

void loop()
{
  //Get the Temperature
  Wire.beginTransmission(TEMP_ADDR); //Start talking
  Wire.write(0);                     //Ask for register zero
  Wire.endTransmission();            //Complete transmission
  Wire.requestFrom(TEMP_ADDR, 1);    //Request 1 byte
```

```
while(Wire.available() == 0);        //Wait for response
int c = Wire.read();                 //Get the temp in C
lcd.setCursor(8,0);                  //Move the cursor
lcd.print(c);                        //Print this new value

//Debounce both buttons
currentDownTempButton = debounce(lastDownTempButton, DOWN_BUTTON);
currentUpTempButton   = debounce(lastUpTempButton, UP_BUTTON);

//Turn down the set temp
if (lastDownTempButton== LOW && currentDownTempButton == HIGH)
{
  set_temp--;
}
//Turn up the set temp
else if (lastUpTempButton== LOW && currentUpTempButton  == HIGH)
{
  set_temp++;
}
//Print the set temp
lcd.setCursor(8,1);
lcd.print(set_temp);
lastDownTempButton = currentDownTempButton;
lastUpTempButton = currentUpTempButton;

//It's too hot!
if (c >= set_temp)
{
  //So that the speaker will only beep one time...
  if (!one_time)
  {
    tone(SPEAKER, 400);
    delay(500);
    one_time = true;
  }
  //Turn off the speaker if it's done
  else
  {
    noTone(SPEAKER);
  }
  //Turn the fan on and update display
  digitalWrite(FAN, HIGH);
  lcd.setCursor(15,1);
  lcd.write(2);
}
//It't not to hot!
else
{
  //Make sure the speaker is off, reset the "one beep" variable
  //Update the fan state, and LCD display
  noTone(SPEAKER);
```

```
      one_time = false;
      digitalWrite(FAN, LOW);
      lcd.setCursor(15,1);
      lcd.write(1);
    }
}
```

You no longer need to have the Arduino and components tethered to the computer to see what the temperature is. If you like, you can plug in a battery or wall power supply and place it anywhere in your room.

> **NOTE** To watch a demo video of this personal thermostat in action, check out www.exploringarduino.com/content/ch10. You can also find this video on the Wiley website shown at the beginning of this chapter.

Taking This Project to the Next Level

You could expand the functionality of this program in all kinds of ways. Here are a few suggestions for further improvements you can make:

- Add a transistor to the fan so that it can draw more current and move more air.
- Use pulse-width modulation (PWM) to control fan speed so that it changes according to how far over the set temperature you are.
- Add LED indicators that display visual alerts.
- Make the speaker alert into a melody instead of a tone.
- Add a light sensor and automatically adjust the backlight brightness of the display using an SPI potentiometer from Chapter 9, "The SPI Bus," based on the brightness of the room.

Summary

In this chapter you learned about the following:

- Parallel LCDs can be interfaced with the Arduino through a standard wiring scheme.
- You can create custom characters for your LCD by generating arbitrary bitmaps.
- You can modify your debounce function from Chapter 2 to debounce multiple buttons.
- You combine multiple sensors, motors, buttons, and displays into one coherent project.

CHAPTER 11

Wireless Communication with XBee Radios

Parts You'll Need for This Chapter

Two Arduinos (Unos and/or Leonardos recommended)

USB cables for programming Arduinos

Power supplies for each Arduino (optionally power over USB)

SparkFun USB XBee Explorer

XBee Series 1 radio (×2)

XBee shields (×2)

Pushbutton

Piezo buzzer

Common cathode RGB LED

10KΩ resistor

10KΩ potentiometer

150Ω resistor

220Ω resistors (×3)

Jumper wires

Breadboards (×2)

CODE AND DIGITAL CONTENT FOR THIS CHAPTER

Code downloads, video, and other digital content for this chapter can be found at www.exploringarduino.com/content/ch11.

In addition, all code can be found at www.wiley.com/go/exploringarduino on the Download Code tab. The code is in the chapter 11 download and individually named according to the names throughout the chapter.

It's time to untether! A common requirement in many microcontroller projects is wireless connectivity. There are many ways to achieve wireless connectivity, but one of the easiest methods with the Arduino is to use XBee radios, which are produced by a company named Digi. XBees act as a wireless serial pass-through, allowing you to use the serial printing and reading commands you've already learned about. This chapter focuses only on XBee communication, but does cover some of the caveats that you must understand when using any form of wireless communication.

XBees make it easy to communicate wirelessly between the Arduino and your computer or between multiple Arduinos. In this chapter, you learn how to facilitate both.

NOTE To follow a video tutorial about using XBee radios, visit www.jeremyblum .com/2011/02/27/arduino-tutorial-9-wireless-communication/. You can also find this video on the Wiley website shown at the beginning of this chapter.

Understanding XBee Wireless Communication

The name says it all: Wireless communication permits two or more devices to talk to each other without wires tethering them together. Wireless transmitters operate by transmitting data in the form of radio waves through free space by a process of electromagnetic radiation at a particular frequency. Different frequencies are used by different transmission technologies to prevent "crowding" of certain parts of the available electromagnetic spectrum. Governmental agencies, such as the Federal Communications Commission (FCC) in the USA, regulate this spectrum and publish rules specifying which frequencies can be used for what. The XBee radio transmits data 2.4GHz. You might recognize this frequency because many devices around your home use it. It falls within the ISM (Industrial, Scientific, and Medical) band, a set of frequencies set aside for unlicensed wireless communication use. Your WiFi router probably operates at this frequency as well. The XBee modules use the IEEE 802.15.4 standard, which specifies a set of operating rules for wireless personal area networks (PANs).

XBees are generally used in a PAN point-to-point or a point-to-multipoint configuration; Figure 11-1 shows examples of both. Point-to-point is useful when you want to simply replace wired serial communication between two remote units. Point-to-multipoint is often used for distributed sensor networks.

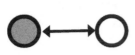 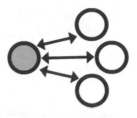

Point to Point   **Point to Multipoint**

Figure 11-1: PAN configurations

XBee Radios

XBee radios can communicate in an application programming interface (API) mode, and a simple serial pass-through mode. In API mode, they can directly transmit digital or analog I/O pin states. This enables you to have a microcontroller-free weather station transmitter, for example. In this chapter, you use the XBees as a simple serial pass-through. Serial data sent into one radio comes out of another and vice versa. Using this method, you can use the XBees as a drop-in replacement for a wired serial connection (either between two Arduinos or between an Arduino and your computer).

XBees have 20 pins and are, for the most part, pin compatible with each other. This chapter uses Series 1 XBees, which use the 802.15.4 standard. They are capable of point-to-point and point-to-multipoint communication, but they do not implement the ZigBee standard, a mesh networking standard found in Series 2/ZB XBee radios. If you aren't sure what kind of XBees you have, you probably have Series 1. They look like the ones in Figure 11-2.

Credit: SparkFun [Photographer Juan Peña], www.sparkfun.com.

Figure 11-2: XBee Series 1 radios

NOTE Series 1 and Series 2 modules are *not* compatible with each other. You can use either one (as long as both radios are the same series), but I strongly recommend using Series 1 if you are just starting out. Series 1 modules require less configuration and are a lot easier to set up.

There are other differences in each series of XBee as well. There are Pro and non-Pro versions of most XBee modules. The Pro versions are completely compatible with their non-Pro counterparts, but consume more power, cost more, are slightly longer, and have a significantly longer range (about 1 mile versus 300 feet). I recommend starting out with the cheaper, non-Pro version, and upgrading later if you find you need more range.

Also, some radios are available in 2.4GHz and 900MHz versions. 900MHz falls in another portion of the ISM band and is legal for personal use in some countries, but not in others. 900MHz, because it is a lower frequency, achieves better range and is better at penetrating walls. The 900MHz modules and 2.4GHz modules cannot communicate with each other.

Finally, the XBee modules come with various antenna options: built-in wire antennas, trace antennas, chip antennas, and external antenna connectors. Pick whichever option suits your needs; you can generally get better range with an external antenna, but it will take up more space.

 This chapter uses non-Pro, Series 1, 2.4GHz XBees with chip antennas in serial pass-through mode. Familiarize yourself with the module pin-out from the datasheet shown in Figure 11-3.

Most of the details will be abstracted away by the XBee shield (explained in the next section), but you should be aware of the fact that the XBee is a 3.3V module; it needs a 3.3V power supply.

WARNING If you supply an XBee radio with 5V on the supply pin, you will ruin the component.

The XBee Radio Shield and Serial Connections

In this chapter, you learn to use the XBee radio in conjunction with a shield that makes it easy to connect the module to your Arduino. A number of XBee Arduino shields are available, so my descriptions here are general so that they apply to any shield you might use. All the shields essentially do the same thing, but with some minor differences, as explained in this section. Figure 11-4 shows examples of the most common XBee shields.

XBee®/XBee-PRO® RF Module Pin
Numbers

(top sides shown - shields on bottom)

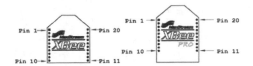

Pin Assignments for the XBee and XBee-PRO Modules
(Low-asserted signals are distinguished with a horizontal line above signal name.)

Pin #	Name	Direction	Description
1	VCC	-	Power supply
2	DOUT	Output	UART Data Out
3	DIN / **CONFIG**	Input	UART Data In
4	DO8*	Output	Digital Output 8
5	**RESET**	Input	Module Reset (reset pulse must be at least 200 ns)
6	PWM0 / RSSI	Output	PWM Output 0 / RX Signal Strength Indicator
7	PWM1	Output	PWM Output 1
8	[reserved]	-	Do not connect
9	DTR / SLEEP_RQ / DI8	Input	Pin Sleep Control Line or Digital Input 8
10	GND	-	Ground
11	AD4 / DIO4	Either	Analog Input 4 or Digital I/O 4
12	**CTS** / DIO7	Either	Clear-to-Send Flow Control or Digital I/O 7
13	ON / **SLEEP**	Output	Module Status Indicator
14	VREF	Input	Voltage Reference for A/D Inputs
15	Associate / AD5 / DIO5	Either	Associated Indicator, Analog Input 5 or Digital I/O 5
16	**RTS** / AD6 / DIO6	Either	Request-to-Send Flow Control, Analog Input 6 or Digital I/O 6
17	AD3 / DIO3	Either	Analog Input 3 or Digital I/O 3
18	AD2 / DIO2	Either	Analog Input 2 or Digital I/O 2
19	AD1 / DIO1	Either	Analog Input 1 or Digital I/O 1
20	AD0 / DIO0	Either	Analog Input 0 or Digital I/O 0

Credit: Digi International, Inc., www.digi.com

Figure 11-3: XBee series 1 pin-out

Arduino Wireless Shield   Sparkfun Xbee Shield   Cooking Hacks XBee Shield

Figure 11-4: Various XBee shields

Credits: Arduino, www.arduino.cc; SparkFun
[Photographer Juan Peña], www.sparkfun.com;
Cooking Hacks, www.cooking-hacks.com

Most XBee shields implement a number of key features, as explained in detail in the following sections.

3.3V Regulator

Most Arduinos (excluding the Due) operate at 5V logic levels; 0V indicates a logical low, and 5V indicates a logical high. The XBee, however, operates at 3.3V logic level, and it must be supplied with 3.3V power. Although the Arduino does have a small 3.3V regulator onboard, it does not supply enough current for the XBee, so most shields implement an LDO (low dropout) linear regulator that drops the 5V supply down to 3.3V for feeding into the VCC pin of the XBee.

Logic Level Shifting

The UART TX and RX pins of the Arduino and the XBee need to be connected; here too, however, you need to consider the fact that the XBee is a 3.3V part. Data transmitted from the XBee to the Arduino does not need to be level shifted (although some shields will do it anyways). This is because 3.3V is still above the threshold to be read as a logical high by the Arduino RX I/O pin. The data transmitted from the Arduino to the XBee, however, must be shifted down to 3.3V before it can be fed into the DI I/O pin of the XBee. Different shields use different methods to accomplish this.

Associate LED and RSSI LED

Most shields have an "associate" LED that blinks whenever the XBee is powered up and in use as a simple serial pass-though. It is generally used when running the XBee in API mode, which you do not do in this chapter.

The RSSI LED, also present on most XBee shields, lights up briefly when data is being received.

UART Selection Jumper or Switch

The XBee radio communicates with your Arduino via a serial Universal Asynchronous Receiver/Transmitter (UART) connection (RX and TX). In the case of the Arduinos other than the Mega and Due, there is only one available UART that is duplexed to the USB serial connection that you use for communicating with your computer for programming and debugging. The Leonardo (and similar boards) has just one UART, but it can be dedicated to the RX/TX pins, because the USB programming interface connects to the microcontroller unit (MCU) directly. In the case of the Uno, this raises a question: How can the XBee module and your computer's interface both be connected to the Arduino's single UART at the same time? When the shield is attached, the connection of the RX and TX pins looks like the diagram shown in Figure 11-5.

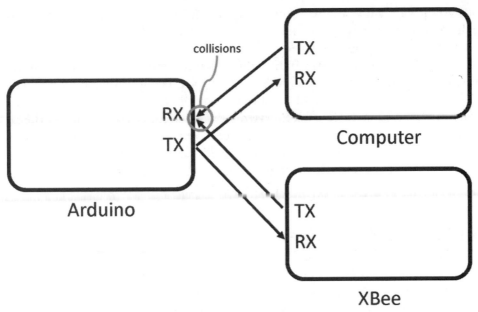

Figure 11-5: Colliding UART communication lines

Note the collision callout in Figure 11-5. Consider what would happen if both the XBee and your computer tried to transmit data to the Arduino. How does the Arduino know where the data is coming from? More importantly, what happens if both try to transmit to the Arduino at the same time? The data will "collide," causing garbled data that cannot be properly interpreted by the Arduino.

Because of this collision condition, and complexities regarding the drivers for these I/O ports, you cannot program the Arduino or talk to it from your computer while the XBee is connected to the Arduino's serial port. You can deal with this in two ways:

- You can unplug the XBee shield every time you want to program your Arduino.

- You can use a jumper or switch on the XBee shield to switch whether or not the XBee is connected through to the Arduino.

When you want to program your Arduino, you need to either remove the XBee shield, or be sure to set your shield's jumper/switch so that the XBee is disconnected.

Hardware vs. Software Serial UART Connection Option

In this chapter, you use only the "hardware" UART port of your Arduino to communicate with your XBee (pins 0 and 1 on your Arduino). As explained in the preceding section, these pins are also used for the USB connection to your computer. Most shields only allow a connection between the XBee and Arduino on the hardware serial UART port. If your shield supports it, you can avoid unplugging your XBee to program to your Arduino by using the SoftwareSerial library. The library allows you to define two arbitrary digital pins on your Arduino to act as RX/TX pins for talking with your XBee. For this to work, your XBee shield must have jumpers that enable you to choose which Arduino pins the RX/TX lines from the XBee connection. The SparkFun XBee shield has a switch that allows to you connect the RX/TX pins to pins 2 and 3 instead of pins 0 and 1. If your shield supports this, you can use the SoftwareSerial commands throughout this chapter in place of the traditional Serial commands when communicating with the XBee radio.

Configuring Your XBees

Before you can actually use your XBees, you need to configure them to talk to each other. Out of the box, XBees can already talk to each other; they are set to a default channel and are in broadcast mode. In other words, they send and receive with any other similarly configured XBee within range. Although this is okay, at some point you may want to use multiple XBee setups within range of each other, change communication speed, or otherwise configure them in a way unique to your setup. Here, you learn how to configure your XBees to speak specifically to each other.

Configuring via a Shield or a USB Adapter

You can program XBees, just like you can program your Arduino, via a USB serial connection. You can program an XBee in two ways. The first option is to use the USB-serial converter that is built in to your Arduino (via the FTDI chip or 8U2/16U2 Atmel chip that was explained in Chapter 6, "USB and Serial Communication"). The second option is to use a dedicated XBee USB adapter. I strongly recommend getting an XBee USB adapter; it will make it easier to handle communication between an Arduino and your computer later in this chapter. In this chapter, I use the popular SparkFun XBee USB Explorer (see Figure 11-6) to program the XBees.

dedicated XBee
USB adapter

Credit: SparkFun [Photographer Juan Peña], www.sparkfun.com

Figure 11-6: SparkFun USB Explorer

Programming Option 1: Using the Uno as a Programmer (Not Recommended)

I do not recommend using an Arduino Uno as the programmer for your XBee; it you can damage your Arduino if you are not careful. If you want to program your XBee using your Arduino, you need to deal with the problem of colliding serial data that was explained in the preceding section. You will need to (carefully) physically remove the ATMega chip from the Arduino. This is possible with the Uno, but not possible with the Uno SMD version or any other board that has the ATMega chip soldered onto the board rather than in a socket.

After removing the ATMega chip, attach the XBee shield and the XBee radio and connect your Arduino to your computer via USB. Now, all serial commands you send will go to the XBee rather than to your ATMega chip. (Check the specific documentation for your board to see whether you need to set a jumper or switch for the communication to happen.)

Programming Option 2: Using the SparkFun USB Explorer (Recommended)

Using an XBee-USB adapter is easy: Plug the XBee into the socket on the adapter, connect it your computer with the USB cable, and you are ready to program. The SparkFun board uses the same FTDI chip that older Arduinos used for serial-USB communication. Later in the chapter, this adapter is used to facilitate wireless communication between your computer and an Arduino with an XBee shield.

Choosing Your XBee Settings and Connecting Your XBee to Your Host Computer

You have an enormous number of configuration options for your XBees, and covering all of them could constitute its own book. Here, we cover the most important values that you need to configure:

- **ID:** Personal area network (PAN) ID. All XBees that you want to talk to each other must be assigned to the same PAN ID.

- **MY**: My address. This is a unique address identifying each XBee within a certain personal area network.

- **DL:** Destination address. This is the unique address of the XBee that you want this XBee to talk/listen to.

- **BD:** Baud rate. The rate at which the radios communicate with. We will use 9600 baud for this value, which is the default.

These values are shown in Figure 11-7 for a two-XBee system using the values that you will configure in the next step.

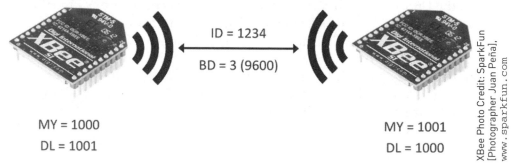

MY = 1000
DL = 1001

MY = 1001
DL = 1000

XBee Photo Credit: SparkFun [Photographer Juan Peña], www.sparkfun.com

Figure 11-7: XBee point-to-point system

Note that the MY and DL values for each XBee are swapped with each other because one XBee's destination address is the other's source address. (The ID that I use in these examples for the PAN is 1234, but you can choose another four-digit hex PAN ID if you desire.) The BD is set to 3, the default value. Instead of setting it to the actual baud rate, you set it to a number that represents the baud rate. The baud values are related to BD values follows:

- 0: 1200 baud
- 1: 2400 baud
- 2: 4800 baud
- 3: 9600 baud (Default)
- 4: 19200 baud
- 5: 38400 baud
- 6: 57600 baud
- 7: 115200 baud

Connect your XBee to your computer using either of the two methods described earlier. Make sure to insert the XBee in the right direction. After connecting it, you need to identify the serial port that it is connected to. You can do this the same way you did for the Arduino in Chapter 1, "Getting Up and Blinking with the Arduino." Note down what serial port the XBee connected to.

Configuring Your XBee with X-CTU

Next, you program your XBees with the values specified in Figure 11-7. If you are using Windows, you can use an application called X-CTU to do this using a graphical interface. I recommend this method if you have access to a Windows computer. If you don't have a Windows computer, skip to the next section, where you learn how to configure your XBees using a serial terminal in Linux or OS X.

A quick Google search for "X-CTU" will return the most up-to-date download link for the application from the Digi website. The installer is also linked from the web page for the chapter: www.exploringarduino.com/content/ch11. Find a download link, then complete the following steps:

1. Download the installer, install X-CTU, and launch the application. Once launched, you should see a window like the one in Figure 11-8. A list of available Com ports appears on the left side of the window.

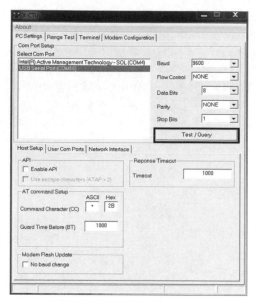

Figure 11-8: Main X-CTU window

2. Select the Com port that your XBee explorer is connected to and click the Test/Query button highlighted in Figure 11-8. If this is a new XBee that is configured using default settings (a 9600 baud rate), the window shown in Figure 11-9 should pop up confirming the current configuration info has been read from the radio.

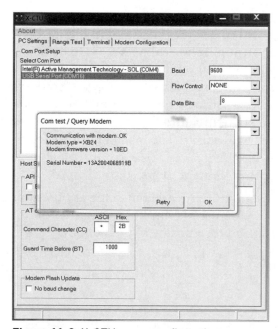

Figure 11-9: X-CTU query confirmation

3. Navigate to the Modem Configuration screen and click the Read button to display all the available configuration options on your XBee and what they are currently set to. The result should look something like Figure 11-10.

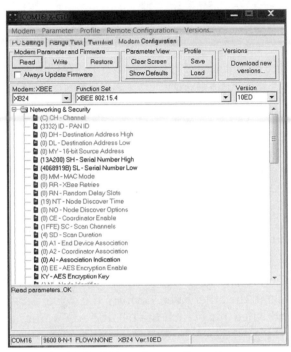

Figure 11-10: X-CTU modem configuration

4. Now, you set the PAN ID, source address, and destination address. You can set many other configuration options as well, but we focus on just these settings in this book. To change a setting, just click it to make it editable. Set the following:

ID   1234

DL   1001

MY   1000

5. Click the Write button at the top of the window to write these values into your XBee. When you do this, those values should turn blue. Figure 11-11 highlights these values.

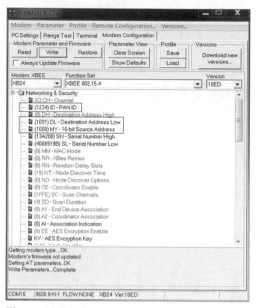

Figure 11-11: Settings written to XBee

You have now configured your first XBee! Now, carefully remove this XBee from the USB explorer and install the other XBee. Perform the same steps previously listed with your second XBee, but switch the DL and MY values so that the XBees talk to each other. Figure 11-12 shows the completed configuration for this second XBee.

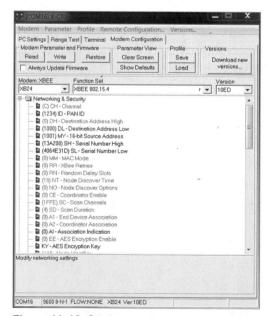

Figure 11-12: Settings written to second XBee

Both of your XBees are now configured and ready for communication with each other. By assigning them a nondefault PAN ID, you reduce the risk that they will interfere with other XBee networks. If you've successfully configured the radios, you can skip to the section "Talking with Your Computer Wirelessly."

Configuring Your XBee with a Serial Terminal

If you don't have Windows, you need to do your XBee configuration through a serial terminal, because X-CTU is Windows only. This process is the same for both Linux and Mac machines. You use the "screen" application that comes bundled with the system accessible. As in the first chapter, use the Arduino integrated development environment (IDE) to figure out what the device name is for your USB-serial adapter when it is plugged it in. You can find the name by looking in the Tools menu, under "Serial Port."

After identifying the device name, open a terminal (you can find the terminal by searching for it in your system's search box) and complete the following steps:

1. In the terminal, enter the command **screen /dev/ttyUSB6 9600** (replacing **/dev/ttyUSB6** with the name of your serial port) and press Enter.

   When you press Enter, a connection is initiated to the XBee serial terminal, and the screen goes blank. Once connected to the radio, as you type the commands, they will *not* appear in the terminal. The XBee does not echo your text back to you.

   First, I explain the programming process, and then I provide a list of commands to enter in the terminal. To program the XBee, you need to complete these steps:

   a. Put the XBee in programming mode.

   b. Set the PAN ID (ATID).

   c. Set the source address (ATMY).

   d. Set the destination address (ATDL).

   e. Write the settings to the XBee's nonvolatile memory (ATWR).

   Once you enter programming mode, entry of the other commands is time sensitive. If you wait too long between entering commands, you'll exit programming mode and have to reenter it. This timeout happens after only a few seconds, so try to be quick. Remember that as you type your commands are not shown. Furthermore, after each command, a carriage return is not added to the terminal, so you will be typing "on top of" your previous commands. Steps 2-7 describe the commands you actually need to enter into the terminal to program your XBee.

2. Type **+++** and wait; do not press Enter. The terminal will reply with an "**OK**" indicating that the XBee has entered programming mode.

3. Type **ATID1234** and press Enter. This sets the PAN ID to 1234.

4. Type **ATMY1000** and press Enter. This sets the source address to 1000.

5. Type **ATDL1001** and press Enter. This sets the destination address to 1001.

6. Type **ATWR** and press Enter. This commits the settings that you just entered to nonvolatile memory. Nonvolatile memory is not deleted when power is removed from the XBee.

7. If you want, you can confirm that the values have been written by entering **ATID**, **ATMY**, or **ATDL** without numbers afterward and pressing Enter. This prints the current values to the display.

NOTE If at any time you are exited from the programming mode, you can reenter it by typing +++ and picking up where you left off.

After completing all the preceding steps, carefully replace the XBee with your other module. Then, run through the same steps, but swap the values for ATMY and ATDL so that the XBees are set up to talk to each other.

Your XBees are now configured, and you're ready to have them talk to each other! If you're having trouble with the configuration, watch the video mentioned at the beginning of this chapter; it walks through the configuration steps visually.

Talking with Your Computer Wirelessly

Now that you know how to configure your XBees, it's time to start using them. First, you use them to replace the USB cable between your computer and your Arduino. You cannot download programs to your Arduino via an XBee connection without hardware modifications, so you still upload and test your programs via a USB connection. Then, you untether and replace the USB connection with a wireless XBee connection.

Powering Your Remote Arduino

Your remote Arduino will not be connected to your computer via USB, so you need to power it somehow. You have a few options for doing this, as described in this section.

USB with a Computer or a 5V Wall Adapter

This connection method defeats the point of going wireless, but you can leave the Arduino plugged into your computer via USB. The USB cable will provide 5V power to your Arduino, and the XBee will communicate with a separate USB XBee Explorer plugged into a different USB port on your computer. This is fine for testing your wireless communication, but is a bit silly for any practical application. If you go this route, make sure to choose the serial port connected to the USB Explorer to receive communication in the serial monitor or in Processing.

You can also use the 5V USB connection with a wall adapter. This makes a bit more sense because you are no longer tethered to same computer that you are programming from. If you have a smartphone, you probably already have one of these adapters; they are commonly used for charging iPhones, Android devices, and other smartphones and tablets. Figure 11-13 shows a standard USB wall adapter for U.S. outlets.

Credit: adafruit Industries, www.adafruit.com

Figure 11-13: 5V USB wall adapter

Batteries

You can also power the Arduino using batteries. One of the most popular methods is to use a 9V battery hooked into the direct current (DC) power jack or the "Vin" input pin. Both of these inputs feed into the Arduino's onboard linear 5V regulator, which generates a clean 5V signal for your microcontroller and other logic. Figure 11-14 shows an example of a 9V battery pack with an integrated switch and DC power jack from adafruit.com.

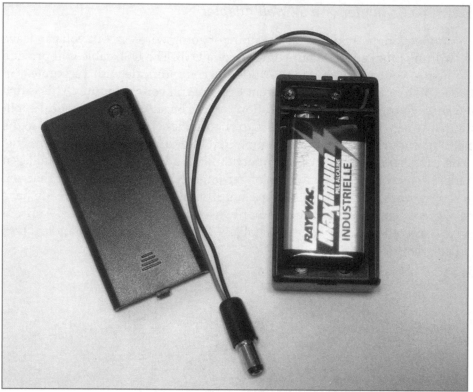

Figure 11-14: 9V battery pack

9V batteries are expensive, so some people prefer to use a AA battery pack. An average AA battery has a nominal voltage of 1.5V. Hence, it's fairly common to put four of these in series to generate about 6V total. Connecting four AA batteries to the Vin pin or the barrel jack input of the Arduino sends power through the voltage regulator, which has a small "dropout" voltage. (A dropout voltage is the minimum voltage that must exist between the input and output voltages.) On the Arduino, the 5V regulator has a dropout of approximately 1V (though this varies with temperature and current consumption). The input from a AA battery pack (with four batteries) is generally around 5.5V. With a 1V drop, you can generally expect that the Arduino logic will be operating around 4.5V. The ATMega is rated to run at this voltage (it can actually run all the way down to 1.8V), but you should be aware that all your logic will be operating at a slightly lower voltage than when you are on USB.

Wall Power Adapters

A third option for powering your remote Arduino is to use a wall adapter. These plug into an ordinary outlet and have a barrel jack connector on the other end for connecting to your Arduino. There are three important specifications you need to check for when choosing a wall power adapter: the physical characteristics of the jack, the supplied voltage, and the maximum current output capabilities.

The Arduino requires a 2.1mm center-positive DC barrel jack plug. In other words, the inside of the jack should be at a positive voltage, and the outside contact should be connected to ground. This is generally indicated on the charger by a symbol that looks like the one in Figure 11-15.

Figure 11-15: Center-positive symbol

Because the Arduino has a built-in voltage regulator, you can use any DC voltage between 7V and 12V. This voltage will also be available on the Vin pin, which can prove useful for powering higher-power devices such as motors.

All DC wall adapters are also rated for the maximum current that they supply. The higher the current, the more things you will be able to power with it. A 1-amp supply is fairly common and provides more than enough power for your Arduino's 5V regulated logic and some additional components.

Revisiting the Serial Examples: Controlling Processing with a Potentiometer

At this point, you're finally ready to start doing some wireless communication. Because XBee is nothing more than a serial pass-through, you can start by testing your setup with the examples you already created in Chapter 6. You need to complete the following steps:

1. Upload the sketch that allows you to change the color of a Processing window using a potentiometer connected to your Arduino.

    Do this before you install the XBee shield on to your Arduino, because of the shared UART complexities that were discussed earlier in the chapter.

If your shield has a jumper or switch to select whether or not the XBee is connected to the UART, you can use that while programming. (Check the documentation for your particular shield if you're unsure.)

The sketch that reads the pot and transmits it to the computer is repeated in Listing 11-1 for your reference.

Listing 11-1: Arduino Code to send Data to the Computer—pot_to_processing/arduino_read_pot

129

```
//Sending POT value to the computer

const int POT=0; //Pot on analog pin 0

int val; //For holding mapped pot value

void setup()
{
  Serial.begin(9600); //Start serial
}

void loop()
{
  val = map(analogRead(POT), 0, 1023, 0, 255); //Read and map POT
  Serial.println(val);                         //Send value
  delay(50);                                   //Delay so we don't
                                               //flood the computer
}
```

2. Unplug the Arduino from your computer and install the XBee shield along with the XBee. Connect a potentiometer to analog input 0 as shown in the wiring diagram in Figure 11-16.

3. Power this Arduino using one of the methods described in the previous section. I chose to use a USB cable with a wall power adapter, but any of the methods described would work fine.

4. Connect your XBee USB Explorer with the other programmed XBee radio to your computer with a USB cable. (Alternatively, you can use another Arduino board connected to an XBee Shield with the ATMega chip removed.) If the radios are configured correctly, you should see the RX light on the USB XBee Explorer flashing rapidly as it receives data.

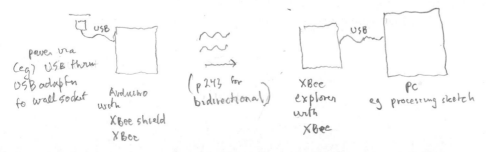

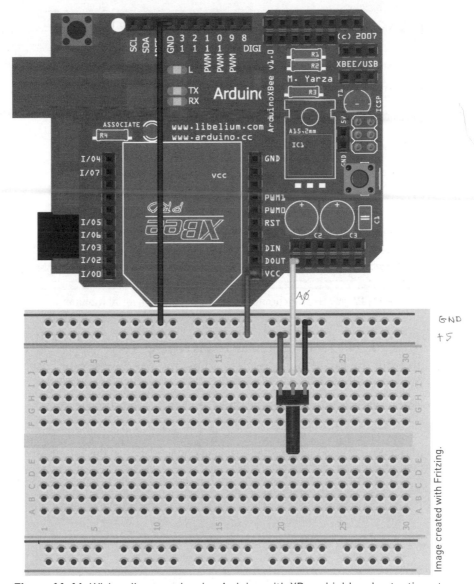

Figure 11-16: Wiring diagram showing Arduino with XBee shield and potentiometer

5. Before using this to control the Processing sketch, you can open a serial
   monitor window from the Arduino IDE to see the input coming in through
   your XBee. Select the serial port that your Explorer is connected to and
   open the serial monitor to see the values streaming in (see Figure 11-17).

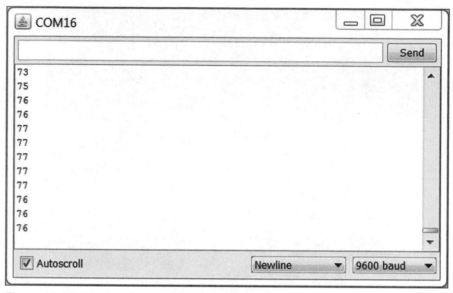

Figure 11-17: Wireless incoming data shown with the serial monitor

6. After you have confirmed that data is coming in, close the serial monitor and run the Processing sketch to adjust the window's color based on the incoming data.

   Before starting the sketch, ensure that you have the proper serial port selected. Listing 11-2 repeats the code.

Listing 11-2: Processing Code to Read Data and Change Color on the Screen— pot_to_ processing/processing_display_color

```
//Processing Sketch to Read Value and Change Color on the Screen

//Import and initialize serial port library
import processing.serial.*;
Serial port;

float brightness = 0; //For holding value from pot

void setup()
{
  size(500,500);                         //Window size
  port = new Serial(this, "COM3", 9600); //Set up serial
  port.bufferUntil('\n');                //Set up port to read
                                         //until newline
}

void draw()
{
```

```
    background(0,0,brightness); //Updates the window
}

void serialEvent (Serial port)
{
  brightness = float(port.readStringUntil('\n')); //Gets val
}
```

When you run the sketch, it should work just as it did when you were connected directly to the Arduino with a USB cable. Run around your house or office (if you are using a battery pack) and control the colors on your screen.

Revisiting the Serial Examples: Controlling an RGB LED

You've now confirmed that you can send data wirelessly from your Arduino to the computer. Next, you use the RGB LED control sketch from Chapter 6 to confirm that you can wirelessly send commands from your computer to your Arduino. After confirming that you can successfully send data between your Arduino and the computer wirelessly, you can design any number of exciting applications; you'll find some ideas listed on the webpage for this chapter.

Again, the first step is to load the appropriate program (see Listing 11-3) on to your Arduino. Use the same program that you used in chapter six. It accepts a string of RGB values and sets an RGB LED accordingly.

Listing 11-3: RGB LED Control via Serial— processing_control_RGB/list_control

```
//Sending Multiple Variables at Once

//Define LED Pins
const int RED   =11;
const int GREEN =10;
const int BLUE  =9;

//Variables for RGB levels
int rval = 0;
int gval = 0;
int bval = 0;

void setup()
{
  Serial.begin(9600); //Serial port at 9600 baud

  //Set pins as outputs
  pinMode(RED, OUTPUT);
  pinMode(GREEN, OUTPUT);
```

```
    pinMode(BLUE, OUTPUT);
}

void loop()
{
  //Keep working as long as data is in the buffer
  while (Serial.available() > 0)
  {
    rval = Serial.parseInt();  //First valid integer
    gval = Serial.parseInt();  //Second valid integer
    bval = Serial.parseInt();  //Third valid integer

    if (Serial.read() == '\n') //Done transmitting
    {
      //set LED
      analogWrite(RED, rval);
      analogWrite(GREEN, gval);
      analogWrite(BLUE, bval);
    }
  }
}
```

Next, wire up the Arduino just as you did in Chapter 6 (with the addition of the wireless shield and XBee radio), as shown in Figure 11-18.

As in the previous section, connect your USB Explorer to your computer and launch the Processing sketch, which is shown in Listing 11-4. Make sure you put the hsv.jpg file into the data folder of the sketch, as you did in Chapter 6 (It is included in the online code download). Before running the sketch, be sure to set the serial port name to the correct value.

Listing 11-4: Processing Sketch to Set Arduino RGB Colors —processing_control_RGB/
processing_control_RGB

```
import processing.serial.*; //Import serial library
PImage img;                 //Image object
Serial port;                //Serial port object

void setup()
{
  size(640,256); //Size of HSV image
  img = loadImage("hsv.jpg"); //Load in background image
  port = new Serial(this, "COM9", 9600); //Open serial port

}

void draw()
{
  background(0);    //Black background
  image(img,0,0);   //Overlay image
}
```

```
void mousePressed()
{
  color c = get(mouseX, mouseY); //Get the RGB color where mouse
                                 //was pressed
  String colors = int(red(c))+","+int(green(c))+","+int(blue(c))+"\n";
  //extract values from color
  print(colors); //Print colors for debugging
  port.write(colors); //Send values to Arduino
}
```

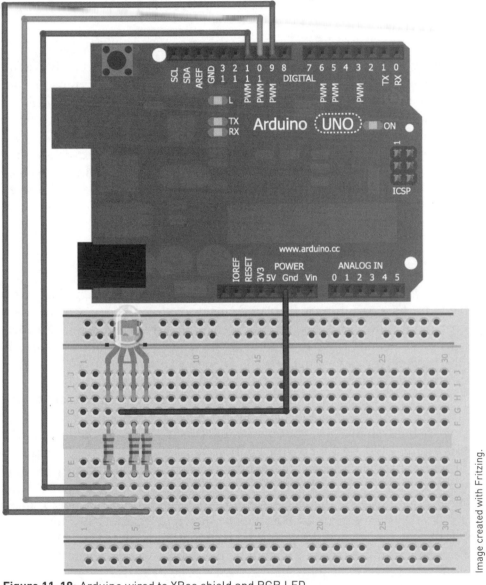

Figure 11-18: Arduino wired to XBee shield and RGB LED

Image created with Fritzing.

When you run this sketch, the color picker should appear just as it did in Chapter 6. Click a color. It will be transmitted to the remote Arduino, and the RGB LED will become the color you've picked. The values transmitted should show up in the Processing terminal as well. At this point, you've completely tested that your XBees can communicate back and forth with a computer. In the next section, you use the techniques that you developed here to communicate directly between two Arduinos.

Talking with Another Arduino: Building a Wireless Doorbell

Facilitating wireless communication between Arduinos is extremely useful. You can use multiple Arduino nodes to create sensor networks, transmit control commands (for a radio-controlled [RC] car, for example), or to facilitate remote monitoring of an electrical system. In this section, you use two Arduinos equipped with XBees to make a doorbell for your home, apartment, or office. A remote Arduino at your door will respond to button presses from a visitor. When a visitor "rings" the doorbell, your other Arduino will light up and make sounds to indicate that you have a visitor. You might want to watch the video demo of the system in action at www.exploringarduino.com/content/ch11 before you build the project.

System Design

The system you'll build consists of two Arduinos. Each will have an XBee shield and a radio. One Arduino can be placed outside of your home or apartment for people to press the button, and the other can be placed anywhere inside to alert you when somebody rings the doorbell. The range of the two units depends on the type of XBees, how many walls are between the two units, and other environmental factors.

Because just making a generic buzzer is boring, the receiving Arduino will flash multicolor lights and alternate tones to get your attention. You can easily customize the system to add your own sound effects. While the outdoor system in this example will be a simple pushbutton, you could replace the pushbutton with an IR sensor, light sensor, or occupancy sensor to automatically determine when somebody is approaching.

When designing a multifaceted system, it's good engineering practice to devise a high-level system design, such as the one shown in Figure 11-19. The level of detail that you use when designing such a diagram is up to you. Designing a simple diagram like the one shown here will help you to devise a plan for building each part of the individual system.

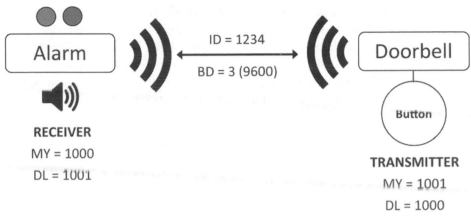

Figure 11-19: Wireless doorbell system diagram

Transmitter Hardware

First, build the hardware for the doorbell component, which will be referred to as the transmitter. You need a button with a pull-down resistor, connected to a digital input on an Arduino with a mounted XBee shield (see Figure 11-20).

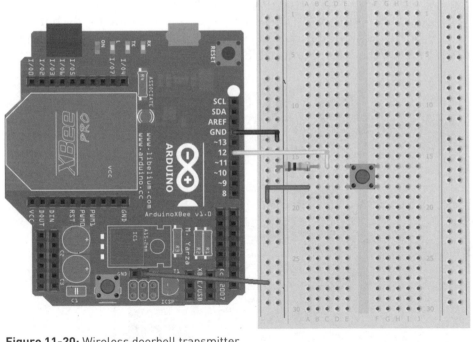

Figure 11-20: Wireless doorbell transmitter

Image created with Fritzing.

It doesn't matter what kind of Arduino you use in your system, but it is important to note that serial communication on boards like the Leonardo works differently than on the Uno. The Leonardo and Micro have a single MCU to control serial communication and program execution, whereas the Uno and Mega have separate processors. To demonstrate these differences, I chose to use a Leonardo for the transmitter. The circuit for either type of board is the same; software differences are addressed next.

Because the transmitter will presumably not be near a computer, choose one of the power options from earlier in the chapter that doesn't require power over USB from a computer. In the video demo, I used a 9V battery connected to the barrel jack connector. If you want this to be a bit more permanent, you might want to power the circuit using a DC wall adapter.

> **TIP** If you are interested in making something a bit more polished, you could buy a large, wired pushbutton and wire it through the wall to the Arduino on the other side.

Receiver Hardware

Next, build the component that will notify you when the transmitter's button is pressed. This will be your receiver. The hardware for this circuit consists of an Arduino with an XBee shield and radio, an RGB LED, resistors, and a small Piezo speaker. Follow the wiring diagram in Figure 11-21. Note that only the red and green LEDs are used in the sketch, so adding a resistor for the blue LED resistor is not necessary. You could also install a potentiometer in-line with the speaker to make the volume adjustable.

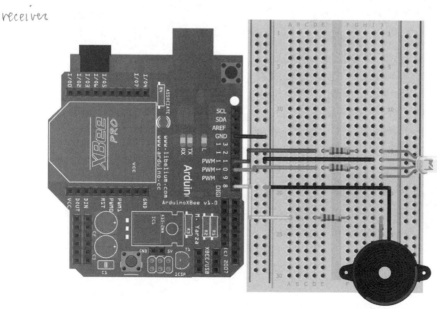

Figure 11-21: Wireless doorbell receiver

You need to pick an Arduino and power supply. While any type of board will work, I am using an Uno. I chose a USB cable connected to a wall adapter for power. You could just as easily use a battery or a USB connection to your computer. You can expand the functionality of the receiver by adding more lights, motors, or controlling a Processing sketch on your computer.

Transmitter Software

Once your hardware is all set up, you need to write the software for both ends of the system. Bear in mind that there are myriad ways to set up this communication scheme, and just one methodology is outlined here.

For this setup, you have the transmitter sending a value every 50ms. It will be '0' when the button is not pressed and '1' when the button is pushed. It's not necessary to debounce the button, because you are not looking for button clicks; the receiver will ring as long as the transmitter button is held down.

The code changes slightly depending on what kind of Arduino you are using. In the case of the Arduino Uno (or any other Arduino that has a separate Atmel or FTDI chip for handling serial communication), the main MCU UART connection is shared between the USB port and the RX/TX pins (pins 0 and 1) on the Arduino. If using an Uno or Mega (or any other Arduino with a separate USB-serial chip), you need to remove the XBee shield to program the Arduino, or adjust the jumpers/switch if your shield has that functionality. On these boards, Serial refers to both USB and UART communication over pins 0 and 1.

If you are using the Leonardo, or another Arduino that has USB communication integrated, you use Serial to talk over USB and Serial1 to talk over the RX/TX pins. You do not need to remove an XBee shield to program a board like the Leonardo because the UART is not shared. The code in Listing 11-5 is written for the Leonardo and other similar Arduinos. If you are using an Uno-based platform, replace references to Serial1 with Serial.

Listing 11-5: Doorbell Transmitter—doorbell/transmitting_arduino

```
//Code running on an Arduino to transmit the doorbell push

const int BUTTON =12; //Button on pin 12

void setup()
{
  //NOTE: On the Leonardo, the RX/TX serial pins are
  //not multiplexed with USB like they are on Uno.
  //This sketch is written for the Leonardo (Serial1 = RX/TX pins)
  //If you are using the Uno, change Serial1 to Serial, here and below
  Serial1.begin(9600); //Start serial
}
```

```
void loop()
{
  Serial1.println(digitalRead(BUTTON)); //Send the button's state
  delay(50); //Small delay so we don't flood the receiver
}
```

In the setup, the serial port connected to the XBee starts to run at 9600 baud. Every 50ms, the value of the digital input is read and printed out to the radio. `digitalRead()` can be placed directly inside of the `println` statement because the output value doesn't need to be used anywhere else in the program.

Receiver Software

The receiver software is more complicated than the transmitter program. The example code provided in Listing 11-6 was written for an Arduino Uno. If you are using a Leonardo-type board, replace `Serial` with `Serial1`.

This software needs to listen to the serial port, determine whether the remote button is being pressed, and modulate light/sound while still listening for new incoming data. The last part is what makes this program tricky; you need to use a "nonblocking" technique so that program doesn't have to call `delay()` at any point. A blocking function is anything that prevents the system from performing other tasks. `delay()` is an example of a blocking function. When it is invoked, nothing else happens in the program until `delay()` has finished. If you were to use a `delay()` statement in a communication scheme like this, you would run into two problems: The receiver's response to the transmitter's signal would not be instantaneous, and the input buffer could overflow because the transmitter may be sending data at a rate faster than the receiver can read it.

The goal is to have the light blink back and forth between red and green, and to have the Piezo's pitch go back and forth between two frequencies. You can't use a `delay()` for the reasons mentioned earlier. Instead of a `delay()`, you use the `millis()` function, which returns the number of milliseconds since the Arduino started running the sketch. The light and speaker switch at a rate of once every 100ms. So, you store the time at which the previous switch was made and look for a new `millis()` value to be at least 100ms greater than the previous switch time. When that happens, you swap the pins for the LED and adjust the frequency. Also in `loop()`, you check the serial buffer for a `'0'` or `'1'` and adjust the lights and sound accordingly.

The `setup()` initializes the program's values. To facilitate switching, you keep track of the pin states of the LEDs. You also keep track of the current frequency and the previous toggle time returned from `millis()`.

Consider the code in Listing 11-6 and load it on to your receiving Arduino. Before uploading the code, remember to set any necessary jumpers or remove the XBee shield to program the board.

Listing 11-6: Doorbell Receiver—doorbell/receiving_arduino

```
//Code running on an Arduino to receive doorbell value

const int RED     =11; //Red LED on pin 11
const int GREEN   =10; //Green LED on pin 10
const int SPEAKER =8;  //Speaker on pin 8

char data;                        //Char to hold incoming serial data
int onLED = GREEN;                //Initially on LED
int offLED = RED;                 //Initially off LED
int freq = 131;                   //Initial speaker frequency
unsigned long prev_time = 0; //Timer for toggling the LED and speaker

void setup()
{
  Serial.begin(9600); //Start serial
}

void loop()
{

  //Handle light and sound toggling
  //If 100ms have passed
  if (millis() >= prev_time + 100)
  {
    //Toggle the LED state
    if (onLED == GREEN)
    {
      onLED = RED;
      offLED = GREEN;
    }
    else
    {
      onLED = GREEN;
      offLED = RED;
    }
    //Toggle the frequency
    if (freq == 261){
        freq = 131;
    } else {
        freq = 261;
    }
    //Set the current time in ms to the
    //Previous time for the next trip through the loop
    prev_time = millis();
  }

  //Check if serial data is available
  if (Serial.available() > 0)
  {
```

```
    //Read byte of data
    data = Serial.read();

    //If the button is pressed, play tone and turn LED on
    if (data == '1')
    {
      digitalWrite(onLED, HIGH);
      digitalWrite(offLED, LOW);
      tone(SPEAKER, freq);
    }
    //If the button is not pressed, turn the sound and light off
    else if (data == '0')
    {
      digitalWrite(onLED, LOW);
      digitalWrite(offLED, LOW);
      noTone(SPEAKER);
    }
  }
}
```

The first `if()` statement in `loop()` checks the elapsed time since it last ran. If it's been at least 100ms, it's time to switch the lights and frequency. By checking the current states, you can alternate values for the light and frequency. You set the `offLED` when the other light gets turned on. At the end of the `if()` statement, the previous time is set to the present time so that the process can be repeated.

The second large `if()` statement in `loop()` checks incoming serial data. When a `'0'` is received, everything gets turned off. When there is a `'1'`, the light and speaker turn on according to the values set earlier in `loop()`.

NOTE Watch a demo video of the wireless Arduino doorbell at www.exploringarduino.com/content/ch11. You can also find this video on the Wiley website shown at the beginning of this chapter.

Summary

In this chapter, you learned about the following:

- There are a wide range of available XBee models.

- You must convert between 5V and 3.3V logic levels to use an XBee with most Arduinos.

- You can configure XBee using either X-CTU on Windows, or the terminal on Linux and Mac.

- There are a variety of options for powering your Arduino that do not require you to stay connected to your computer via USB.

- You can communicate wirelessly between your computer and an Arduino using XBees.

- You can communicate wirelessly between two Arduinos using XBees.

- The `millis()` function can be used with state variables to create "non blocking" code that implements time delays.

Advanced Topics and Projects

In This Part

Hardware and Timer Interrupts

Parts You'll Need for This Chapter

Arduino (Uno recommended)

USB cables for programming Arduino

Pushbutton

Piezo buzzer

Common cathode RGB LED

$10k\Omega$ resistor

100Ω resistor

150Ω resistor

220Ω resistors (×3)

10uF electrolytic capacitor

74HC14 hex inverting Schmitt trigger IC

Jumper wires

Breadboard

CODE AND DIGITAL CONTENT FOR THIS CHAPTER

Code downloads, video, and other digital content for this chapter can be found at www
.exploringarduino.com/content/ch12.

In addition, all code can be found at www.wiley.com/remtitle
.cgi?isbn=1118549368 on the Download Code tab. The code is in the chapter 12
download and individually named according to the names throughout the chapter.

Up to this point, every Arduino program you've written has been synchronous. This presents a few problems, namely that using delay() can preclude
your Arduino from doing other things. In the preceding chapter, you created
a software timer using millis() to avoid the synchronous blocking nature of
delay(). In this chapter, you take this idea a step further by adding both timer
and hardware interrupts. Interrupts make it possible to execute code asynchronously by triggering certain events (time elapsed, input state change, and so on).
Interrupts, as their name implies, allow you to stop whatever your Arduino is
currently doing, complete a different task, and then return to what the Arduino
was previously executing. In this chapter, you learn how to execute interrupts
when timed events occur or when input pins change state. You will use this
knowledge to build a "nonblocking" hardware interrupt system, as well as a
sound machine using timer interrupts.

> **NOTE** Follow a video tutorial about interrupts and hardware debouncing:
> www.jeremyblum.com/2011/03/07/arduino-tutorial-10-interrupts-
> and-hardware-debouncing. **You can also find this video on the Wiley website
> shown at the beginning of this chapter.**

Using Hardware Interrupts

Hardware interrupts are trigged depending on the state (or change in state), of
an input I/O pin. Hardware interrupts can be particularly useful if you want to
change some state variable within your code without having to constantly poll
the state of a button. In some previous chapters, you used a software debounce
routine along with a check for the button state each time through the loop. This
works great if the other content in your loop does not take a long time to execute.

Suppose, however, that you want to run a procedure in your loop that takes
awhile. For example, perhaps you want to slowly ramp up the brightness of an
LED or the speed of a motor using a for() loop with some delay() statements.
If you want button presses to adjust the color or speed of such an LED fade, you
will miss any presses of the button that occur while the delay() is happening.
Ordinarily, human reaction time is slow enough that you can execute many
functions within the loop() of an Arduino program, and can poll a button once
every time you go through the loop without missing the button press. However,
when there are "slow" components to your code within the loop(), you risk
missing external inputs.

That's where interrupts come in. Select pins on your Arduino (or all pins on the Due) can function as external hardware interrupts. Hardware within the ATMega knows the state of these pins and can report their values to your code asynchronously. Hence, you can execute your main program, and have it "interrupted" to run a special function whenever an external interrupt event is detected. This interrupt can happen anywhere in the program's execution. Figure 12-1 shows what this process could look like in practice.

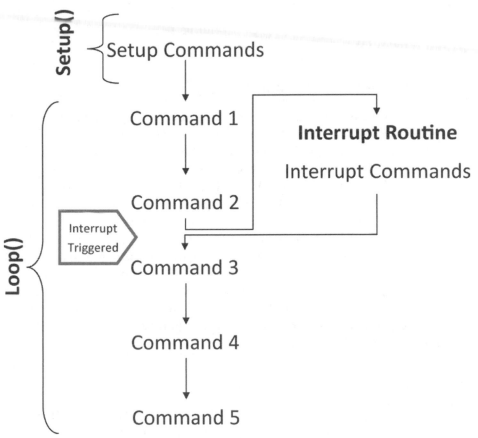

Figure 12-1: How an external interrupt affects program flow

Knowing the Tradeoffs Between Polling and Interrupting

Hardware interrupts are an alternative to repeatedly polling external inputs in `loop()`. They are not better or worse; instead, there are tradeoffs between using the two. When designing a system, you must consider all your options and choose the appropriate one for your application. This section describes the main differences between polling inputs and using interrupts so that you can decide for yourself which option is best for your particular project.

Ease of Implementation (Software)

Thanks to the excellent programming language that has been constructed for the Arduino, attaching external interrupts in software is actually very straightforward. Using polling to detect inputs to the Arduino is still easier because all you have to do is call `digitalRead()`. If you don't need to use hardware interrupts, don't bother to use them over polling, because it does require you to write a little more code.

Ease of Implementation (Hardware)

For most digital inputs, the hardware for an input that triggers via polling or interrupting is exactly the same, because you are just looking for a state change in the input. However, in one situation you need to adjust your hardware if you are using an edge-triggered interrupt: bouncy inputs. As discussed in Chapter 2, "Digital Inputs, Outputs, and Pulse-Width Modulation," many buttons (something you will commonly want to use to trigger an input) bounce when you press them. This can be a significant problem because it will cause the interrupt routine to trigger multiple times when you want it to trigger only once. What's worse, it is not possible to use the software debouncing function that you had previously written because you cannot use a `delay()` in an interrupt routine. Therefore, if you need to use a bouncy input with a hardware interrupt, you need to first debounce it with hardware. If your input does not bounce (like a rotary encoder) you don't have to worry, and your hardware will be no different than it was with a polling setup.

Multitasking

One of the primary reasons for using interrupts is to enable pseudo-multitasking. You can never achieve true multitasking on an Arduino because there is only one microcontroller unit (MCU), and because it can execute only one command at a time. However, because it executes commands so quickly, you can use interrupts to "weave" tasks together so that they appear to execute simultaneously. For instance, using interrupts, you can be dimming LEDs with `delay()` while appearing to simultaneously respond to a button input that adjusts the fade speed or color. When polling an external input, you can only read the input once you get to a `digitalRead()` in your program loop, meaning that having "slower" functions in your program could make it hard to effectively listen for an input.

Acquisition Accuracy

For certain fast acquisition tasks, interrupting is an absolute necessity. For example, suppose that you are using a rotary encoder. Rotary encoders are commonly mounted on direct current (DC) motors and send a pulse to the microcontroller every time some percentage of a revolution is completed. You can use them to create a feedback system for DC motors that allows you to keep track of their position, instead of just their speed. This enables you dynamically adjust speed based on torque requirements or to keep track of how much a DC motor has moved. However, you need to be absolutely sure that every pulse is captured by the Arduino. These pulses are fairly short (much shorter than a pulse created by you manually pushing a button) and can potentially be missed if you check for them by polling within `loop()`. In the case of a rotary encoder that triggers only once per revolution, missing a pulse causes your program to believe that the motor is moving at half of its actual speed! To ensure that you capture timing for important events like this, using a hardware input is a must. If you are using a slowly changing input (like a button), polling might suffice.

Understanding the Arduino's Hardware Interrupt Capabilities

With most Arduino boards, you can use only certain pins as interrupts. Interrupts are referred to by an ID number that corresponds to a particular pin. The exception is the Due, on which all the pins can act as interrupts, and you reference them by pin number. If you are not using the Due, consult Table 12-1 to determine what pins on your Arduino can act as interrupts and what ID number they are.

Table 12-1: Available Hardware Interrupts on Various Arduinos

BOARD	INT 0	INT 1	INT 2	INT 3	INT 4	INT 5
Uno, Ethernet	Pin 2	Pin 3	-	-	-	-
Mega2560	Pin 2	Pin 3	Pin 21	Pin 20	Pin 19	Pin 18
Leonardo	Pin 3	Pin 2	Pin 0	Pin 1	-	-

These IDs are used in conjunction with `attachInterrupt()`. The first argument is the ID (in the case of the boards in Table 12-1) or the pin number (in the case of the Due). If, on the Uno, you want to attach an interrupt to physical pin 2 on the board, the first argument of `attachInterrupt()` would be 0 because pin 2 is attached to interrupt 0 on the Uno. The Uno (and other ATMega328-based boards) support just two external interrupts, whereas the Mega and the Leonardo support more external interrupts.

Hardware interrupts work by "attaching" interrupt pins to certain functions. So, the second argument of `attachInterrupt()` is a function name. If you want to toggle the state of a Boolean variable every time an interrupt is triggered, you might write a function like this, which you pass to `attachInterrupt()`:

```
void toggleLed()
{
    var = !var;
}
```

When this function is called, the Boolean `var` is toggled to the opposite of its previous state, and the rest of your program continues running where it left off.

The final argument passed to `attachInterrupt()` is the trigger mode. Arduino interrupts can be triggered on `LOW`, `CHANGE`, `RISING`, or `FALLING`. (The Due can also be triggered on `HIGH`.) `CHANGE`, `RISING`, and `FALLING` are the most common things to trigger on because they cause an interrupt to execute exactly one time when an external input changes state, like a button going from `LOW` to `HIGH`. The transition from `LOW` to `HIGH` is `RISING`, and from `HIGH` to `LOW` is `FALLING`. It is less common to trigger on `LOW` or `HIGH` because these cause the interrupt to fire continuously as long as that state is true, effectively blocking the rest of the program from running.

Building and Testing a Hardware-Debounced Button Interrupt Circuit

To test out your newfound knowledge, you construct a circuit with an RGB LED and a hardware-debounced pushbutton. The LED fades up and down on a selected color. When the button is pressed, the LED immediately changes the fade color to another one, while using `delay()` to accomplish the fading.

Creating a Hardware-Debouncing Circuit

As you learned in the Chapter 2, most buttons actually "bounce" up and down when you press them. This action presents a serious problem when you are using hardware interrupts because it might cause an action to be triggered more times than you intended. Luckily, you can debounce a button in hardware so that you always get a clean signal going into your microcontroller.

First, take a look at an ordinary button signal hooked up using a pull-up resistor. Using a pull-up resistor instead of a pull-down does exactly what you would expect: By default, the button state is pulled high by the resistor; when the button is pressed, it connects ground to the I/O pin and input goes low.

You use a pull-up circuit instead of a pull-down in this example and invert the output later. Figure 12-2 shows the button signal being probed with an oscilloscope. When I press the button, it bounces up and down before finally settling at a low state.

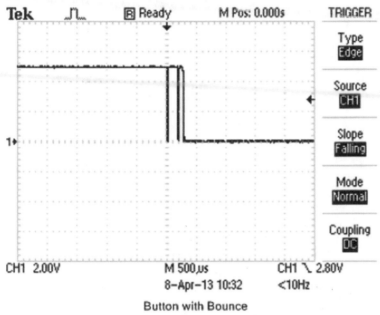

Button with Bounce

Figure 12-2: Ordinary pushbutton bouncing before settling

If you trigger an interrupt off this signal, it executes the interrupt function three times in a row. But, using something called a resistor-capacitor network (commonly called an RC circuit), you can prevent this.

If you connect a capacitor across the terminal of the switch and a resistor in series with the switch, it creates a resistor-capacitor network. While the switch is not pressed, the capacitor charges through the resistors. When you push the button, the capacitor starts to discharge, and the output goes high. If the button bounces up and down for a few milliseconds, the resistors recharge the capacitor while the switch momentarily opens, allowing it to maintain the voltage level at the output. Through this process, you get a signal that transitions between high and low only one time in a period determined by the values of the resistor and capacitor. Such a circuit would look like the one shown in Figure 12-3.

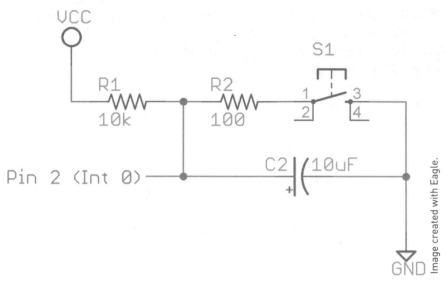

Figure 12-3: Creating a debounce circuit: adding a capacitor and a resistor

Adding the resistor in series with the switch (R2 in Figure 12-3) is not completely necessary; without it, the capacitor would discharge (almost) instantly and would still be recharged quickly enough by R1. However, this rapid discharge over the switch could damage cheap buttons. Including the 100Ω resistor decreases the discharge time and keeps all your components safe. This, however, adds a discharge curve to your output. You can see this effect in the oscilloscope in Figure 12-4.

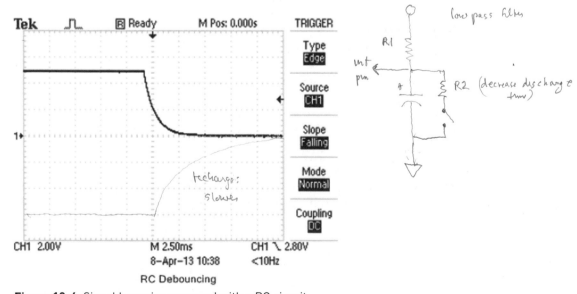

Figure 12-4: Signal bouncing removed with a RC circuit

The RC circuit that you just created will make a "curved" input signal to the Arduino's I/O pin. Our interrupt is looking for an edge, which is detected when a shift from high to low or from low to high occurs at a certain speed. The "sharpness" of this edge is called the *hysteresis* of the signal edge, and it might not be sharp enough with the smoothing caused by the capacitor. You can increase the sharpness of this falling signal with a Schmitt trigger. *Schmitt triggers* are integrated circuits (ICs) that create a sharp edge when the input signal surpasses a certain threshold. The output from the trigger can then be fed right into the Arduino's I/O pin. In this case, you use an inverting Schmitt trigger, the 74HC14 IC. This chip has six separate inverting Schmitt triggers in it, but you use only one. Inspect the datasheet image of the IC in Figure 12-5.

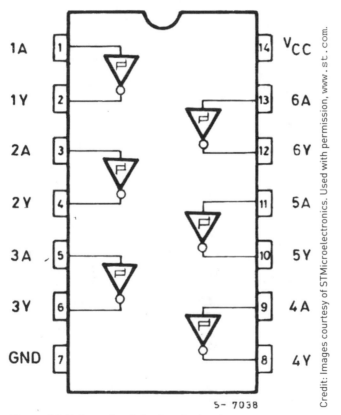

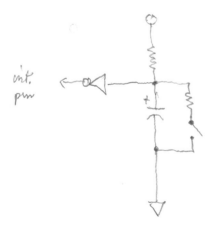

Figure 12-5: Inverting Schmitt trigger pin-out

Credit: Images courtesy of STMicroelectronics. Used with permission, www.st.com.

The output from your debounce circuit will go through one of these inverting Schmitt triggers before finally being fed into the Arduino. The resulting circuit diagram looks Figure 12-6.

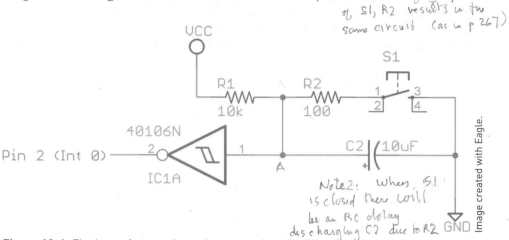

Note1: interchanging posns of S1, R2 results in two same circuit (as in p 267)

Note2: When S1 is closed there will be an RC delay discharging C2 due to R2

Figure 12-6: Final step for creating a debounce circuit: adding an inverting Schmitt trigger

Because this is an inverting trigger, the signal will also be flipped. So, when the button is held down, the final signal will be a logical high, and vice versa. So, in the next step, when you write the code, you want to look for a rising edge to detect when the button is first pressed. The final output signal looks like a nice, clean, bounce-free signal (see Figure 12-7).

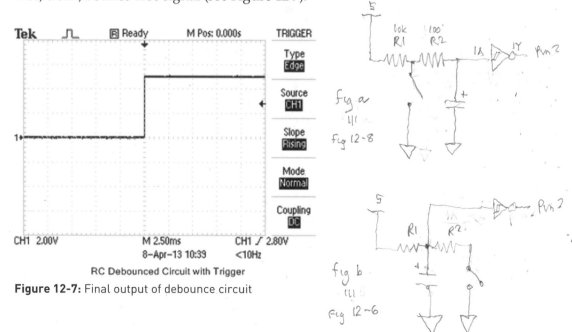

Figure 12-7: Final output of debounce circuit

fig a
fig 12-8

fig b
Fig 12-6

You've now got a nice clean signal that you can feed into your hardware interrupt function!

Assembling the Complete Test Circuit

From a schematic level, you now understand how to wire up a button debouncer. For the tests that you'll run momentarily, you use an RGB LED in tandem with a button to test your hardware-debouncing and interrupt code. Wire up a complete circuit as shown in the wiring diagram in Figure 12-8.

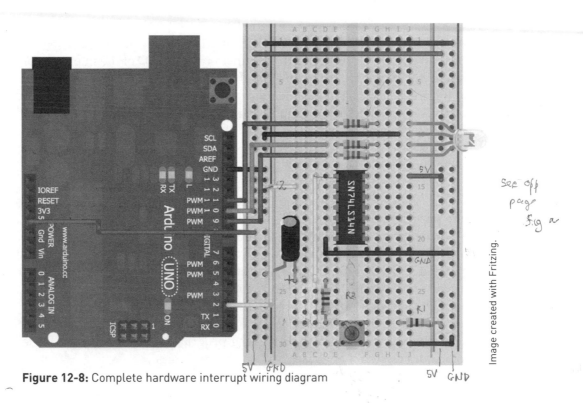

Figure 12-8: Complete hardware interrupt wiring diagram

Image created with Fritzing.

Writing the Software

It's now time to write a simple program to test both your debouncing and the hardware interrupt capabilities of the Arduino. The most obvious and useful implementation of hardware interrupts on the Arduino is to allow you to listen for external inputs even while running timed operations that use `delay()`. There are many scenarios where this might happen, but a simple one occurs when fading an LED using pulse-width modulation (PWM) via `analogWrite()`. In this sketch, you have one of the three RGB LEDs always fading up and down slowly from 0 to 255 and back again. Every time you press the button, the color that is being faded immediately changes. This would not be possible using polling because you would only be checking the button state after completing a fade cycle; you would almost certainly miss the button press.

First, you need to understand *volatile* variables. Whenever a variable will be changing within an interrupt, it must be declared as *volatile*. This is necessary to ensure that the compiler handles the variable correctly. To declare a variable as volatile, simply add `volatile` before the declaration:

```
volatile int selectedLED = 9;
```

To ensure that your Arduino is listening for an interrupt, you use `attachInterrupt()` in `setup()`. The inputs to the function are the ID of the interrupt (or the pin number for the Due), the function that should be run when an interrupt occurs, and the triggering mode (`RISING`, `FALLING`, and so on). In this program, the button is connected to interrupt 0 (pin 2 on the Uno), it runs the `swap()` function when triggered, and it triggers on the rising edge:

```
attachInterrupt(0, swap, RISING);
```

You need to write `swap()` and add it to your program; this is included in the complete program code shown in Listing 12-1. That's all you have to do! After you've attached the interrupt and written your interrupt function, you can write the rest of your program to do whatever you want. Whenever the interrupt is triggered, the rest of program pauses, the interrupt function runs, and then your program resumes where it left off. Because interrupts pause your program, they are generally very short and do not contain delays of any kind. In fact, `delay()` does not even work inside of an interrupt-triggered function. Understanding all of this, you can now write the following program to cycle through all the LED colors and switch them based on your button press.

Listing 12-1: Hardware Interrupts for Multitasking—hw_multitask.ino

```
//Use Hardware-Debounced Switch to Control Interrupt

//Button pins
const int BUTTON_INT =0;   //Interrupt 0 (pin 2 on the Uno)
const int RED        =11; //Red LED on pin 11
const int GREEN      =10; //Green LED on pin 10
const int BLUE       =9;  //Blue LED on pin 9
```

```
//Volatile variables can change inside interrupts
volatile int selectedLED = RED;

void setup()
{
  pinMode (RED, OUTPUT);
  pinMode (GREEN, OUTPUT);
  pinMode (BLUE, OUTPUT);
  //The pin is inverted, so we want to look at the rising edge
  attachInterrupt(BUTTON_INT, swap, RISING);
}

void swap()
{
  //Turn off the current LED
  analogWrite(selectedLED, 0);
  //Then, choose a new one.
  if (selectedLED == GREEN)
    selectedLED = RED;
  else if (selectedLED == RED)
    selectedLED = BLUE;
  else if (selectedLED == BLUE)
    selectedLED = GREEN;
}

void loop()
{
  for (int i = 0; i<256; i++)
  {
    analogWrite(selectedLED, i);
    delay(10);
  }
  for (int i = 255; i>= 0; i--)
  {
    analogWrite(selectedLED, i);
    delay(10);
  }
}
```

When you load this up, your RGB LED should start fading back and forth on one color. Every time you press the button, a new color will take over, with the same brightness as the previous color.

NOTE You can watch a demo video of the Hardware Interrupted Arduino with button debouncing at www.exploringarduino.com/content/ch12. You can also find this video on the Wiley website shown at the beginning of this chapter.

Using Timer Interrupts

Hardware interrupts are not the only kind of interrupt you can trigger on an Arduino; there are also timer-based interrupts. The ATMega328 (the chip used in the Uno) has three hardware timers, which you can use for all kinds of different things. In fact, the default Arduino library already uses these timers to increment `millis()`, operate `delay()`, and enable PWM output with `analogWrite()`. Although not officially supported by the Arduino programming language (yet), you can also take manual control of one of these timers to initiate timed functions, generate arbitrary PWM signals on any pin, and more. In this section, you learn how to use a third-party library (the TimerOne library) to take manual control of the 16-bit Timer1 on the ATMega328-based Arduinos. Similar libraries are available for doing these tricks on the Leonardo, and other Arduino boards, but this section focuses on the Uno.

> **NOTE** Timer1 is used to enable PWM output on pins 9 and 10; so when you use this library, you will be unable to run `analogWrite()` on those pins.

Understanding Timer Interrupts

Just like a timer on your watch, timers on the Arduino count up from zero, incrementing with every clock cycle of the oscillating crystal that drives the Arduino. Timer1 is a 16-bit timer, meaning that it can count up from zero to 2^{16}-1, or 65,535. Once that number is reached, it resets back to zero and starts counting again. How quickly it reaches that number depends on the clock divider. With no divider, the clock would go through 16 million cycles per second (16MHz), and would overflow and reset this counter many times per second. However, you can "divide" the clock, an approach taken by many underlying Arduino functions and libraries. The TimerOne library abstracts away much of the complexity of dealing with the timer, allowing you to simply set a trigger period. Using the timer, a function can be triggered every set number of microseconds.

Getting the Library

To get started, download the TimerOne library, either from the Exploring Arduino web page for this chapter or directly from `https://code.google.com/p/arduino-timerone/downloads`. Unzip it (but keep it within a folder called `TimerOne`), and copy it to your Arduino libraries folder. The default location of the folder will differ based on your operating system:

- **Windows:** `Documents/Arduino/libraries`
- **Mac:** `Documents/Arduino/libraries`
- **Linux:** `/home/YOUR_USER_NAME/sketchbook/libraries`

If the Arduino integrated development environment (IDE) was open when you copied the TimerOne folder, make sure you restart it so that the library is loaded. You are now ready to take control of Timer1 with your Arduino.

Executing Two Tasks Simultaneously(ish)

It's important to keep in mind that there is no such thing as "true" simultaneous execution on an Arduino. Interrupts merely make it seem like multiple things are happening at the same time, by allowing you to switch between multiple tasks extremely quickly. Using the TimerOne library you just installed, you make an LED blink using the timer while you execute other functions within `loop()`. At the end of the chapter, you will execute serial print statements in the main loop with delays, while using timer interrupts to control lights and sounds simultaneously. To confirm that the library is installed properly, you can load the program shown in Listing 12-2 on to an Arduino Uno (with no other components connected). It should blink the onboard LED connected to pin 13. This LED will blink on and off every second and is controlled by the timer. If you put any other code in `loop()`, it will appear to execute simultaneously.

Listing 12-2: Simple Timer Interrupt Blink Test—timer1.ino

```
//Using Timer Interrupts with the Arduino
#include <TimerOne.h>
const int LED=13;

void setup()
{
  pinMode(LED, OUTPUT);
  Timer1.initialize(1000000); //Set a timer of length 1,000,000
                              //microseconds (1 second)
  Timer1.attachInterrupt(blinky); //Runs "blinky" on each
                                  //timmer interrupt
}

void loop()
{
  //Put any other code here.
}

//Timer interrupt function
void blinky()
{
  digitalWrite(LED, !digitalRead(LED)); //Toggle LED State
}
```

When you call `Timer1.initialize`, you are setting the period of the timer in microseconds. In this case, it has been set to trigger every 1 second. (There are a million microseconds in 1 second.) When you run `Timer1.attachInterrupt()`, you can choose a function that will be executed every time the specified period elapses. Obviously, the function you call should take less time to execute than the time between executions.

Now that you can implement both timer and hardware interrupts, you can develop hardware that takes advantage of both of them. You will do this in the next section.

Building an Interrupt-Driven Sound Machine

To finalize and confirm your understanding of hardware and timer interrupts, you build a "sound machine" that enables you to step through and listen to multiple octaves of each note on a musical major scale. The system uses a hardware-debounced pushbutton interrupt to select the note played (C, A, B, and so forth). A timer interrupt steps through all the octaves of the note in order until the next note is selected with the push button. In `loop()`, you can run a simple serial debugging interface that prints the current key and pitch to the screen of your computer. The notes start at octave 2 (it doesn't sound very good below that) and go up toward octave 6.

Computing the frequency of each octave is easy once you know the initial frequency. Consider C, for example. C2, where we will be starting, has a frequency of about 65Hz. To get to C3 (130Hz), multiply the frequency of C2 by 2. To get C4, multiply by 2 again, for 260Hz. The frequency of each step can be computed as a power of 2 related to the initial frequency. Knowing this, you can construct a timer interrupt that increases by the power of 2 with each time step.

You can switch between notes in the same way you switched between LED colors in the earlier example with the pushbutton. Assign base frequencies to each note, and switch which base frequency is used for `tone()` every time the button is pressed.

Sound Machine Hardware

The hardware setup here is very simple. Keep the debounced button wired as you had it in the RGB LED example, and add a speaker to pin 12 through a 150Ω resistor. I used a piezo speaker, but you can use a larger speaker as well. The circuit should look the one shown in Figure 12-9.

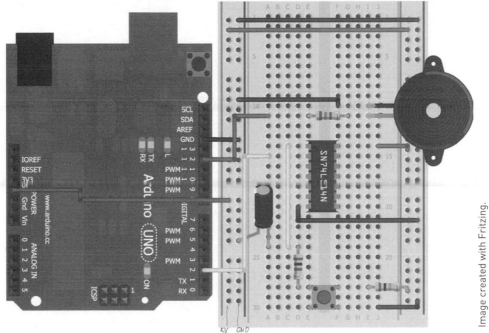

Figure 12-9: Sound machine wiring diagram

Image created with Fritzing.

Sound Machine Software

The software for the sound machine utilizes software and hardware interrupts in addition to serial communication and `tone()` to control a speaker. Load the code from Listing 12-3 on to your Arduino and press the button on the breadboard to cycle through base frequencies. You can open the serial monitor to see the frequency currently playing.

Listing 12-3: Sound Machine Code—fun_with_sound.ino

```
//Use Hardware and Timer Interrupts for Fun with Sound

//Include the TimerOne library
#include <TimerOne.h>

//Button pins
const int BUTTON_INT =0;  //Interrupt 0 (pin 2 on the Uno)
const int SPEAKER    =12; //Speaker on pin 12

//Music keys
#define NOTE_C 65
#define NOTE_D 73
#define NOTE_E 82
#define NOTE_F 87
```

```
#define NOTE_G 98
#define NOTE_A 110
#define NOTE_B 123

//Volatile variables can change inside interrupts
volatile int key = NOTE_C;
volatile int octave_multiplier = 1;        // both : use 16 rather than 1

void setup()
{
  //Set up serial
  Serial.begin(9600);

  pinMode (SPEAKER, OUTPUT);
  //The pin is inverted, so we want to look at the rising edge
  attachInterrupt(BUTTON_INT, changeKey, RISING);

  //Set up timer interrupt
  Timer1.initialize(500000); // (.5 seconds)
  Timer1.attachInterrupt(changePitch); //Runs "changePitch" on each
                                       //timer interupt
}

void changeKey()                // # change freq by changing key
{
  octave_multiplier = 1;        // reset to base octave
  if (key == NOTE_C)
    key = NOTE_D;
  else if (key == NOTE_D)
    key = NOTE_E;
  else if (key == NOTE_E)
    key = NOTE_F;
  else if (key == NOTE_F)
    key = NOTE_G;
  else if (key == NOTE_G)
    key = NOTE_A;
  else if (key == NOTE_A)
    key = NOTE_B;
  else if (key == NOTE_B)
    key = NOTE_C;
}

//Timer interrupt function        # change freq by keeping key, going up an octave
void changePitch()
{
  octave_multiplier = octave_multiplier * 2;
  if (octave_multiplier > 16) octave_multiplier = 1;
  tone(SPEAKER,key*octave_multiplier);
}                    pin        freq
                                      optional: duration
void loop()
```

95-102

```
{
  Serial.print("Key: ");
  Serial.print(key);
  Serial.print(" Multiplier: ");
  Serial.print(octave_multiplier);
  Serial.print(" Frequency: ");
  Serial.println(key*octave_multiplier);
  delay(100);
}
```

You can easily find the music keys defined at the beginning with a search on the Internet. They are the frequencies of the second octave of those notes. Note that the `key` and `octave_multiplier` must be declared as volatile integers because they are going to be changed within interrupt routines. `changeKey()` is called every time the button interrupt is triggered. It changes the octave's base value by moving from key to key. `changePitch()` calls `tone()` to set the frequency for the speaker. It is triggered every .5 seconds by the timer interrupt. Each time it is triggered, it doubles the frequency of the original note until it reaches 16 times its original frequency. It then loops back around and starts again at the base frequency for the current note. Within `loop()`, the current key, multiplier, and frequency are printed to the serial monitor every .1 seconds.

NOTE To watch a demo video of the sound machine, check out www.exploringarduino.com/content/ch12. You can also find this video on the Wiley website shown at the beginning of this chapter.

Summary

In this chapter you learned about the following:

- There are tradeoffs between polling inputs and using interrupts.
- Different Arduinos have different interrupt capabilities. The Due can interrupt on any I/O pin, but other Arduinos have particular interrupt-enabled pins.
- Buttons can be debounced in hardware using an RC circuit and a Schmitt trigger.
- The Arduino can be made to respond to inputs asynchronously by attaching interrupt functions.
- You can install a third-party timer library to adder timer interrupt functionality to the Arduino.
- You can combine timer interrupts, hardware interrupts, and polling into one program to enable pseudo-simultaneous code execution.

Data Logging with SD Cards

Parts You'll Need for This Chapter

Arduino (Uno recommended)

USB cable

Arduino power supply (DC, USB, or battery pack)

IR distance sensor

Real-time clock breakout (or self-assembled RTC circuit)

SD card shield

SD card

Jumper wires

Breadboard

Computer with SD card reader

CODE AND DIGITAL CONTENT FOR THIS CHAPTER

Code downloads, video, and other digital content for this chapter can be found at www.exploringarduino.com/content/ch13.

In addition, all code can be found at www.wiley.com/go/exploringarduino on the Download Code tab. The code is in the chapter 13 download and individually named according to the names throughout the chapter.

There are countless examples of Arduinos being used to log weather conditions, atmospheric conditions from weather balloons, building entry data, electrical loads in buildings, and much more. Given their small size, minimal power consumption, and ease of interfacing with a vast array of sensors, Arduinos are an obvious choice for building data loggers, which are devices that record and store information over a period of time. Data loggers are often deployed into all kinds of environments to collect environmental or user data and to store it into some kind of nonvolatile memory, such as an SD card. In this chapter, you learn everything you could want to know about interfacing with an SD card from an Arduino. You learn how to both write data to a file and how to read existing information off an SD card. You use a real-time clock to add accurate timestamps to your data. You also learn briefly about how to display the data on your computer after you have retrieved it.

NOTE To follow a video tutorial about data logging, check out www.jeremyblum .com/2011/04/05/tutorial-11-for-arduino-sd-cards-and-datalogging/. You can also find this video on the Wiley website shown at the beginning of this chapter.

NOTE To follow a more advanced tutorial about logging location from a GPS receiver, check out www.jeremyblum.com/2012/07/16/tutorial-15-for-arduino-gps-tracking/. You can also find this video on the Wiley website shown at the beginning of this chapter.

Getting Ready for Data Logging

Data logging systems are very simple. They generally consist of some kind of acquisition system, such as analog sensors, to obtain data. They also contain some kind of memory for storing sizeable quantities of that data over a long period of time.

This chapter highlights a few common ways that you can use an SD card with your Arduino to record useful data. However, there are many uses for data logging. Here is a brief list of projects in which you could use it:

- A weather station for tracking light, temperature, and humidity over time
- A GPS tracker and logger that keeps a record of where you've been over the course of a day
- A temperature monitor for your desktop computer to report data about what components are getting the hottest
- A light logger that keeps track of when, and for how long, the lights are left on in your home or office

Later in this chapter, you create a data logging system that uses an infrared (IR) distance sensor to create a log of when people enter and exit a room.

Formatting Data with CSV Files

CSV, or comma-separated value, files will be the format of choice for storing data with your SD card. CSV files are easy to implement with a microcontroller platform and can easily be read and parsed by a wide range of desktop applications, making them well suited for this kind of task. A standard CSV file generally looks something like this:

```
Date,Time,Value1,Value2
2013-05-15,12:00,125,255
2013-05-15,12:30,100,200
2013-05-15,13:00,110,215
```

Rows are delimited by new lines, and columns are delimited by commas. Because commas are used to distinguish columns of data, the main requirement is that your data cannot have commas within it. Furthermore, each row should generally always have the same number of entries. When opened with a spreadsheet program on your computer, the preceding CSV file would look something like this.

Table 13-1: An Imported CSV File

DATE	TIME	VALUE1	VALUE2
2013-05-15	12:00	125	255
2013-05-15	12:30	100	200
2013-05-15	13:00	110	215

Because CSV files are just plain text, your Arduino can easily write to them using familiar `print()` and `println()`-style commands. Conversely, Arduinos can also parse CSV files with relative ease by looking for newline and command delimiters to find the right information.

Preparing an SD Card for Data Logging

Before you start logging data with your Arduino, prepare the SD card you plan to use. Which kind of SD card you use will depend on the kind of shield you are using. Some will use full-size SD cards, others will use micro SD cards. Most micro SD cards ship with an adapter that lets you plug them into standard-sized SD card readers. To complete the exercises in this chapter, you need an SD card reader for your computer (either built in or external).

Most new SD cards will already be properly formatted and ready to use with an Arduino. If your card is not new, or already has things on it, first format the card in either FAT16 (sometimes just called FAT) or FAT32 format. Cards less than or equal 2GB should be formatted as FAT16, and larger cards should be formatted as FAT32. In this chapter, the examples use a 2GB micro SD card formatted as FAT16. Note that formatting the card removes everything on it, but doing so ensures that it is ready for use with your Arduino. If your SD card is new, you can skip these steps and come back to complete them only if you have issues accessing the card from the Arduino when you run the sketch later in this chapter.

Formatting your SD card from Windows is easy:

1. Insert the SD card into your card reader; it should then appear in My Computer (see Figure 13-1).

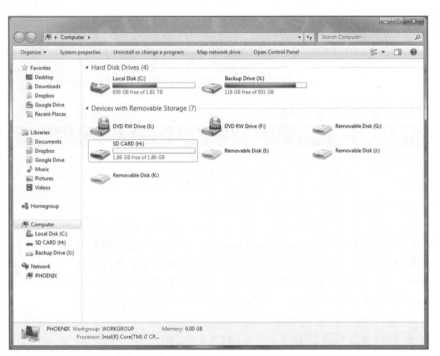

Figure 13-1: SD card shown in My Computer

2. Right-click the card (it will probably have a different name), and select the Format option (see Figure 13-2). A window will appear with options for formatting the card.

Figure 13-2: Format option selected

3. Choose the file system type (FAT for cards 2GB and under, FAT32 for larger cards), use the default allocation size, and choose a volume label. (I chose LOG, but you can choose whatever you want.) Figure 13-3 shows the configuration for a 2GB card.

Figure 13-3: Format option window

4. Click the Start button to format the SD card.

On a Mac, the process is similarly straightforward:

1. Use the Finder to locate and open the Disk Utility application.

2. Click on the SD card in the left panel, and click on the Erase tab. Choose MS-DOS(FAT) for the format.

3. Click Erase. This will format the card as FAT16 regardless of its capacity. (Macs cannot natively format cards as FAT32.)

On Linux, you can format the card from the terminal. Most Linux distros will mount the card automatically when you insert it:

1. Insert the card, and a window should pop up showing the card.

2. Open a terminal, and type in **df** to get a list of the mounted media. The result should look like Figure 13-4.

   The last entry should be your SD card. On my system, it was mounted as /dev/mmcblk0p1, but on yours might differ.

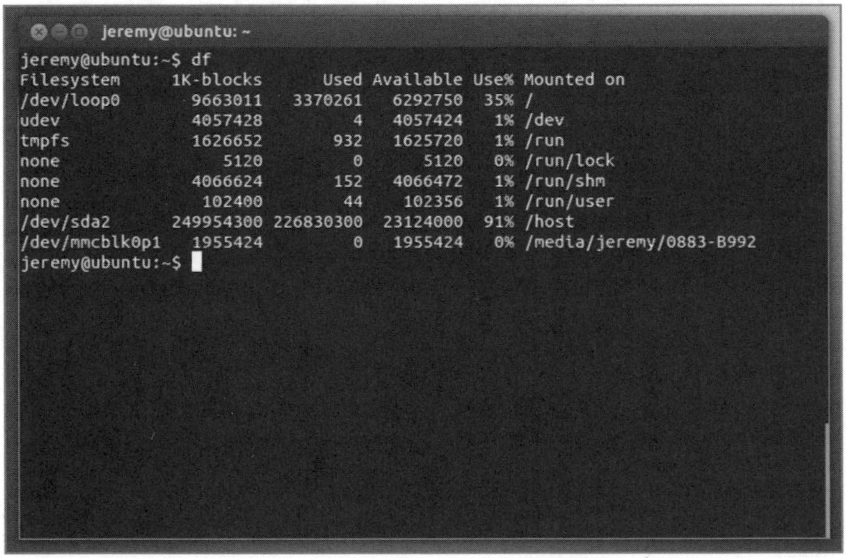

```
jeremy@ubuntu: ~
jeremy@ubuntu:~$ df
Filesystem     1K-blocks       Used Available Use% Mounted on
/dev/loop0       9663011    3370261   6292750  35% /
udev             4057428          4   4057424   1% /dev
tmpfs            1626652        932   1625720   1% /run
none                5120          0      5120   0% /run/lock
none             4066624        152   4066472   1% /run/shm
none              102400         44    102356   1% /run/user
/dev/sda2      249954300  226830300  23124000  91% /host
/dev/mmcblk0p1   1955424          0   1955424   0% /media/jeremy/0883-B992
jeremy@ubuntu:~$ 
```

Figure 13-4: Linux df command

3. Unmount the card before you format it by using the **umount** command. The argument will be the name of your SD card (see Figure 13-5).

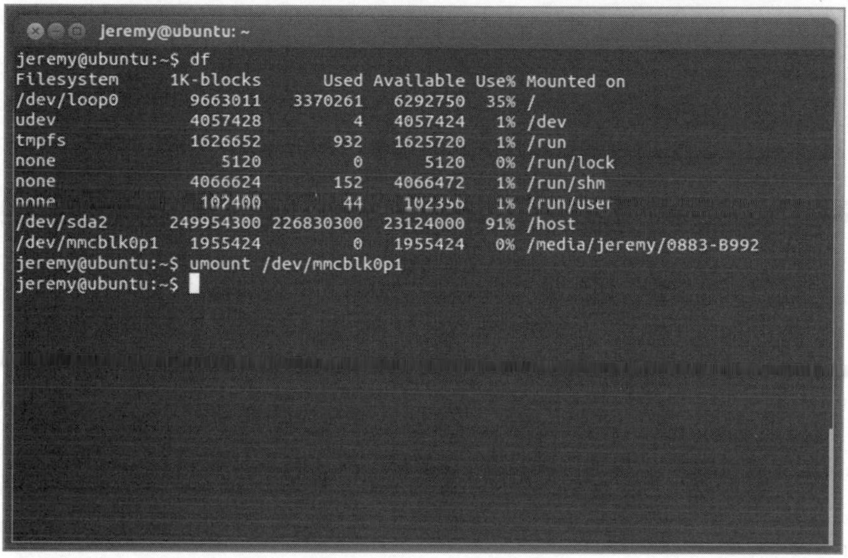

Figure 13-5: Unmounting the SD card in Linux

4. Format the card using the **mkdosfs** command. You may need to run the command as a super user (using the **sudo** command). You will pass the -F flag, specifying to use a FAT file system. You can include either 16 or 32 as the flag argument to choose FAT16 or FAT32. To format a card that was mounted as /dev/mmcblk0p1, you use the command **sudo mkdosfs -F 16 /dev/mmcblk0p1** (see Figure 13-6).

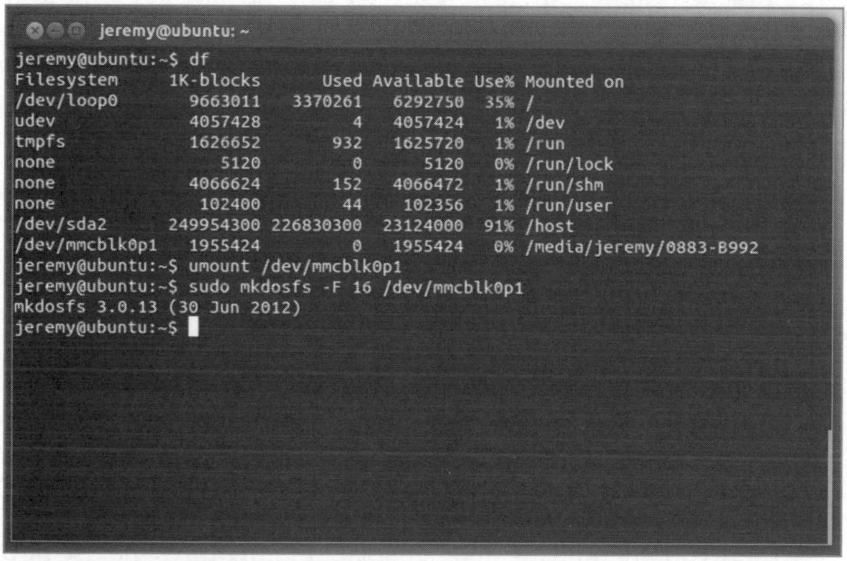

Figure 13-6: Formatting the SD card in Linux

Your SD card should now be formatted and ready to go! You're now ready to start interfacing with the SD card via an SD card shield.

Interfacing the Arduino with an SD Card

SD cards, like the XBee radios that you used in Chapter 11, "Wireless Communication with XBee Radios," are 3.3V devices. Therefore, it's important to connect to SD cards through a shield that properly handles the logic level shifting and voltage supply to your SD card. Furthermore, SD communication can be accomplished using the serial peripheral interface (SPI) bus, something that you should already be familiar with after having read Chapter 9, "The SPI Bus." The Arduino language comes with a handy library (the SD library) that abstracts away the lower-level SPI communication and allows you to easily read and write files stored on your SD card. You use this library throughout the chapter.

SD Card Shields

You have a tremendous number of options for adding data logging capabilities to your Arduino. It is impossible to provide documentation for every shield available, so this discussion keeps the examples general enough to apply to most shields with SD card connection capabilities. This section identifies some of the more popular shields and the pros and cons of using each one.

All shields have the following things in common:

- They connect to SPI pins via either the 6-pin programming header or via multiplexed digital pins. These are pins 11, 12, and 13 on the Uno, and pins 50, 51, and 52 on Mega boards. The Leonardo's SPI pins are located on the in-circuit serial programming (ICSP) header only.

- They designate a chip select (CS) pin, which may or may not be the default CS pin (10 on non-Mega boards, 53 on Mega boards).

- They supply 3.3V to the SD card and will level-shift the logic levels.

Here's a list of the most common shields:

- **Cooking Hacks Micro SD shield** (www.exploringarduino.com/parts/cooking-hacks-SD-shield): This shield is used to illustrate the examples in this chapter. This is the smallest shield of those listed here (not a full-sized shield), and it can be connected to either a row of header pins (8–13 on the Uno), or to your Arduino's ICSP 6-pin header. When connected to pins 8–13, the default pin 10 is connected to CS. When connected to the ISP header, the CS pin can be connected to any pin you want. This is useful if you are utilizing another shield that requires the use of pin 10. This board ships with a 2GB SD card (see Figure 13-7).

Credit: Cooking Hacks, www.cooking-hacks.com

Figure 13-7: Cooking Hacks MicroSD shield

■ **Official Arduino Wireless SD shield** (www.exploringarduino.com/parts/
arduino-wireless-shield): This is the first of several "official" Arduino
shields with SD card support. This shield includes circuitry for adding
both an XBee radio and an SD card to your Arduino, making it easy to
combine lessons from this chapter with lessons from Chapter 11. On this
shield, the SD card CS pin is connected to pin 4 of the Arduino. You must
keep pin 10 as an output, and also specify that pin 4 is your CS when running your sketch with this shield (see Figure 13-8).

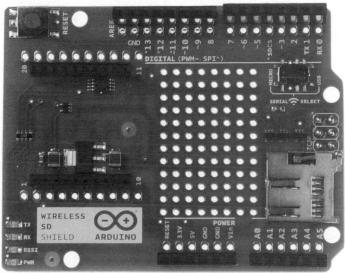

Credit: Arduino, www.arduino.cc

Figure 13-8: Arduino Wireless SD shield

■ **Official Arduino Ethernet SD shield** (www.exploringarduino.com/parts/ arduino-ethernet-shield) **:** The Arduino Ethernet shield allows your Arduino to connect to a wired network. It implements an SD card interface, as well, although its primary purpose is to allow for the storage of files to be accessed over the network. Both the Ethernet controller and the SD card are SPI devices on this shield; the Ethernet controller CS is connected to pin 10, and the SD card CS is connected to pin 4 (see Figure 13-9).

Figure 13-9: Arduino Ethernet SD shield

■ **Official Arduino Wi-Fi SD shield** (www.exploringarduino.com/parts/ arduino-wifi-shield) **:** This shield also implements network connectivity, but it takes advantage of a Wi-Fi radio to do so. For the same reasons as the Ethernet shield, it also houses an SD card reader/writer. As with the Ethernet shield, the Wi-Fi controller CS is pin 10, and the SD card CS is pin 4. You must take care to not attempt to simultaneously enable both devices; only one CS line can be active at a time (low logic level), as with all SPI configurations (see Figure 13-10).

Figure 13-10: Arduino Wi-Fi SD shield

▪ **adafruit data logging shield** (`www.exploringarduino.com/parts/ adafruit-data-logging-shield`): This shield is particularly well suited to the experiments that you will be doing later in this chapter because it includes both a real-time clock (RTC) chip and an SD card interface. This shield connects the SD card to the default pin CS and connects a real-time clock chip to the I²C bus (see Figure 13-11).

Credit: adafruit Industries, www.adafruit.com

Figure 13-11: adafruit data logging shield

■ **SparkFun MicroSD shield** (`www.exploringarduino.com/parts/spark-fun-microSD-shield`): This shield is, like the Cooking Hacks shield, is a minimalist shield that only has an SD card slot. However, it also has a prototyping area to allow you to solder on additional components. It connects the SD card's CS pin to pin 8 on the Arduino, so you must specify this when using the SD card library with this shield (see Figure 13-12).

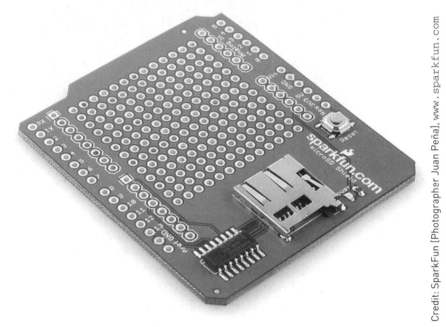

Figure 13-12: SparkFun MicroSD shield

Credit: SparkFun [Photographer Juan Peña], www.sparkfun.com

SD Card SPI Interface

As mentioned earlier, your Arduino communicates with the SD card over an SPI interface. This necessitates the use of a MOSI (master output, slave input), MISO (master input, slave output), SCLK (serial clock), and CS (chip select) pin. You use the SD card Arduino library to complete the following examples. It assumes that you are using the hardware SPI pins on your Arduino and either a default or custom CS pin. The SD card library must have the default CS pin set as an output to function correctly, even if you are using a different CS pin. In the case of the Uno, this is pin 10; in the case of the Mega, this is pin 53. The following examples use the Uno with the default CS pin 10.

Writing to an SD Card

First, you use the SD card library to write some sample data to your SD card. Later in the chapter, you capture some sensor data and write that directly to the SD card. The data is stored in a file called log.csv that you can later open up on your computer. Importantly, if you formatted your card FAT16, the filenames you use must be in 8.3 format. This means that the extension must be three characters, and the filename must be eight characters or fewer.

Ensure that your SD shield is mounted correctly to your Arduino and that you have an SD card inserted. When mounted, the Cooking Hacks SD shield looks like Figure 13-13. (The pins are inserted into pins 8–13, and the jumper is on the right side when viewed from this angle.)

Figure 13-13: Mounted SD card shield

For the sake of debugging, you will take advantage of the reporting functionality of many of the SD card functions. For example, to initialize communication with an SD card, you call the following function in your setup:

```
if (!SD.begin(CS_pin))
{
 Serial.println("Card Failure");
```

```
 return;
}
Serial.println("Card Ready");
```

Note that instead of just calling `SD.begin(CS_pin)`, it is executed within an `if` statement. This tries to initialize the SD card and it returns a status. If it returns `true`, the program moves on, and a success message is printed to the serial terminal. If it returns `false`, a failure message is reported, and the `return` command halts further execution of the program.

You use a similar approach when you are ready to write a new line of data to a log file. If you want to write "hello" to a new line in the file, the code would look like this:

```
File dataFile = SD.open("log.csv", FILE_WRITE);
if (dataFile)
{
  dataFile.println("hello");
  dataFile.close(); //Data isn't written until we close the connection!
}
else
{
  Serial.println("Couldn't open log file");
}
```

This first line creates a new file (or opens the file if it exists) called log.csv on the SD card. If the file is opened/created successfully, the `dataFile` variable will be `true`, and the write process will be initiated. If it is `false`, an error is reported to the serial monitor. Writing new lines to a file is easy: Just execute `dataFile.println()` and pass what you want to write to a new line. You can also use `print()` to prevent appending a newline character to the end. This is sent to a buffer, and only actually added to the file once the `close` command is called on the same `File`.

Now, you can bring all this knowledge together into a simple program that will create a log.csv file on your SD card and write a comma-separated timestamp and phrase every 5 seconds. On each line of the CSV file, you record the current time from `millis()` and a simple phrase. This might not seem very useful, but it is an important step to test before you start adding actual measurements in the coming examples. The code should look something like Listing 13-1.

Listing 13-1: SD Card Write Test—write_to_sd.ino

```
//Write to SD card

#include <SD.h>
```

```
//Set by default for the SD card library
//MOSI = pin 11
//MISO = pin 12
//SCLK = pin 13
//We always need to set the CS Pin
const int CS_PIN = 10;

//We set this high to provide power
const int POW_PIN =8;

void setup()
{
  Serial.begin(9600);
  Serial.println("Initializing Card");
  //CS pin is an output
  pinMode(CS_PIN, OUTPUT);

  //Card will draw power from pin 8, so set it high
  pinMode(POW_PIN, OUTPUT);
  digitalWrite(POW_PIN, HIGH);

  if (!SD.begin(CS_PIN))
  {
    Serial.println("Card Failure");
    return;
  }
  Serial.println("Card Ready");
}

void loop()
{
  long timeStamp = millis();
  String dataString = "Hello There!";

  //Open a file and write to it.
  File dataFile = SD.open("log.csv", FILE_WRITE);
  if (dataFile)
  {
    dataFile.print(timeStamp);
    dataFile.print(",");
    dataFile.println(dataString);
    dataFile.close(); //Data isn't actually written until we
                      //close the connection!

    //Print same thing to the screen for debugging
    Serial.print(timeStamp);
    Serial.print(",");
    Serial.println(dataString);
  }
  else
```

```
  {
    Serial.println("Couldn't open log file");
  }
  delay(5000);
}
```

You want to note a few important things here, especially if you are not using the same Cooking Hacks MicroSD card shield:

- `CS_PIN` should be set to whatever pin you have your SD card CS hooked up to. If it is not 10, you must also add `pinMode(10, OUTPUT)` within `setup()`; otherwise, the SD library will not work.

- This particular shield draws power from pin 8 (as opposed to being connected directly to a 5V supply). Therefore, `POW_PIN` must be set as an output and set `HIGH` in the setup function to power up the SD card shield.

- Each time through the loop, the `timestamp` variable is updated with the current time elapsed in milliseconds. It must be of type `long` because it will generate a number larger than 16 bits (the standard size of an Arduino integer type).

As you saw earlier, the filename is opened for writing and data is appended in a comma-separated format. The same data is also printed out to the serial terminal for debugging purposes. This is not explicitly necessary, and you will not use it once you have the logger "in the field" taking data. However, it is useful for confirming that everything is working. If you open the serial terminal, you should see something like Figure 13-14.

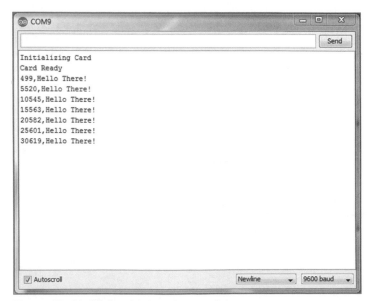

Figure 13-14: SD Card debugging output

If you receive errors, make sure that your shield is plugged in, that the SD card is inserted fully, and that the card has been properly formatted. You can confirm that the data is being written correctly by removing the SD card, inserting it into your computer, and opening it up with a spreadsheet program (see Figure 13-15). Note how the comma-separated data is automatically placed into rows and columns based on the location of the delimiting commas and newlines.

	A	B
1	10	Hello There!
2	5030	Hello There!
3	10049	Hello There!
4	15067	Hello There!
5	20085	Hello There!
6	25104	Hello There!
7	30123	Hello There!
8	35141	Hello There!
9	40160	Hello There!
10	45178	Hello There!
11	50197	Hello There!
12	55218	Hello There!
13	60239	Hello There!
14	65258	Hello There!
15	70277	Hello There!
16	75295	Hello There!
17	80313	Hello There!

Figure 13-15: Logged data in a spreadsheet

Reading from an SD Card

Now it's time to learn about reading from SD cards. This is not used quite as commonly for data logging, but it can prove useful for setting program parameters. For instance, you could specify how frequently you want data to be logged. That's what you do next.

Insert the SD card into your computer and create a new TXT file called `speed` `.txt` on the SD card. In this file, simply enter the refresh time in milliseconds that you want to use. In Figure 13-16, you can see that I set it to 1000ms, or 1 second.

Figure 13-16: Creating the speed command file

After choosing a desired refresh speed, save the file on the SD card and put it back in your Arduino shield. You now modify your program to read this file, extract the desired field, and use it to set the refresh speed for data logging.

To open a file for reading, you use the same `SD.open` command that you used earlier, but you do not have to specify the `FILE_WRITE` parameter. Because the `File` class that you are using inherits from the stream class (just like the `Serial` class), you can use many of the same useful commands, such as `parseInt()`, that you've used in previous chapters. To open and read the update speed from the file, all you have to do is this:

```
File commandFile = SD.open("speed.txt");
if (commandFile)
{
  Serial.println("Reading Command File");
```

```
  while(commandFile.available())
  {
    refresh_rate = commandFile.parseInt();
  }
  Serial.print("Refresh Rate = ");
  Serial.print(refresh_rate);
  Serial.println("ms");
}
else
{
  Serial.println("Could not read command file ");
  return;
}
```

This opens the file for reading and parses out any integers read. Because you defined only one variable, it grabs that one and saves it to the refresh rate variable, which would need to be defined earlier in the program. You can have only one file open at a time, and it's good practice to close a file when you're finished reading from, or writing to a card.

You can now integrate this into your writing program from earlier to adjust the recording speed based on your speed.txt file, as shown in Listing 13-2.

Listing 13-2: SD Reading and Writing—sd_read_write.ino

```
//SD read and write

#include <SD.h>

//Set by default for the SD card library
//MOSI = pin 11
//MISO = pin 12
//SCLK = pin 13
//We always need to set the CS pin
const int CS_PIN =10;
const int POW_PIN =8;

//Default rate of 5 seconds
int refresh_rate = 5000;

void setup()
{
  Serial.begin(9600);
  Serial.println("Initializing Card");
  //CS pin is an output
  pinMode(CS_PIN, OUTPUT);

  //Card will draw power from pin 8, so set it high
  pinMode(POW_PIN, OUTPUT);
```

```
    digitalWrite(POW_PIN, HIGH);

    if (!SD.begin(CS_PIN))
    {
      Serial.println("Card Failure");
      return;
    }
    Serial.println("Card Ready");

    //Read the configuration information (speed.txt)
    File commandFile = SD.open("speed.txt");
    if (commandFile)
    {
        Serial.println("Reading Command File");

        while(commandFile.available())
        {
          refresh_rate = commandFile.parseInt();
        }
        Serial.print("Refresh Rate = ");
        Serial.print(refresh_rate);
        Serial.println("ms");
        commandFile.close(); //Close the file when finished
    }
    else
    {
      Serial.println("Could not read command file.");
      return;
    }
}

void loop()
{
  long timeStamp = millis();
  String dataString = "Hello There!";

  //Open a file and write to it.
  File dataFile = SD.open("log.csv", FILE_WRITE);
  if (dataFile)
  {
    dataFile.print(timeStamp);
    dataFile.print(",");
    dataFile.println(dataString);
    dataFile.close(); //Data isn't actually written until we
                      //close the connection!

    //Print same thing to the screen for debugging
    Serial.print(timeStamp);
    Serial.print(",");
    Serial.println(dataString);
```

```
  }
  else
  {
    Serial.println("Couldn't open log file");
  }
  delay(refresh_rate);
}
```

When you now run this program, data should be written at the rate you specify. Looking at the serial terminal confirms this (see Figure 13-17).

Figure 13-17: Data logging at rate specified by the command file

Using a Real-Time Clock

Nearly every data logging application will benefit from the use of a real-time clock. Using a real-time clock within your system allows you to timestamp measurements so that you can more easily keep track of when certain events occurred. In the previous section, you simply used the `millis()` function to keep track of the time elapsed since the Arduino turned on. In this section, you use a dedicated real-time clock integrated circuit to keep accurate time so that when you save data to the SD card it corresponds to the time the data was taken.

Understanding Real-Time Clocks

Real-time clocks do exactly what their name implies. You set the time once, and they keep very accurate time, even accounting for leap years and things of that nature. This example uses the popular DS1307 real-time clock integrated circuit.

Using the DS1307 Real-Time Clock

The real-time clock communicates with your Arduino over an I^2C connection and connects to a coin cell battery that will allow it to keep time for several years. A crystal oscillator connected to the real-time clock enables precision timekeeping. To make things easier, I suggest using the adafruit DS1307 breakout board (www.exploringarduino.com/parts/adafruit-DS1307-breakout); it combines the IC, the oscillator, a coin cell battery, a decoupling capacitor, and the I^2C pull-up resistors into a nice package that can easily be mounted on your Arduino (see Figure 13-18).

Figure 13-18: Real-time clock breakout mounted on an Arduino

The rest of these instructions assume that you are using this breakout board. However, you can just as easily assemble these components on a breadboard and wire them directly to your Arduino. The crystal is a 32.768kHz unit, and the I^2C pull-up resistors are 2.2kilohms. The battery is a standard 3.0V coin cell. If you choose to assemble it yourself, you can buy all these components and put them on a breadboard as shown in Figure 13-19.

Image created with Fritzing.

Figure 13-19: Real-time clock circuit assembled on breadboard

Using the RTC Arduino Third-Party Library

As in the preceding chapter, you again use a third-party library to extend the Arduino's capabilities. In this case, it's to facilitate easy communication with the real-time clock (RTC) chip. Unsurprisingly, the library is called *RTClib*. The library was originally developed by JeeLabs, and was updated by adafruit Industries. A link to download the library can be found on the web page for this chapter: www.exploringarduino.com/content/ch13. Download the library and add it to your Arduino user library folder, just as you did in the preceding chapter. Make sure that the folder name has no dashes in it; underscores are okay.

The library is easy to use. The first time you run the example code, you use the RTC.adjust function to automatically grab the current date/time from your computer at the time of compilation and use that to set up the clock. From this point on, the RTC runs autonomously, and you can obtain the current time/date from it by executing the RTC.now() command. In the next section, you use this functionality to enable real-time logging.

Using the Real-Time Clock

Now it is time to combine the SD card and real-time clock, along with the RTC library that you just downloaded, to enable logging using actual time-stamps. You update your sketch once again to use the RTC values rather than the `millis` values.

Installing the RTC and SD Card Modules

First, ensure that both your SD card shield and RTC are connected to your Arduino. If you are using the Cooking Hacks SD shield and the adafruit RTC shield, it should look something like Figure 13-20.

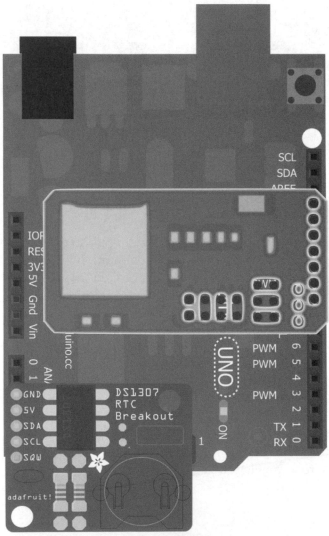

Figure 13-20: Arduino with mounted SD card and RTC breakout boards

Note that the last pin on the RTC is hanging off the Arduino; it is a square wave generated by the RTC that you will not be using. In code, you need to pull A2 to ground and A3 to 5V to ensure that the RTC breakout is powered. If you assembled your own RTC circuit on a breadboard, your setup will look a bit different.

Updating the Software

Now, you add the RTC functionality into the software. You need to add a few things to your previous program to get the RTC integrated:

- Include the RTC libraries
- Power the RTC module
- Initialize the RTC object
- Set the RTC time using the computer time if it is unset
- Write the actual timestamps to the log file

Furthermore, in this code revision, I added a column header that is printed every time the code starts. This way, even if you are appending to an existing CSV file, you an easily find each time that the log was restarted.

WARNING If, when you run your program, you notice that it simply stops after a short while, you may be running out of RAM. In most cases, this can be attributed to strings that take up a large amount of RAM, especially within your `Serial`
`.print` and `Serial.println` statements. You can resolve this problem by removing serial printing statements, or by telling the Arduino to store these strings in flash memory instead of in RAM. You can store strings in flash memory by wrapping the serial print string in `F()`, like this: `Serial.println(F("Hello"));`. This method was used Listing 13-3.

The updated program is shown in Listing 13-3, using the RTC as a clock for datalogging. It moves the majority of the strings into flash memory to save RAM using the technique explained in the previous warning section.

Listing 13-3: SD Reading and Writing with an RTC— sd_read_write_rtc.ino

```
//SD read and write with RTC

#include <SD.h>    //For talking to SD Card
#include <Wire.h>  //For RTC
#include "RTClib.h" //For RTC

//Define pins
```

```
//SD card is on standard SPI pins
//RTC is on Standard I2C Pins
const int CS_PIN      =10;
const int SD_POW_PIN  =8;
const int RTC_POW_PIN =A3;
const int RTC_GND_PIN =A2;

//Default rate of 5 seconds
int refresh_rate = 5000;

//Define an RTC object
RTC_DS1307 RTC;

//Initialize strings
String year, month, day, hour, minute, second, time, date;

void setup()
{
  Serial.begin(9600);
  Serial.println(F("Initializing Card"));

  //CS pin and pwr/gnd pins are outputs
  pinMode(CS_PIN,    OUTPUT);
  pinMode(SD_POW_PIN, OUTPUT);
  pinMode(RTC_POW_PIN, OUTPUT);
  pinMode(RTC_GND_PIN, OUTPUT);

  //Setup power and ground pins for both modules
  digitalWrite(SD_POW_PIN, HIGH);
  digitalWrite(RTC_POW_PIN, HIGH);
  digitalWrite(RTC_GND_PIN, LOW);

  //Initiate the I2C bus and the RTC library
  Wire.begin();
  RTC.begin();

  //If RTC is not running, set it to the computer's compile time
  if (! RTC.isrunning())
  {
    Serial.println(F("RTC is NOT running!"));
    RTC.adjust(DateTime(__DATE__, __TIME__));
  }

  //Initialize SD card
  if (!SD.begin(CS_PIN))
  {
    Serial.println(F("Card Failure"));
    return;
  }
  Serial.println(F("Card Ready"));
```

```
    //Read the configuration information (speed.txt)
    File commandFile = SD.open("speed.txt");
    if (commandFile)
    {
      Serial.println(F("Reading Command File"));

      while(commandFile.available())
      {
        refresh_rate = commandFile.parseInt();
      }
      Serial.print(F("Refresh Rate = "));
      Serial.print(refresh_rate);
      Serial.println(F("ms"));
      commandFile.close();
    }
    else
    {
      Serial.println(F("Could not read command file."));
      return;
    }


    //Write column headers
    File dataFile = SD.open("log.csv", FILE_WRITE);
    if (dataFile)
    {
      dataFile.println(F("\nNew Log Started!"));
      dataFile.println(F("Date,Time,Phrase"));
      dataFile.close(); //Data isn't actually written until we
                        //close the connection!

      //Print same thing to the screen for debugging
      Serial.println(F("\nNew Log Started!"));
      Serial.println(F("Date,Time,Phrase"));
    }
    else
    {
      Serial.println(F("Couldn't open log file"));
    }

}


void loop()
{
  //Get the current date and time info and store in strings
  DateTime datetime = RTC.now();
  year  = String(datetime.year(),  DEC);
  month = String(datetime.month(), DEC);
  day   = String(datetime.day(),   DEC);
  hour  = String(datetime.hour(),  DEC);
  minute = String(datetime.minute(), DEC);
```

```
     second = String(datetime.second(), DEC);

     //Concatenate the strings into date and time
     date = year + "/" + month + "/" + day;
     time = hour + ":" + minute + ":" + second;

     String dataString = "Hello There!";

     //Open a file and write to it.
     File dataFile = SD.open("log.csv", FILE_WRITE);
     if (dataFile)
     {
       dataFile.print(date);
       dataFile.print(F(","));
       dataFile.print(time);
       dataFile.print(F(","));
       dataFile.println(dataString);
       dataFile.close(); //Data isn't actually written until we
                         //close the connection!

       //Print same thing to the screen for debugging
       Serial.print(date);
       Serial.print(F(","));
       Serial.print(time);
       Serial.print(F(","));
       Serial.println(dataString);
     }
     else
     {
       Serial.println(F("Couldn't open log file"));
     }
     delay(refresh_rate);
   }
```

The RTC library is imported by the sketch via `#include "RTClib.h"` and an RTC object is created with `RTC_DS1307 RTC;`. The RTC is an I²C device, and relies on the Wire library, so that needs to be included, too. This is the same library you used in Chapter 8, "The I²C Bus." In `setup()`, `RTC.isrunning()` checks to see if the RTC is not already running. If it isn't, the date and time are set based on the compile time, determined by your computer's clock. Once this is set, the time will not be reset as long as the battery stays connected to the RTC. Also in `setup()`, a column header is inserted into the log file, adding a note that the logging has been restarted. This is useful for appending to the log file each time you restart the system.

During each pass through the loop, the `datetime` object is set to the current date and time. You can then extract the year, month, hour, and so on from this object and convert them to strings that you can concatenate into the `date` and `time` variables. These variables are printed to the serial console and to the SD card log file.

After running this sketch on your Arduino for a little while, use your computer to read the SD card and to open the log file; it should be populated with the date and time and look something like Figure 13-21. Your spreadsheet software may automatically change the dates into your local formatting.

	A	B	C
1			
2	New Log Started!		
3	Date	Time	Phrase
4	4/8/2013	23:24:05	Hello There!
5	4/8/2013	23:24:07	Hello There!
6	4/8/2013	23:24:09	Hello There!
7	4/8/2013	23:24:11	Hello There!
8	4/8/2013	23:24:14	Hello There!
9	4/8/2013	23:24:16	Hello There!
10	4/8/2013	23:24:18	Hello There!
11	4/8/2013	23:24:20	Hello There!
12	4/8/2013	23:24:22	Hello There!
13	4/8/2013	23:24:24	Hello There!
14	4/8/2013	23:24:26	Hello There!
15	4/8/2013	23:24:28	Hello There!
16	4/8/2013	23:24:30	Hello There!
17	4/8/2013	23:24:32	Hello There!
18	4/8/2013	23:24:34	Hello There!
19	4/8/2013	23:24:36	Hello There!
20	4/8/2013	23:24:38	Hello There!

Figure 13-21: Spreadsheet output from RTC SD card test

Building an Entrance Logger

Now that you have all the basic skills down, you can put them to use to build an entrance logger for your room. You use the distance sensor from some of your previous projects to create a basic motion sensor that can keep track of when people enter or exit through a doorway. The logger will keep track of the times of these events on the SD card for you to review later.

Logger Hardware

All you need to do is to add an analog distance sensor to your existing setup. If you're using the same setup as me, you do not even need a breadboard; just connect the proper wires to power, ground, and A0 (for the analog signal output from the sensor). With everything attached, it should look like Figure 13-22.

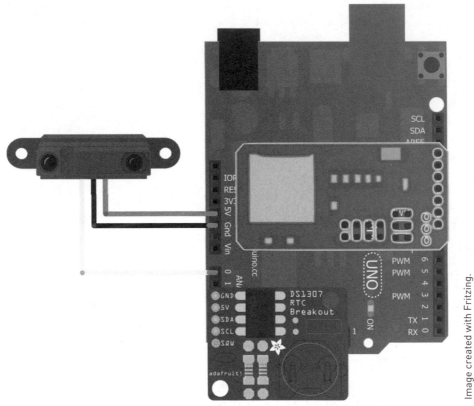

Figure 13-22: Entrance logger hardware

For this to actually work well, you want to mount the IR distance sensor and Arduino on a wall so that the IR beam cuts horizontally across the door. This way, anybody walking through the door must pass in front of the IR distance sensor. Don't affix anything to your wall until you've written the software in the next step and uploaded it. I suggest using easily removable painters tape to hold it to your wall so that you don't damage anything. Once set up, the system should look something like Figure 13-23.

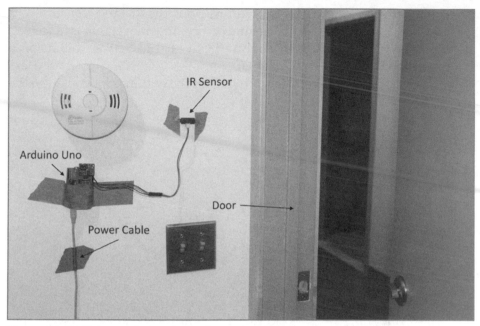

Figure 13-23: Entrance logger trained on a door

Logger Software

For the entrance logger, reading configuration variables from the SD card is not particularly useful, so you can remove those parts of the code. You want to add some code to check the state of the distance and to see whether its readings have changed drastically between pollings. If they have, you can assume that something moved in front of the distance sensor and that somebody must have entered or exited the room.

You also need to choose a "change threshold." For my setup, I found that an analog reading change of more than 75 between pollings was a good indication of movement. (Your setup will probably be different. It's a good idea to check the values of your system once you have the physical setup fixed.) You want to make sure you're checking the distance sensor frequently enough that you capture movement every time. However, it doesn't make sense to run it so often that you end up with millions of readings for a day's worth of logging.

I recommend that you write to the SD card every time movement is detected, but that you only periodically write to the SD card when there is no movement. This methodology strikes a good balance between storage space required and accuracy. Because you care the most about having accurate timing for when somebody passes the sensor, that detection is recorded with a higher temporal resolution than when nothing is happening in front of the sensor. This technique is implemented in Listing 13-4. The Arduino polls the distance sensor every 50ms (and writes a 1 to the "active" column every time movement is detected). If movement is not being detected, it only writes a 0 to the "active" column once every second (as opposed to every 50ms).

Listing 13-4 shows the completed software for the entrance logger, given the improvements just described.

Listing 13-4: Entrance Logger Software—entrance_logger.ino

```
//Logs Room Entrance Activity

#include <SD.h>    //For talking to SD Card
#include <Wire.h>  //For RTC
#include "RTClib.h" //For RTC

//Define pins
//SD Card is on Standard SPI Pins
//RTC is on Standard I2C Pins
const int CS_PIN      =10; //SS for SD Shield
const int SD_POW_PIN  =8;  //Power for SD Shield
const int RTC_POW_PIN =A3; //Used as digital output
const int RTC_GND_PIN =A2; //Used as digital output
const int IR_PIN      =0; //Analog input 0

//Define an RTC object
RTC_DS1307 RTC;

//Initialize strings
String year, month, day, hour, minute, second, time, date;

//Initialize distance variables
int raw = 0;
int raw_prev = 0;
boolean active = false;
int update_time = 0;

void setup()
{
  Serial.begin(9600);
  Serial.println(F("Initializing Card"));

  //CS pin, and pwr/gnd pins are outputs
  pinMode(CS_PIN,    OUTPUT);
  pinMode(SD_POW_PIN, OUTPUT);
  pinMode(RTC_POW_PIN, OUTPUT);
  pinMode(RTC_GND_PIN, OUTPUT);

  //Setup power and ground pins for both modules
  digitalWrite(SD_POW_PIN, HIGH);
```

```
    digitalWrite(RTC_POW_PIN, HIGH);
    digitalWrite(RTC_GND_PIN, LOW);

    //Initiate the I2C bus and the RTC library
    Wire.begin();
    RTC.begin();

    //If RTC is not running, set it to the computer's compile time
    if (! RTC.isrunning())
    {
      Serial.println(F("RTC is NOT running!"));
      RTC.adjust(DateTime(__DATE__, __TIME__));
    }

    //Initialize SD card
    if (!SD.begin(CS_PIN))
    {
      Serial.println(F("Card Failure"));
      return;
    }
    Serial.println(F("Card Ready"));

    //Write column headers
    File dataFile = SD.open("log.csv", FILE_WRITE);
    if (dataFile)
    {
      dataFile.println(F("\nNew Log Started!"));
      dataFile.println(F("Date,Time,Raw,Active"));
      dataFile.close(); //Data isn't actually written until we
                        //close the connection!

      //Print same thing to the screen for debugging
      Serial.println(F("\nNew Log Started!"));
      Serial.println(F("Date,Time,Raw,Active"));
    }
    else
    {
      Serial.println(F("Couldn't open log file"));
    }

}

void loop()
{
  //Get the current date and time info and store in strings
  DateTime datetime = RTC.now();
  year  = String(datetime.year(),  DEC);
  month = String(datetime.month(), DEC);
  day   = String(datetime.day(),  DEC);
  hour  = String(datetime.hour(),  DEC);
```

```
   minute = String(datetime.minute(), DEC);
   second = String(datetime.second(), DEC);

   //Concatenate the strings into date and time
   date = year + "/" + month + "/" + day;
   time = hour + ":" + minute + ":" + second;

   //Gather motion data
   raw = analogRead(IR_PIN);
   //If the value changes by more than 75 between readings,
   //indicate movement.
   if (abs(raw-raw_prev) > 75)
     active = true;
   else
     active = false;
   raw_prev = raw;

   //Open a file and write to it.
   if (active || update_time == 20)
   {
     File dataFile = SD.open("log.csv", FILE_WRITE);
     if (dataFile)
     {
       dataFile.print(date);
       dataFile.print(F(","));
       dataFile.print(time);
       dataFile.print(F(","));
       dataFile.print(raw);
       dataFile.print(F(","));
       dataFile.println(active);
       dataFile.close(); //Data isn't actually written until we
                         //close the connection!

       //Print same thing to the screen for debugging
       Serial.print(date);
       Serial.print(F(","));
       Serial.print(time);
       Serial.print(F(","));
       Serial.print(raw);
       Serial.print(F(","));
       Serial.println(active);
     }
     else
     {
       Serial.println(F("Couldn't open log file"));
     }
     update_time = 0;
   }
   delay(50);
   update_time++;
}
```

Data Analysis

After loading this code on to your Arduino, set it up at your door and let it run for a while. When satisfied with the amount of data you have collected, put the SD card in your computer and load the CSV file with your favorite spreadsheet program. Assuming that you only logged over the course of one day, you can now plot the time column against the activity column. Whenever there is no activity, the activity line graph remains at zero. Whenever somebody enters or exits the room, it jumps up to one, and you can see exactly when it happened.

The procedure for creating a plot will vary with different graphing applications. To make it easy for you, I've created a preformatted online spreadsheet that will do the plotting for you. You must have a Google account to use it. Visit the web page for this chapter (www.exploringarduino.com/content/ch13) and follow the link to the graph-generation spreadsheet. It will prompt you to create a new spreadsheet in your Google Drive account. Once this completes, just copy your data in place of where the template data is, and the graph will update for you automatically. Figure 13-24 shows what a graph of data over a few minutes might look like.

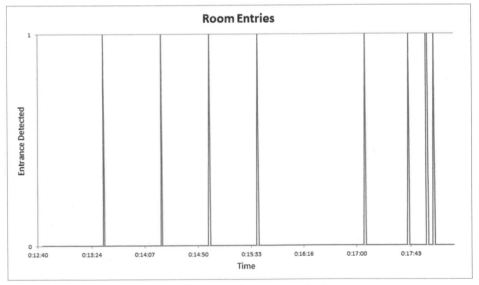

Figure 13-24: Entrance logger data graphed over several minutes

Summary

In this chapter you learned about the following:

- CSV files use newlines and commas as delimiters to easily store data in a plain text format.
- You can format an SD card in Windows, Mac, or Linux.
- There are a plethora of available SD card shields, each with unique features.
- You can use the SD Library to write to and read from a file on an SD card.
- You can build an RTC and write software that utilizes it to insert timestamps.
- You can overcome RAM limitations by storing strings in flash memory.
- You can detect movement by looking for changing analog values produced by a distance sensor.
- You can graph data from a data logger using a spreadsheet on your computer.

Connecting Your Arduino to the Internet

Parts You'll Need for This Chapter

Arduino (Uno recommended)

USB cable

Arduino Ethernet shield

Photoresistor

10kΩ resistor

TMP36 temperature sensor

RGB LED

220Ω resistors (×3)

150Ω resistor

Speaker or buzzer

Ethernet cable

Access to a wired router

Jumper wires

Breadboard

CODE AND DIGITAL CONTENT FOR THIS CHAPTER

Code downloads, video, and other digital content for this chapter can be found at www
.exploringarduino.com/content/ch14.

In addition, all code can be found at www.wiley.com/go/exploringarduino on
the Download Code tab. The code is in the chapter 14 download and individually
named according to the names throughout the chapter.

This is it, the final frontier (and chapter). Short of launching your Arduino
into space, connecting it to the Internet is probably the closest that you will get
to making the whole world your playground. Internet connectivity, in general,
is an extremely complex topic; you could easily write entire volumes of books
about the best way to interface the Arduino with the "Internet of things," as it is
now often called. Because it is infeasible to cover the multitude of ways you can
interface your Arduino with the web, this chapter focuses on imparting some
knowledge with regard to how network connectivity works with your Arduino
and how you can use the Arduino Ethernet shield to both serve up web pages
and to broadcast data to the web. Specifically, you learn about traversing your
network topology, how a web page is served, and how to use a third-party data
logging service to connect your Arduino to the "Internet of things."

The Web, the Arduino, and You

Explaining all the workings of the web is a bit ambitious for one chapter in a
book, so for this chapter, you can essentially think of your Arduino's relation
to the Internet using the diagram shown in Figure 14-1.

First, you work only in the realm of your local network. When working within
your local network, you can talk to your Arduino via a web browser only if they
are both on the same local network. Then, you will explore ways in which you
can traverse your router to access functionality from your Arduino anywhere
in the world (or at least anywhere you can get an Internet connection).

Networking Lingo

Before you get your feet wet with networking your Arduino, let's get some
lingo straight. The following are words, concepts, and abbreviations that you
will need to understand as you work through this chapter.

IP Address

An Internet Protocol (IP) address is a unique address that identifies each device
that connects to the Internet. In the case of your home network, there are actually two kinds of IP addresses you need to worry about: the local IP address
and the global IP address. If your home or office has a router (like the one in

Figure 14-1), everything within your local network has a local IP address that is visible only to other devices within your network. Your router/modem has one public-facing global IP addresses that is visible to the rest of the Internet. If you want to get data between somewhere else on the Internet and a device behind a router, you need to use Network Address Translation (NAT).

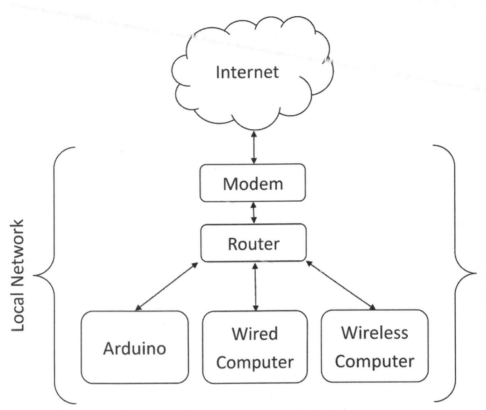

Figure 14-1: A simplified view of the web and your local network

Network Address Translation

There are not enough IP addresses to have one for every device in the world. Furthermore, users often do not want their computers and other networked devices visible to the rest of the world. For this reason, routers are used to create isolated networks of computers with local IP addresses. However, when you do want one of these machines to be accessible from the rest of the Internet, you need to use NAT through the router. This allows a remote device to send a request to your router asking to talk to a device in your local network. When you connect your Arduino to the larger web later in this chapter, you use a form of NAT.

MAC Address

MAC addresses, unlike IP addresses, are globally unique. (Well, they are supposed to be, but in practice they often are not.) MAC addresses are assigned to every physical network interface and do not change. For instance, when you buy a computer, the Wi-Fi module inside has a unique MAC address, and the Ethernet adapter has a unique MAC address. This makes MAC addresses useful for identifying physical systems on a network.

HTML

HTML, or Hypertext Markup Language, is the language of the web. To display a web page from your Arduino, you will write some simple HTML that creates buttons and sliders for sending data.

HTTP

HTTP, or Hypertext Transfer Protocol, defines the protocol for communicating across the World Wide Web, and is most commonly used in browsers. HTTP defines a set of header information that must be sent as part of a message across the web. This header defines how a web page will display in addition to whether the request was successfully received and acknowledged.

GET/POST

GET and POST define two ways for transferring information to a remote web server. If you've ever seen a URL that looks like www.jeremyblum.com/?s=arduino, you've seen a GET request. GET defines a series of variables following a question mark in the URL. In this case, the variable s is being set to Arduino. When the page receives this URL, it identifies this variable, performs the search, and returns the results page.

A POST is very similar, but the information is not transmitted in a visible medium through the URL. Instead, the same variables are transmitted transparently in the background. This is generally used to hide sensitive information or to ensure that a page cannot be linked to if it contains unique information.

DHCP

DHCP, or Dynamic Host Configuration Protocol, makes connecting devices to your local network a breeze. Odds are that whenever you've connected to a Wi-Fi (or wired) network you haven't had to manually set an IP address at which the router can connect to you. So, how does the router know to route packets to you?

When you connect to the network, a DHCP request is initiated with the router that allows the router to dynamically assign you an available IP address. This makes network setup much easier because you don't have to know about your network configuration to connect to it. However, it can make talking to your Arduino a bit tougher because you need to find out what IP it was assigned.

DNS

DNS stands for Domain Name System. Every website that you access on the Internet has a unique IP address that is the location of the server on the web. When you type in www.google.com, a DNS server looks at a table that informs it of the IP address associated with that "friendly" URL. It then reports that IP back to your computer's browser, which can, in turn, talk to Google's server. DNS allows you to type in friendly names instead of remembering the IP addresses of all your favorite websites. DNS is to websites as your phone's contact list is to phone numbers.

Clients and Servers

In this chapter, you learn about how to use the Ethernet shield to make the Arduino act as either a client or a server. All devices connected to the Internet are either clients or servers, though some actually fill both roles. A *server* does as the name implies: When information is requested from it, it serves it up to the requesting computer over the network. This information can come in many forms; it could be a web page, database information, email, or a plethora of other things. A *client* is the device that requests data, and obtains a response. When you browse the Internet from your computer, your computer's web browser is acting as a client.

Networking Your Arduino

For all the examples in this chapter, you use your Arduino paired with the official Arduino Ethernet shield. There are multiple revisions of this shield, but these examples are tested to work on the most recent version of the shield with the WIZnet Ethernet controller chip. Significantly older versions of the shield used a different chip, and are not guaranteed to work with these examples. You may also use the Arduino Ethernet, a single-board Arduino that combines the Ethernet connectivity on to the Arduino board.

> **TIP** I have found that the Ethernet shield works more reliably than the Arduino Ethernet.

✳   Attach the Ethernet shield to your Arduino, and connect the shield's Ethernet port to an available Ethernet port on your home router using an Ethernet cable. This should be an ordinary Ethernet crossover cable (nearly all cables will be labeled as "crossover" on the sheathing). Connect the USB cable to your computer and Arduino for programming. If your router is not near the computer that you want to use for programming, program it first, and then connect it to the router. However, some of the examples depend on debugging information shown via the serial monitor. If you want your system to operate without a serial connection, you might want to connect it to an LCD for displaying the IP address, which you will otherwise be displaying via the serial terminal later in the chapter. You can use your knowledge from Chapter 10, "Liquid Crystal Displays," to print information to the LCD instead of the serial terminal if you want; that is not covered in this chapter.

Controlling Your Arduino from the Web

First, you configure your Arduino to act as a web server. Using some HTML forms, and the integrated Ethernet libraries, you have your Arduino automatically connect to the network and serve a web page that you can access to control some of its I/O pins. You expose buttons to the web interface for toggling the colors in an RGB LED and controlling a speaker's frequency. The program that you write for this purpose is extensible, allowing you to add control of additional devices as you become more comfortable working with the Arduino.

Setting Up the I/O Control Hardware

First, set up some test hardware connected to your Arduino server so that you can control it from the web. For this example, you connect an RGB LED and a piezo or ordinary speaker. Wire it up as shown in Figure 14-2. Recall that Pins 4, 10, 11, 12, and 13 are used for communication with the Ethernet chip and SD card, so you cannot use those pins for general I/O. You connect your RGB LED to pins 5, 6, and 7. The speaker connects to pin 3.

Designing a Simple Web Page

It's useful to design a simple web page separately from the Arduino before trying to get the Arduino to serve it up so that you can ensure that it looks the way you want. Your web page will have simple buttons for toggling each LED, and will have a slider for adjusting the frequency at which a speaker is playing. It will use HTML `form` elements to render these components, and it will use the HTTP GET protocol to send commands from the browser to the server. As you design the website, it won't actually be hooked up to a server, so interacting with it will not elicit any action from the Arduino, or anything else.

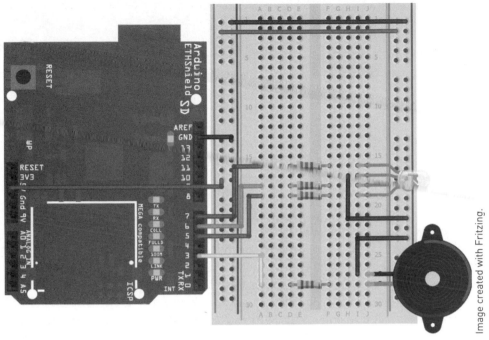

Figure 14-2: Arduino server wired to RGB LED and speaker

Open up your favorite text editor (I recommend Notepad++ for Windows because it highlights and color codes your HTML when you save as an HTML file) and create a new file with a `.html` extension. It doesn't matter what you name the file; `test.html` will work fine. This will be a very bare-bones website, so do not worry about making this a fully "compliant" HTML website; it will be missing some tags that are normally used, such as `<body>` and `<head>`. These missing tags will not affect how the page is rendered in the browser. In your new HTML file, enter the markup from Listing 14-1.

Listing 14-1: HTML Form Page—server_form.html

```
<form action='' method='get'>
  <input type='hidden' name='L' value='7' />
  <input type='submit' value='Toggle Red' />
</form>

<form action='' method='get'>
  <input type='hidden' name='L' value='6' />
  <input type='submit' value='Toggle Green' />
</form>

<form action='' method='get'>
```

```
  <input type='hidden' name='L' value='5' />
  <input type='submit' value='Toggle Blue' />
</form>

<form action='' method='get'>
  <input type='range' name='S' min='0' max='1000' step='100' value='0'/>
  <input type='submit' value='Set Frequency' />
</form>
```

This HTML page includes four form elements. `<form>` specifies the beginning of a form, and `</form>` specifies the end. Within each form are `<input />` tags that specify what data will be passed to the server when the form is submitted. In the case of the LED toggle buttons, a variable called `L` will be passed to the server via a GET method with a value equivalent to the I/O pin number that you will be toggling. The empty `action` element in the `form` tag indicates that the same page should be reloaded when the variable is passed to the server. The `hidden input` specifies that value will just be passed when the Submit button is pressed. For the frequency slider, we are using a new HTML5 `input` element called `range`. This will make a range slider. You can move the slider (in increments of 100) to select a frequency that will be transmitted as the value of a variable called `s`. In older browsers, this slider might render as an input box rather than a slider, if they don't yet support the `range` element. To see what the page will look like, open it up with your favorite browser (I recommend Google Chrome). In Chrome, you need to press Ctrl+O (Windows) or Cmd+O (OSX) to get an Open dialog box. Open the HTML file you just made in your browser (see Figure 14-3).

Figure 14-3: Web page content test in Chrome.

If you press any of the buttons, you should see a variable GET statement appended to the address in your browser's URL bar.

Writing an Arduino Server Sketch

Now, you need to take the HTML you've developed, and integrate it into a larger Server sketch that will handle connecting to the network, responding to client requests with the page you designed, and responding to GET statements from the page forms.

Connecting to the Network and Retrieving an IP via DHCP

Thanks to the wonders of DHCP, connecting to the network with the Arduino Ethernet shield is a snap. Before showing you the code, let's look at what is going to happen. At the top of your program, you should include the serial peripheral interface (SPI) and Ethernet libraries, define the MAC address of your Ethernet shield (it will be on a sticker on the shield), and create an instance of `EthernetServer`. Within the `setup()`, you begin an Ethernet session with the MAC address you've defined and start the web server. You can optionally supply a static IP address when initiating the Ethernet session, but by leaving that argument out, the Arduino will connect via DCHP and return the assigned IP address via the serial terminal. You can then use that IP address to connect to Arduino and view the web page it will be hosting.

Replying to a Client Response

The main loop is responsible for a number of actions. To handle moving through all these various action states, a number of "state variables" are used throughout the loop to keep track of what actions have been performed and what still needs to happen for successful communication with the client to take place.

The Arduino will always be checking for client connections (from your laptop, for example) to the server. When a client connects, the Arduino replies with two things: the HTTP response header and the HTML-formatted web page that was requested. The response header tells your browser what kind of information is about to be sent. When you have tried to visit a nonexistent web page, you've probably gotten the dreaded "404 Response." The 404 header indicates to the browser that the server could not find the requested page. A "200 Response," in contrast, indicates that the request has been received and that the HTML will be transmitted to the browser. So, on the Arduino, you want to send a "200 Response" to the browser and follow that up with a definition of the Content-Type (HTML, in this case). This complete header looks like this:

```
HTTP/1.1 200 OK
Content-Type: text/html
```

This header must be followed by a blank line, then the content of your HTML page that you wrote earlier. This same program is also used to reply to GET requests. To identify GET requests, you need to look for the question mark character in the URL that specifies what parameters have been selected and sent. If the ? is found, the program waits until it receives a variable name. In the case of the HTML you wrote earlier, the command for LED control is an L, and the command for the speaker frequency adjustment is an s. Depending on which of these is in the URL, the program parses integers out of the URL and controls the peripheral accordingly. After this has happened, a `break` command is used to exit the code from the connected client loop, and it starts listening for a new client connection to do the whole process over again.

Putting It Together: Web Server Sketch

Given all the requirements listed in the previous sections, you can now construct a server program for the Arduino. These programs tend to be fairly nontrivial because they require the use of several state variables that track the interaction between the client and server. The sketch in Listing 14-2 works great for accomplishing the tasks of controlling an RGB LED and speaker. If you want to add additional functionality with more GET variables, it should be fairly straightforward to do so. The areas where you can insert this extra functionality are called out in the code comments.

Listing 14-2: Web Server Code—control_led_speaker.ino

```
//Arduino Web Server
//Some code adapted under MIT License from
//http://bildr.org/2011/06/arduino-ethernet-pin-control/

#include <Ethernet.h>
#include <SPI.h>

const int BLUE    =5;
const int GREEN   =6;
const int RED     =7;
const int SPEAKER =3;

//For controlling LEDS and the speaker
//If you want to control additional things, add variables to
//control them here.
int freq = 0;
int pin;

//Set to your MAC address!
//It should be on your sticker. If you can't find it,
//make one up, or use this one.
byte mac[] = { 0x90, 0xA2, 0xDA, 0x00, 0x4A, 0xE0 };

//Start the server on port 80
EthernetServer server = EthernetServer(80); //port 80

boolean receiving = false; //To keep track of whether we are
                           //getting data.

void setup()
{
  Serial.begin(9600);
```

```
  pinMode(RED, OUTPUT);
  pinMode(GREEN, OUTPUT);
  pinMode(BLUE, OUTPUT);

  //Connect with DHCP
  if (!Ethernet.begin(mac))
  {
    Serial.println("Could not Configure Ethernet with DHCP.");
    return;
  }
  else
  {
    Serial.println("Ethernet Configured!");
  }

  //Start the server
  server.begin();                    // start listening for clients
  Serial.print("Server Started.\nLocal IP: ");
  Serial.println(Ethernet.localIP());

}

void loop()
{
  EthernetClient client = server.available();   // Gets a client that is connected to the
                                                 // server and has data available for reading

  if (client)       // Evaluates to true when connected client has data available for
  {                 // reading

    //An HTTP request ends with a blank line
    boolean currentLineIsBlank = true;
    boolean sentHeader = false;

    while (client.connected())       // Is a client connected?
    {
      if (client.available())        // I/o available from client?
      {
        char c = client.read(); //Read from the incoming buffer

        if(receiving && c == ' ') receiving = false; //Done receiving
        if(c == '?') receiving = true; //Found arguments

        //This looks at the GET requests     // ex:  ?L=5
        if(receiving)
        {
          //An LED command is specified with an L
          if (c == 'L')
          {
            Serial.print("Toggling Pin ");
            pin = client.parseInt();   // arduino's parseInt() skips initial non-numeric
            Serial.println(pin);       // chars to find a string [-]dddd
```

@ 325

2

3

4

5

6

toggle action

```
        digitalWrite(pin, !digitalRead(pin));    // eg: read HIGH, write LOW
        break;
6     }
      //A speaker command is specified with an S
      else if (c == 'S')
6     {
        Serial.print("Setting Frequency to ");    ← client.read();
        freq = client.parseInt();
        Serial.println(freq);
        if (freq == 0)
          noTone(SPEAKER);
        else
95        tone(SPEAKER, freq);
        break;                    ← "S = <freq>"    then break?
6     }
      //Add similarly formatted else if statements here
      //TO CONTROL ADDITIONAL THINGS
5   }  // IF(receiving)

    //Print out the response header and the HTML page
    if(!sentHeader)
5   {
        //Send a standard HTTP response header
        client.println("HTTP/1.1 200 OK");
        client.println("Content-Type: text/html\n");
                                    \ adds \n
        //Red toggle button
        client.println("<form action='' method='get'>");
        client.println("<input type='hidden' name='L' value='7' />");
        client.println("<input type='submit' value='Toggle Red' />");
        client.println("</form>");

        //Green toggle button
        client.println("<form action='' method='get'>");
        client.println("<input type='hidden' name='L' value='6' />");
        client.println("<input type='submit' value='Toggle Green' />");
        client.println("</form>");

        //Blue toggle button
        client.println("<form action='' method='get'>");
        client.println("<input type='hidden' name='L' value='5' />");
        client.println("<input type='submit' value='Toggle Blue' />");
        client.println("</form>");

        //Speaker frequency slider
        client.println("<form action='' method='get'>");
        client.print("<input type='range' name='S' min='0' max='1000'
        step='100' value='0'/>");
        client.println("<input type='submit' value='Set Frequency' />");
        client.println("</form>");
```

```
          //Add additional forms forms for controlling more things here.

          sentHeader = true;
      } // if (! sentHeader)

      if (c == '\n' && currentLineIsBlank) break;

      if (c == '\n')
      {
        currentLineIsBlank = true;
      }
      else if (c != '\r')
      {
        currentLineIsBlank = false;
      }
    } // if (client.available()) ... client transmission over
  } // while (client.connected())
  delay(5); //Give the web browser time to receive the data.
  client.stop(); //Close the connection: // When client object @ 323 goes out of scope
  } // if (client)                        // the connection persists. End it with client.stop()
} // loop ()
```

This code executes all the functionality that was described in the previous sections. Be sure to change the MAC address listed in this code to the MAC address printed on the sticker on your Arduino shield. If you cannot locate that address, it may still work with the wrong address; you can use the one that is already listed in the code. Load it on to your Arduino and launch the serial monitor. Ensure that your Arduino is plugged into your network and that your router has DHCP enabled (most do). After a few seconds, the DHCP connection should succeed, and you will see a message that informs you of the IP address that it has been assigned (see Figure 14-4).

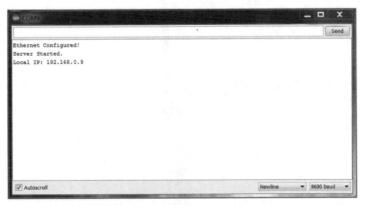

Figure 14-4: DHCP IP acquisition confirmation via serial

In the case shown in Figure 14-4, the Arduino was assigned local IP address 192.168.0.9. This number will almost certainly differ on your network, so be sure to check what it is! Note this IP address; you will now need to use it to access the web interface that you have just launched.

Controlling Your Arduino via the Network

Now that the server code is running, and your Arduino is connected to the network with a valid IP, you can access it with a browser and control it. First, you do so over your local network, and then you learn how you can take advantage of port forwarding in your router to access it from outside of your local network.

Controlling Your Arduino over the Local Network

To confirm that the web interface is working properly, ensure that your computer is attached to the same network as your Arduino (via Wi-Fi or Ethernet). Open your favorite browser, and enter the IP address from the previous section into the URL bar. This should open an interface that looks just like the HTML page you created earlier. Try pressing the buttons to toggle the various LED colors on and off. Move the slider and hit the frequency adjustment button to set the frequency of the speaker. You should see and hear the Arduino responding. If you've left the serial monitor open, you'll also see it displaying debug info as it receives commands. Notice the GET commands being passed to the Arduino server through the browser's URL bar (see Figure 14-5).

Figure 14-5: Arduino control web page and serial debugging

After you're satisfied with controlling the lights and sounds over the local network, you can follow the steps in the next section to enable control from anywhere in the world.

NOTE To watch a demo video of the Arduino being controlled over a local network, check out www.exploringarduino.com/content/ch14. You can also find this video on the Wiley website shown at the beginning of this chapter.

Using Port Forwarding to Control your Arduino from Anywhere

The steps in the previous section enable you to control your Arduino from anywhere within your local network. This is because the IP address that you are connecting to is a local address that sits behind your router. If you want to control your Arduino from computers outside of your local network, you need to take advantage of advanced technologies that will allow you to *tunnel* to your device through your router from the outside world. To do this, you need to implement three steps:

1. Reserve the local DHCP address used by your Arduino.
2. Forward an external port on your router to an internal port pointing at your Arduino.
3. Connect your router to a dynamic DNS updating service.

WARNING The steps in this section are advanced and will differ (maybe drastically) depending on what kind of router you have. I will generalize, but I also assume some existing knowledge of router administration. I recommend searching the web for instructions specific to your router for each of the steps listed. If this is your first time logging in to your router's administration panel, I don't suggest doing these steps; you could potentially mess up your network setup. Some routers may not even support all the functions required to enable port forwarding and dynamic DNS updating. If you are not familiar at all with network administration, stick to local web access for now.

Logging In to Your Router

First, log in to your router's administration panel. The admin panel URL is the gateway IP address for your network. In almost all home network configurations, this is the first three decimal-separated values of your Arduino's local IP, followed by a 1. If, for example, your Arduino's IP was 192.168.0.9, your gateway address is probably (but not necessarily) 192.168.0.1. Try typing that address into your browser to see whether you get a login screen. Enter the login credentials for your router admin page; these are not the same as your wireless login credentials. (If you never changed them from the default values, you might be able to find them in your router's setup manual.)

If that IP address does not work, you need to determine it manually. On Windows, you can open a command prompt and type `ipconfig`. You want to use the Default Gateway address for your active network connection. If you are on a Mac, access System Preferences, go to Network, click the Advanced button, go to the TCP/IP tab, and use the Router Address. If you are in Linux, open a terminal, type `route -n,` and use the last Gateway Address listing that is nonzero.

Reserving Your Arduino's DHCP Address

Once in your router's admin console, look for an option to reserve DHCP addresses. By reserving a DHCP address, you are ensuring that every time a device with a particular MAC address connects to the router it will be assigned the same local IP. Reserved IP addresses are never given to clients with a MAC address other than the specified address, even if that reserved client is not presently connected to the router. By reserving your Arduino's DHCP IP address, you ensure that you'll always be able to forward web traffic to it in the next step.

Once you find the option, reserve whatever IP address your Arduino is currently using by assigning it to the MAC address that you set in the sketch earlier. Be sure to apply the setting, which may require restarting your router. You can confirm that this works by restarting your router and the Arduino and seeing if your Arduino gets the same IP when it reconnects.

You can also accomplish the same effect by giving your Arduino a static IP (not using DHCP) in the sketch. The Arduino website describes how to do this: http://arduino.cc/en/Reference/EthernetIPAddress.

Forwarding Port 80 to Your Arduino

Now that you have an unchanging local IP address for your Arduino, you need to pipe incoming web traffic to that internal IP address. Port forwarding is the act of listening for traffic on a certain port of router and always forwarding that traffic to a specific internal IP address. Port 80 is the default port for HTTP communication, so that is what you will use. Locate the right option in your router administration panel and forward external port 80 to internal port 80 on the IP that you just assigned to your Arduino. If the router specifies a range for the ports, just make the range 80-80. Now, all traffic to your router on port 80 will go to your Arduino.

Using a Dynamic DNS Updating Service

The last step is to figure out how to access your router from elsewhere in the world. If you are working on a commercial network (or you pay a lot for your home's Internet connection), you might have a static global IP address. This is rare for residential Internet connections, but still possible; check with your Internet service provider (ISP). If that is the case, just type **what is my ip** into Google, and it will tell you what your global IP is. If you know you have a static IP, you can access that IP from anywhere in the world and traffic on it should forward to your Arduino. If you want, you can even buy a domain name and set up your domain name's DNS servers to point to that IP address.

However, the odds are good that you have a dynamic global IP address. Your ISP probably changes your IP once every few days or weeks. So, even if you figure out what your global IP is today, and access your Arduino via this IP, it might stop working tomorrow. There is a clever way around this, which is to use dynamic IP services. These services run a small program on your router that periodically checks your global IP address and reports it back to a remote web server. This remote web server then updates a subdomain that you own (such as `myarduino.dyndns.org`) to always point to your global IP, even when it changes. DynDNS is a service that has software built in to most modern routers. Search your router administration page to see which dynamic DNS services it supports. Some are free; some charge a nominal yearly fee. You can follow the setup instructions in your router's admin panel to create an account with one of these services and to connect it to your router. After doing this, you can access your Arduino remotely, even with a dynamically changing global IP address. In case your router does not support any dynamic DNS services, remember that some also offer clients that will run on computers within your network rather than on the router directly.

Once you have determined your public IP address (or obtained a dynamically updating URL), you can enter that into your browser, and you should connect to your Arduino. Give the address to a friend so they can test remotely!

Sending Live Data to a Graphing Service

In the preceding section, you learned how to turn your Arduino into a web server that exposed a web interface for controlling its I/O pins over the local network or the Internet. However, an equally common reason for connecting your Arduino to the Internet is to make networked sensor nodes. Sensor nodes generally only transmit information, instead of listening for commands. Because, in this scenario, the Arduino will be initializing a request out to a known entity on the web (in this case you will use an online graphing service), you do not have to fuss at all with forwarding IP addresses, memorizing the IP address, and so forth.

This section uses an online graphing interface called *Xively* (previously called *Cosm*) to facilitate the creation of live graphs with your Arduino.

Building a Live Data Feed on Xively

For this example, you use the Xively web service to facilitate graphing of some sensors hooked up to your Internet-enabled Arduino. By connecting to the Xively site, you eliminate much of the hard work that you would ordinarily need to do to display your data on the web.

Creating a Xively Account

To start, visit `www.xively.com` and sign up for a free account. Follow the link in the confirmation email you receive and log in to the website.

Creating a Data Feed

Once your account is set up, click the Develop button at the top of the page to create a feed. Press the "+ Add Device" button. A screen like the one shown in Figure 14-6 will prompt you to name your feed and add a description. You can also choose to make your feed public or private.

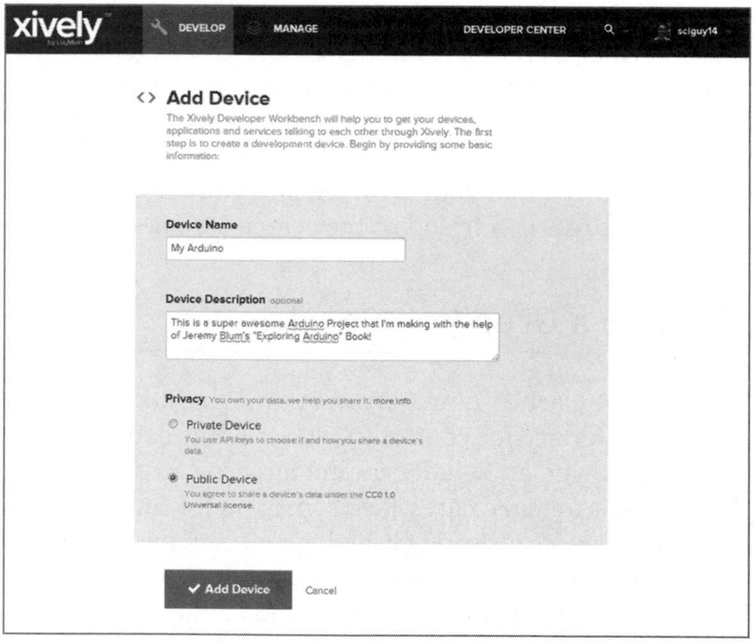

Figure 14-6: Xively feed addition

Enter the requested details and then click Add Device. A new page will appear with relevant connection information for your new feed. Leave this page open, because you will need the information from this page when you configure your Arduino sketch later in this section.

Installing the Xively and HttpClient Libraries

Xively provides a convenient Arduino library that makes it easier to get your Arduino talking to the web through their service. The Xively library depends on the HttpClient library, so you will need to download that as well. Both libraries are available on GitHub, a popular code hosting website. Visit the following two links and click the ZIP download button to download the code repositories: `https://github.com/xively/xively-arduino` and `https://github.com/amcewen/HttpClient`. (These download links can also be found on the web page for this chapter: `www.exploringarduino.com/content/ch14`.) For now, save these ZIP files on your desktop. Then complete the following steps:

1. Unzip the files and rename the library folders so that they do not contain dashes (GitHub adds dashes to the folder names automatically). I recommend renaming the "HttpClient-master" folder to "HttpClient" and the "Xively-Arduino-master" folder to "xively."

2. Move these folders to your Arduino libraries directory, as you did in the "Getting the Library" section of Chapter 12, "Hardware and Timer Interrupts."

3. Open the Arduino integrated development environment (IDE) (you'll need to restart it if it was open when you copied the libraries) and navigate to File > Examples. Confirm that you see "HttpClient" and "xively" in the Examples list. This confirms that the libraries were installed successfully.

For your first experiment with Xively, you'll use their handy example sketch, which broadcasts the state of one analog sensor to web. In the example menu of your Arduino IDE, open the DatastreamUpload example under the "xively" heading. This should open a new sketch. (This sketch is also included in the code download package for this chapter.) Because you'll be modifying the example sketch, use the File > Save As option to save this sketch to your own directory before continuing. A quick glance at the example file reveals that it will be transmitting the analog value that is read by analog input pin 2:

```
// Analog pin which we're monitoring (0 and 1 are used by the
// Ethernet shield)
int sensorPin = 2;
```

Knowing this, you'll wire up your Arduino accordingly in the next section, with the Ethernet shield equipped. You'll come back to this sketch once you've wired your Arduino.

Wiring Up Your Arduino

Next, wire an analog sensor to analog pin 2 of your Arduino. The example sketch that you just downloaded is configured to read an analog input on analog pin 2 and broadcast it up to your Xively account. To keep things simple, grab a photoresistor and 10k resistor and wire them to analog input 2 as a voltage divider, just as you did in Chapter 3, "Reading Analog Sensors" (see Figure 14-7). Once it's wired up, plug your Arduino into the computer and your network.

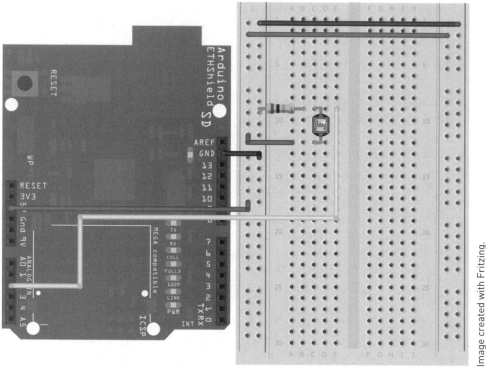

Figure 14-7: Arduino with Ethernet shield wired to photoresistor

Configuring the Xively Sketch and Running the Code

You've already installed the appropriate libraries and opened the example sketch. You now need to configure, compile, and run the code on your Arduino. First, you will configure the sketch to talk to the feed on your Xively account.

You need to change only three values in the sketch to get it to work with your Arduino and your Xively feed: the MAC address of your Arduino Ethernet Shield, your Xively API key, and your Feed ID. The MAC address will be the same MAC address that you used for previous examples. (As before, if you cannot find your

MAC address, just use the default one that comes in the example sketch.) Your API key and Feed ID can be found on the Xively web page that you kept open from before. Find the "API Keys" section (see Figure 14-8).

API Keys

Auto-generated My Arduino device key for feed

1242622121

qkjXS1oUKqbCG-hqh3fw4WlsdvOSAKx4ZXZYSWhGUWdxcz0g

permissions READ,UPDATE,CREATE,DELETE

private accesss

➕ **Add Key**

Figure 14-8: Xively Feed and API Info

This section provides the Feed ID (the first number) and the API key (the second number) to insert into your sketch. The following code snippets show the lines of code that you will need to update with the appropriate values. Listing 14-3 shows an example of the complete sketch with all the values inserted (your values will be different than the ones shown in the listing).

Replace the MAC Address with your own:

```
// MAC address for your Ethernet shield
byte mac[] = { 0xDE, 0xAD, 0xBE, 0xEF, 0xFE, 0xED };
```

Replace the Xively API key with your own:

```
// Your Xively key to let you upload data
char xivelyKey[] = "YOUR_XIVELY_API_KEY";
```

Replace the Feed ID (15552 in the example) with your own (yours may have a different number of digits):

```
// Finally, wrap the datastreams into a feed
XivelyFeed feed(15552, datastreams, 1 /* number of datastreams */);
```

Listing 14-3 shows the completed program.

Listing 14-3: Xively Datastream Upload—xively.ino

```
#include <SPI.h>
#include <Ethernet.h>
#include <HttpClient.h>
#include <Xively.h>

// MAC address for your Ethernet shield
byte mac[] = { 0x90, 0xA2, 0xDA, 0x00, 0x4A, 0xE0 };

// Your Xively key to let you upload data
char xivelyKey[] = "qkjXS1oUKqbCG-hqh3fw4WIsdvOSAKx4ZXZYSWhGUWdxcz0g";

// Analog pin which we're monitoring (0 and 1 are used by the
// Ethernet shield)
int sensorPin = 2;

// Define the strings for our datastream IDs
char sensorId[] = "sensor_reading";
XivelyDatastream datastreams[] = {
  XivelyDatastream(sensorId, strlen(sensorId), DATASTREAM_FLOAT),
};
// Finally, wrap the datastreams into a feed
XivelyFeed feed(1242622121, datastreams, 1 /* number of datastreams */);

EthernetClient client;
XivelyClient xivelyclient(client);

void setup() {
  // Put your setup code here, to run once:
  Serial.begin(9600);

  Serial.println("Starting single datastream upload to Xively...");
  Serial.println();

  while (Ethernet.begin(mac) != 1)
  {
    Serial.println("Error getting IP address via DHCP, trying again...");
    delay(15000);
  }
}

void loop() {
  int sensorValue = analogRead(sensorPin);
  datastreams[0].setFloat(sensorValue);

  Serial.print("Read sensor value ");
  Serial.println(datastreams[0].getFloat());

  Serial.println("Uploading it to Xively");
  int ret = xivelyclient.put(feed, xivelyKey);
```

```
Serial.print("xivelyclient.put returned ");
Serial.println(ret);

Serial.println();
delay(15000);
}
```

Upload the code to your Arduino, and you'll be ready to transmit. When your Arduino connects for the first time, the Xively server automatically adds the feed to the web page you had open earlier.

In the code, you're creating an object that contains all the information of your feed. This appears as an array, named `datastreams[]`. This contains the sensor name and type (in this case, a float). The feed gets wrapped into a `XivelyFeed` object, which has the feed ID, the datastream information, and the number of datastreams that are in the array.

Displaying Data on the Web

Once you start running the sketch on the Arduino, data will be transmitted immediately. Open the serial monitor to observe the status of your transmissions. If you do not see a return status of "200" in the serial monitor, you probably copied the wrong API key or Feed ID. Check those values and try again. Once you know that data is being properly transmitted, return to the Xively website; the `sensor_reading` data stream should now be automatically updating every 15 seconds. Click on the `sensor_reading` link to see a live graph of the data coming from your photoresistor. After the graph has been running for a while, it may look something like Figure 14-9. (The serial monitor is also shown so you can see how they match up.) That's all there is to it. Your Arduino will continue to communicate with and update your feed on the Xively server.

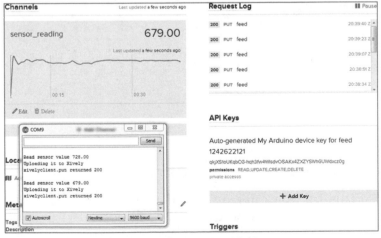

Figure 14-9: Light data being displayed on Xively

Adding Feed Components

Having one sensor feed to Xively is great, but what if you want to add more sensors? Thankfully, adding additional data is quite easy! You add an analog temperature sensor to your Arduino to complement the readings from your light sensor. You could also add any other kind of sensor—even digital I²C and SPI sensors.

Adding an Analog Temperature Sensor

Using the TMP36 temperature sensor that you used in Chapter 3, add a simple analog temperature sensor to the circuit, as in Figure 14-10. This sensor will be read by analog input 3.

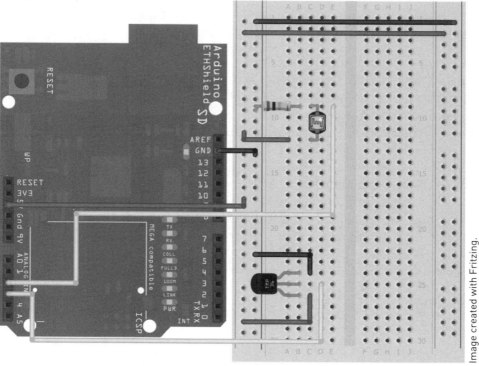

Figure 14-10: Adding a TMP36 temperature sensor

Adding Additional Sensor Readings to the Datastream

You now need to insert the data from this sensor into the stream of data that is sent to the Xively server. Essentially, you just need to add an additional datastream to the code everywhere you see the first datastream. You may also choose to rename to the datastream IDs to something more understandable, like `light_reading` and `temp_reading`. The code in Listing 14-4 should resemble the code you used before, but is now writing two datastreams. Note that you still need to enter in your API key, Feed ID, and MAC address from your previous program into this code; otherwise, it will not work.

Listing 14-4: Xively Datastream Upload Code Updated to Read Multiple Sensors—xively2.ino

```
#include <SPI.h>
#include <Ethernet.h>
#include <HttpClient.h>
#include <Xively.h>

// MAC address for your Ethernet shield
byte mac[] = { 0x90, 0xA2, 0xDA, 0x00, 0x4A, 0xE0 };

// Your Xively key to let you upload data
char xivelyKey[] = "qkjXS1oUKqbCG-hqh3fw4WIsdvOSAKx4ZXZYSWhGUWdxcz0g";

// Analog pin which we're monitoring (0 and 1 are used by the
// Ethernet shield)
int lightPin = 2; //Temperature sensor
int tempPin  = 3; //Light sensor

// Define the strings for our datastream IDs
char lightId[] = "light_reading";
char tempId[]  = "temp_reading";
XivelyDatastream datastreams[] = {
  XivelyDatastream(lightId, strlen(lightId), DATASTREAM_FLOAT),
  XivelyDatastream(tempId, strlen(tempId), DATASTREAM_FLOAT),
};
// Finally, wrap the datastreams into a feed
XivelyFeed feed(1242622121, datastreams, 2 /* number of datastreams */);

EthernetClient client;
XivelyClient xivelyclient(client);

void setup() {
  // Put your setup code here, to run once:
  Serial.begin(9600);

  Serial.println("Starting double datastream upload to Xively...");
  Serial.println();

  while (Ethernet.begin(mac) != 1)
```

```
    {
      Serial.println("Error getting IP address via DHCP, trying again...");
      delay(15000);
    }
  }
}

void loop() {
  int lightValue = analogRead(lightPin);
  datastreams[0].setFloat(lightValue);

  Serial.print("Read light value ");
  Serial.println(datastreams[0].getFloat());

  int tempValue = analogRead(tempPin);
  datastreams[1].setFloat(tempValue);

  Serial.print("Read temp value ");
  Serial.println(datastreams[1].getFloat());

  Serial.println("Uploading it to Xively");
  int ret = xivelyclient.put(feed, xivelyKey);
  Serial.print("xivelyclient.put returned ");
  Serial.println(ret);

  Serial.println();
  delay(15000);
```

First, note that all previous references to `sensor` have been updated to `light`. Now that you are transmitting information from two sensors, it is good coding practice to differentiate between them properly. A `tempId[]` data stream was added and inserted into the `datastreams[]` object. The `XivelyFeed` object definition was updated to indicate that there are now two datastreams instead of one. Within the `loop()`, the lines that were previously printing sensor information about the light sensor have been duplicated to print the same information about the temperature sensor. Note that the light information is listed first in the `datastreams` object, so it is referenced as `datastreams[0]`. The temperature information is listed second in the `datastreams` object, so it is referenced as `datastreams[1]`.

When you run this code on your Arduino, the web interface automatically updates itself to reflect your new datastreams. You might want to delete your old `sensor_reading` datastream, as `light_reading` is now being updated instead. After several minutes of updates, your graphs should look something like Figure 14-11.

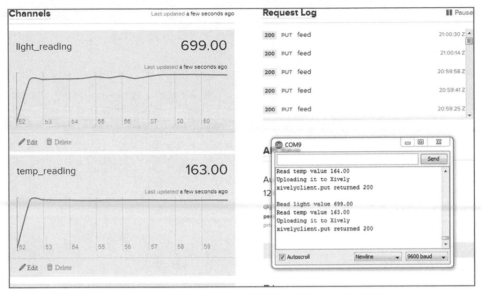

Figure 14-11: Xively graphs for multiple sensors

You have now successfully used your Arduino as both a webserver and a client to a remote web service. Try adding digital sensors, visual feedback, and more to make your system truly interactive.

Summary

In this chapter you learned about the following:

- The Internet has a lot of acronyms. You learned the meanings of IP, DHCP, DNS, MAC, and more.

- You learned the differences between clients and servers.

- You learned enough basic HTML to write a form for controlling your Arduino over the web.

- You ran a web server from your Arduino.

- You can control I/O pins on your Arduino over the Internet.

- You learned how to connect your Arduino to the Xively graphing server.

- You learned how to display data from multiple sensors online.

Deciphering the ATMega Datasheet and Arduino Schematics

At the heart of all Arduinos is an Atmel microcontroller. This appendix does not summarize the features of all the microcontrollers in all the Arduinos, but it is a useful exercise to investigate an ATMega datasheet to get a better idea about how it works. Further, taking a look at the open source schematics for the Arduino Uno will make it easier to understand how an Arduino actually works.

Reading Datasheets

One of the most important skills that you can develop as an engineer is the ability to read datasheets. Just about any electronic component that you can buy has an associated datasheet that contains info about the technical limits of the part, instructions on how to use its capabilities, and so forth.

Breaking Down a Datasheet

Consider the datasheet for the Atmel ATMega 328p, for instance. Recall that the ATMega 328p is the microcontroller unit (MCU) used in the Arduino Uno and many Arduino clones. Finding a datasheet can often be the trickiest part. I recommend just doing a Google search for "ATMega 328p datasheet" and looking for the first PDF link from Atmel. The datasheets for the MCUs used in the Arduinos can also be found on the hardware page for each board on the www.Arduino.cc website. When you have the datasheet in hand, start by reviewing the first page (see Figure A-1). In most cases, the first page tells you all you need to know about the features of that MCU.

Features

- High Performance, Low Power AVR® 8-Bit Microcontroller
- Advanced RISC Architecture
  - 131 Powerful Instructions – Most Single Clock Cycle Execution
  - 32 x 8 General Purpose Working Registers
  - Fully Static Operation
  - Up to 20 MIPS Throughput at 20 MHz
  - On-chip 2-cycle Multiplier
- High Endurance Non-volatile Memory Segments
  - 4/8/16/32K Bytes of In-System Self-Programmable Flash progam memory (ATmega48PA/88PA/168PA/328P)
  - 256/512/512/1K Bytes EEPROM (ATmega48PA/88PA/168PA/328P)
  - 512/1K/1K/2K Bytes Internal SRAM (ATmega48PA/88PA/168PA/328P)
  - Write/Erase Cycles: 10,000 Flash/100,000 EEPROM
  - Data retention: 20 years at 85°C/100 years at 25°C[1]
  - Optional Boot Code Section with Independent Lock Bits
    In-System Programming by On-chip Boot Program
    True Read-While-Write Operation
  - Programming Lock for Software Security
- Peripheral Features
  - Two 8-bit Timer/Counters with Separate Prescaler and Compare Mode
  - One 16-bit Timer/Counter with Separate Prescaler, Compare Mode, and Capture Mode
  - Real Time Counter with Separate Oscillator
  - Six PWM Channels
  - 8-channel 10-bit ADC in TQFP and QFN/MLF package
    Temperature Measurement
  - 6-channel 10-bit ADC in PDIP Package
    Temperature Measurement
  - Programmable Serial USART
  - Master/Slave SPI Serial Interface
  - Byte-oriented 2-wire Serial Interface (Philips I²C compatible)
  - Programmable Watchdog Timer with Separate On-chip Oscillator
  - On-chip Analog Comparator
  - Interrupt and Wake-up on Pin Change
- Special Microcontroller Features
  - Power-on Reset and Programmable Brown-out Detection
  - Internal Calibrated Oscillator
  - External and Internal Interrupt Sources
  - Six Sleep Modes: Idle, ADC Noise Reduction, Power-save, Power-down, Standby, and Extended Standby
- I/O and Packages
  - 23 Programmable I/O Lines
  - 28-pin PDIP, 32-lead TQFP, 28-pad QFN/MLF and 32-pad QFN/MLF
- Operating Voltage:
  - 1.8 - 5.5V for ATmega48PA/88PA/168PA/328P
- Temperature Range:
  - -40°C to 85°C
- Speed Grade:
  - 0 - 20 MHz @ 1.8 - 5.5V
- Low Power Consumption at 1 MHz, 1.8V, 25°C for ATmega48PA/88PA/168PA/328P:
  - Active Mode: 0.2 mA
  - Power-down Mode: 0.1 µA
  - Power-save Mode: 0.75 µA (Including 32 kHz RTC)

8-bit AVR® Microcontroller with 4/8/16/32K Bytes In-System Programmable Flash

**ATmega48PA
ATmega88PA
ATmega168PA
ATmega328P**

Rev. 8161D–AVR–10/09

Figure A-1: The first page of the ATMega 328p datasheet

From a quick glance at the datasheet, you can learn a considerable amount about the microcontroller. You can ascertain that it has 32KB of programmable flash memory, that it can be reprogrammed about 10,000 times, and that it can operate from 1.8V to 5.5V (5V in the case of the Arduino). You can also learn how many inputs/outputs (I/Os) it has, what special functions it has built in (like hardware serial peripheral interface [SPI] and I²C interfaces), and what resolution its analog-to-digital converter (ADC) is.

> **NOTE** This datasheet is actually hundreds of pages, and there could probably be an entire book dedicated just to interpreting it, so I won't go much further here. However, throughout the remainder of this appendix, I do point out several more important topics to look out for.

Datasheets as long as this one generally have PDF bookmarks built in that make it easier to find what you're looking for. Of particular interest for your Arduino adventures may be information about I/O ports, the timers, and the various hardware serial interfaces. As one more example, consider Figure 13-1 from the datasheet's I/O section in the PDF, which is shown here as Figure A-2 for your convenience.

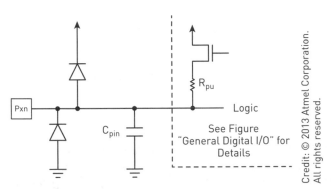

Figure A-2: I/O pins diagram

Diagrams like this one can be found throughout the datasheet, and can give you a deeper insight into how your Arduino is actually working. In this example, you can see that the I/O pins all have protection diodes to protect them from excessively high or negative voltages. It's also important to observe that there is a known pin capacitance, which could have significant implications when trying to determine the rise and fall times when switching the value of a pin.

Understanding Component Pin-outs

All datasheets will include the pin-out for the device in question, which clearly illustrates the functions of each pin. Particularly for microcontrollers, pins may have multiple functions, so understanding the pin-out can be critical for grasping what each pin can and cannot do. Consider the pin-out of the ATMega 328p (see Figure A-3). Understanding the pin-out of the microcontroller at its heart will make it easier to understand the Arduino Uno schematic, which you'll look at in the next section.

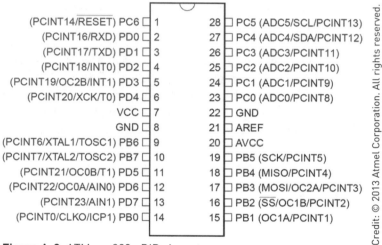

Figure A-3: ATMega 328p DIP pin-out

Note that the pin-out indicates how you can find the pin number on the actual chip. The half circle at the top of the pin-out corresponds to a similar half circle on the actual integrated circuit. Look at the chip in your Arduino and you'll see this half circle; now you know that the pin immediately to its left is pin 1.

You'll also probably notice some abbreviations that you may not be familiar with. They are defined here:

- VCC refers to voltage supply to the chip. In the case of the Arduino, VCC is 5V.

- AVCC is a separate supply voltage for the ADC. For the Arduino, it is also 5V.

- AREF is broken out to a pin. So, you can choose an arbitrary voltage below 5V to act as the reference for the ADC if you desire.

- GND is, of course, the ground connection.

The rest of the pins are all general-purpose I/O. Each is mapped to a unique pin number in the Arduino software so that you don't have to worry about the port letter and number.

The labels in parentheses represent alternative functions for each pin. For example, pins PD0 and PD1 are also the Universal Synchronous/Asynchronous Receiver/Transmitter (USART) Receive (RX) and Transmit (TX) pins, respectively. Pins PB6 and PB7 are the crystal connection pins (XTAL). In the case of the Arduino Uno, an external 16 MHz ceramic resonator is connected to these pins, so you cannot use these for general-purpose I/O. If you have trouble deciphering the pin labels, you can usually learn more about what they mean by searching the rest of the datasheet for those terms. The Arduino website has a diagram illustrating how the ATMega pins are connected to numbered pins on the Arduino board. You can find it at `http://arduino.cc/en/Hacking/ PinMapping168`, and it is shown in Figure A-4.

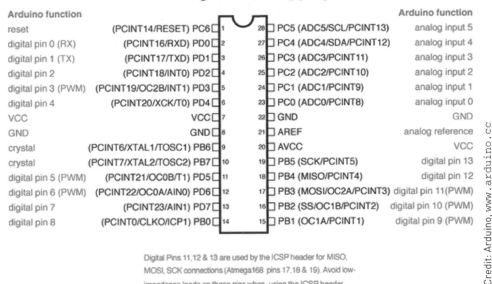

Figure A-4: Arduino ATMega Pin Mapping

Understanding the Arduino Schematic

Perhaps one of the best ways to learn about electrical design is to analyze the schematics of existing products, such as the Arduino. Figure A-4 shows the schematic for the Arduino Uno.

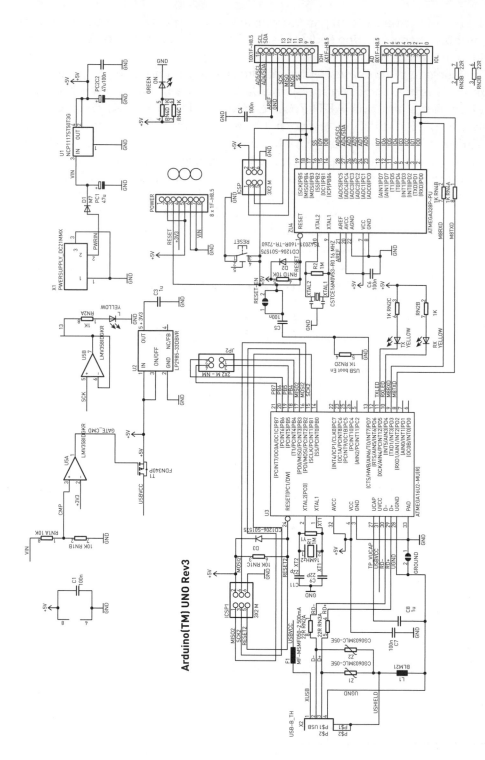

Figure A-5: Arduino Uno Rev 3 schematic

Credit: Arduino, www.arduino.cc

Can you match all the parts to the parts that you can see on your Arduino Uno? Start with the main MCU (Part ZU4 in the schematic), the ATMega328p, and all the breakout pins. Here, you can easily identify which ATMega ports/pins map to the pins that are available to you in the integrated development environment (IDE). Earlier in this appendix, you observed that PD0 and PD1 were connected to the USART TX and RX pins. In the Arduino schematic, you can indeed confirm that these pins connect to the corresponding pins on the 16U2 (8U2 on revisions 1 and 2) USB-to-Serial converter chip. You also know that there is an LED connected (through a resistor) to pin 13 of the Arduino. In the schematic, you can see that pin 13 is connected to pin PB5 on the ATMega. But where is the LED? By using net names, you can indicate an electrical connection between two points on a schematic without actually drawing all the lines. Having every wire shown in a schematic might get confusing very quickly. In the case of PB5, you can see that the wire coming out of the MCU is labeled *SCK*, and that there is a similarly labeled wire at the top of the schematic feeding through a buffer into a resistor and the familiar debug LED.

Most schematics that you'll find are done in a style similar to this one, with lots of labeled nets that connect without direct wires. Continue to analyze the Arduino schematic until you understand where all the signals are going. See how many components you can match to the actual board.

Index

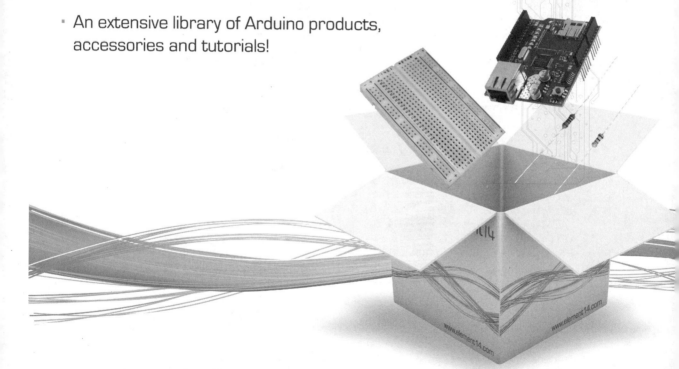